Innovation and Entrepreneurship in the Academia

This book aims to contribute to the understanding and evaluation of the processes through which innovative knowledge is created and translated to entrepreneurial technological advantage in higher education institutions.

The chapters included in this edited volume discuss new trends related to the impact of policies on innovation and entrepreneurial activity in universities, by providing a variety of insights from both an individual and an institutional perspective and with reference to a number of different contexts and units of analysis. The integration of both qualitative and quantitative approaches, and the multidisciplinary approach that characterizes this volume makes it possible to provide an in-depth understanding of today's dynamics.

The volume will be of relevance to scholars, students and researchers interested in Entrepreneurship, Higher Education, Economics and Technology Management.

The chapters in this book were originally published as a special issue of the journal *Industry & Innovation*.

Erik E. Lehmann is Full Professor and holding the Chair of Management and Organization at the University of Augsburg, and Director of the CisAlpino Institute of Comparative Studies in Europe (CCSE) at the University of Augsburg, Germany.

Michele Meoli is Associate Professor of Corporate Finance at the Department of Economics and Technology Management at the University of Bergamo, and Deputy Director of the CisAlpino Institute for Comparative Studies in Europe (CCSE) at the University of Bergamo, Italy.

Stefano Paleari is Full Professor of Finance and Public Management at the Department of Economics and Technology Management at the University of Bergamo. He is President of the CISAlpino Institute for Comparative Studies in Europe (CCSE) at the University of Bergamo, Italy.

Innovation and Entrepreneurship in the Academia

Edited by
Erik E. Lehmann, Michele Meoli and Stefano Paleari

Routledge
Taylor & Francis Group
LONDON AND NEW YORK

First published 2022
by Routledge
2 Park Square, Milton Park, Abingdon, Oxon, OX14 4RN

and by Routledge
605 Third Avenue, New York, NY 10158

Routledge is an imprint of the Taylor & Francis Group, an informa business

British Library Cataloguing-in-Publication Data
A catalogue record for this book is available from the British Library

ISBN13: 978-1-032-15878-5 (hbk)
ISBN13: 978-1-032-15879-2 (pbk)
ISBN13: 978-1-003-24605-3 (ebk)

DOI: 10.4324/9781003246053

Typeset in Minion Pro
by codeMantra

Publisher's Note
The publisher accepts responsibility for any inconsistencies that may have arisen during the conversion of this book from journal articles to book chapters, namely the inclusion of journal terminology.

Disclaimer
Every effort has been made to contact copyright holders for their permission to reprint material in this book. The publishers would be grateful to hear from any copyright holder who is not here acknowledged and will undertake to rectify any errors or omissions in future editions of this book.

Contents

Citation Information

The chapters in this book were originally published in the journal, *Industry and Innovation*, volume 28, issue 3 (2021). When citing this material, please use the original page numbering for each article, as follows:

Chapter 1
Innovation, entrepreneurship and the academic context
Erik E. Lehmann, Michele Meoli and Stefano Paleari
Industry and Innovation, volume 28, issue 3 (2021) pp. 235–246

Chapter 2
The impact of the abolishment of the professor's privilege on European university-owned patents
Catalina Martínez and Valerio Sterzi
Industry and Innovation, volume 28, issue 3 (2021) pp. 247–282

Chapter 3
A burden of knowledge creation in academic research: evidence from publication data
Sascha Schweitzer and Jan Brendel
Industry and Innovation, volume 28, issue 3 (2021) pp. 283–306

Chapter 4
How the university ecosystem shapes the innovation capacities of undergraduate students – evidence from Germany
Carolin Bock, Daniel Dilmetz, Benjamin S. Selznick, Lini Zhang and Matthew J. Mayhew
Industry and Innovation, volume 28, issue 3 (2021) pp. 307–342

Chapter 5
Transformative change in higher education: entrepreneurial universities and high-technology entrepreneurship
James A. Cunningham and Matthias Menter
Industry and Innovation, volume 28, issue 3 (2021) pp. 343–364

Chapter 6

Looking inside the determinants and the effects of entrepreneurial innovation projects in an emerging economy
Maribel Guerrero and David Urbano
Industry and Innovation, volume 28, issue 3 (2021) pp. 365–393

For any permission-related enquiries please visit:
http://www.tandfonline.com/page/help/permissions

Notes on Contributors

Carolin Bock, Department of Law and Economics, Institute of Entrepreneurship, TU Darmstadt, Germany.

Jan Brendel, Faculty of Law and Economics, University of Bayreuth, Germany.

James A. Cunningham, Newcastle Business School, Northumbria University, Newcastle upon Tyne, UK.

Daniel Dilmetz, Department of Law and Economics, Institute of Entrepreneurship, TU Darmstadt, Germany.

Maribel Guerrero, Newcastle Business School and Northumbria Centre for Innovation Regional Transformation and Entrepreneurship (iNCITE), Northumbria University, Newcastle upon Tyne, UK; School of Business and Economics, Universidad del Desarrollo, Santiago de Chile, Chile.

Erik E. Lehmann, Faculty of Business and Economics, University of Augsburg, Germany.

Catalina Martínez, Science and Innovation Department, Institute of Public Goods and Policies, CSIC, Madrid, Spain.

Matthew J. Mayhew, Department of Educational Studies, Ohio State University, Columbus, USA.

Matthias Menter, Faculty of Economics and Business Administration, Friedrich Schiller University Jena, Germany.

Michele Meoli, Department of Management, Information and Production Engineering, University of Bergamo, Italy.

Stefano Paleari, Department of Management, Information and Production Engineering, University of Bergamo, Italy.

Sascha Schweitzer, Faculty of Law and Economics, University of Bayreuth, Germany.

Benjamin S. Selznick, Faculty of Strategic Leadership, James Madison University, Harrisonburg, USA.

Valerio Sterzi, GRETHA UMR CNRS 5113, Université de Bordeaux, Avenue Léon Duguit – PESSAC, France.

David Urbano, Department of Business and Centre for Entrepreneurship and Social Innovation Research (CREIS), Universitat Autònoma De Barcelona, Spain.

Lini Zhang, School of Economics and Management, Shanghai Institute of Technology, China.

Innovation, entrepreneurship and the academic context

Erik E. Lehmann, Michele Meoli and Stefano Paleari

ABSTRACT

This special issue aims to contribute to the understanding and evaluation of the processes through which innovative knowledge is created and translated to entrepreneurial technological advantage in higher education institutions. The papers presented here discuss new trends related to the impact of policies on innovation and entrepreneurial activity in universities, by providing a variety of insights from both an individual and an institutional perspectives and with reference to a number of different contexts and units of analysis.

1. Introduction

In the complex, emerging and uncertain post-COVID-19 world, entrepreneurship is playing the role of an adaptive wildcard. The way entrepreneurs seize new opportunities and take risks increases the range of options available to the world as it navigates towards a greener and fairer society (Ketchen and Craighead 2020). From this perspective, university entrepreneurship has a crucial role to play in resetting the foundations of the economic and social system for a more equitable, sustainable and resilient future (Thomas et al. 2020). It is no surprise that, in the rush to bring the world a solution for the pandemic-induced emergency, universities and academic spin-offs are serving in a pioneering role in the search for a vaccine and in creating room for hope. The very best example are BionTec, an academic spin-off at the Johannes-Gutenberg University of Mainz, founded by two research scientists who announced the first vaccine against COVID-19, and CureVac, an academic spin-off at the University of Tübingen, who followed with their own announced vaccine shortly thereafter.

Indeed, even before the COVID-19 crisis, higher education institutions have played a crucial role in the production and dissemination of knowledge through their missions of education, research and service to society, normally in the form of innovation. Besides publishing scientific articles and educating candidates for the labour market, they also contribute to economic growth and competitiveness by creating opportunities that can be commercially exploited (e.g. Fritsch and Schwirten 1999; McKelvey and Zaring 2017; Goel, Göktepe-Hultén, and Grimpe 2017; Lehmann 2015). This trend towards universities acting as a catalyst for entrepreneurial activity is at the heart of the academic entrepreneurship phenomenon (Etzkowitz et al. 2000). In fact, universities can be regarded as entrepreneurial hubs with multiple and integrated knowledge-based functions that range from the traditional development of pure knowledge and technology, to contributions to innovative ecosystems, to their role as a catalyst for innovation performance and community engagement (McKelvey and Zaring 2017; Smith and Bagchi-Sen 2006).

The justification to use academic and intellectual resources for entrepreneurial activities is found in the efficacy of academics to be creative and to contribute to our knowledge society (Audretsch, Lehmann, and Wright 2014). Academic excellence in the three university missions is thus a prerequisite for generating not only international acclaim but also for the continuing progress and entrepreneurial advancement of societies. Being able to optimally generate and use these resources of academia helps to attract attention by policy makers, university managers and business developers (Grimpe and Hussinger 2013).

First, concerning the traditional education mission, academic excellence can be brought forward by both supporting creative, entrepreneurial thinkers as well as equipping them with necessary skills to establish new businesses. Engaging in innovative activities is not limited to new business creation but can also be found in corporate entrepreneurship. Second, excellence in the research mission can be traced in terms of bibliometric analyses of scholarly output and by making use of suitable indicators of local and/or global spillovers. Third, higher education institutions contribute directly to the development of innovative technologies that generate social and economic welfares. Being (or becoming) excellent in academia is thus crucial for the furtherance of society at large since knowledge creation, university–industry relations and science-based entrepreneurial firms are key components (and byproducts) of academic excellence.

This special issue aims to contribute to the understanding and evaluation of how academic excellence affects the processes through which innovative knowledge is created and translated into a technological advantage. The papers presented in this issue discuss new trends related to (a) individual attributes and dispositions on science-based entrepreneurship; (b) the overall university system as a further enabling factor for spinoff creation; and (c) the role of the context. In all cases, the contributions presented in the special issue refer to a variety of trends, allowing for a better understanding of the interaction between individual, institutional and context-level dynamics.

This editorial paper is articulated as follows. In Section 2 we summarise the state of the art on individual, institutional and context attributes affecting innovation, as well as their interactions, identifying the main streams of literature to which the papers in this special issue contribute. In Section 3, the contributions to this special issue are presented according to the aforementioned classification. Last, Section 4 provides conclusions and highlights avenues for future research.

2. Innovation and entrepreneurship in the academic context

Understanding the determinants of innovation and technology entrepreneurship has become a major concern for public policymakers and university managers seeking to release currently unexploited opportunities hidden in individuals, shelved technologies and resource combinations (Audretsch, Lehmann, and Warning 2005; Audretsch, Hülsbeck, and Lehmann 2011). We draw from the recent literature on academic innovation and entrepreneurship to document the features that determine the innovation output and the establishment of science-based entrepreneurial firms, identifying individual entrepreneurial behaviour and motivations, the institutional setting, the role of the context, as well as the interaction among these different factors.

2.1. Individual entrepreneurial behaviour and motivations

Extant literature emphasises the impact of individual attributes and dispositions on academic innovation and entrepreneurship. The many-sided nature of the resources and assets researchers needs to become entrepreneurs is addressed by D'este and Perkmann (2011). Their study examines what motivates academics to engage with industry using both informal collaboration and formal models of interaction. Four motivations are identified: commercial exploitation of technology or knowledge; learning intended as expected benefits from gaining new insights, receiving feedback on research and accessing new knowledge through engagement with industry; access to private funding complementing public research monies; and access to in-kind resources, such as industry-provided equipment, materials and data for research.

In general, scientists who decide to invest a large amount of time or even shift their career path in order to create a business are likely to have a viable business plan (Zhang 2009). Indeed, the academics involved in creating new ventures may not be motivated solely or primarily by an entrepreneurial vision (i.e. to maximise profits). For example, they may be attracted mainly by the prospect of enhancing their academic position. Fini, Grimaldi, and Sobrero (2009) argue that the enhancement of academic status is perceived to be the most important incentive for fostering the creation of a new company. The existence of non-financial motivations for the creation of firms is highlighted by the entrepreneurship literature's classification of 'push' and 'pull' factors. In the pull approach or 'opportunity' entrepreneurship, incentives for the creation of firm are driven directly or indirectly by the desire to increase the founder's wealth (Baumol 1990); in the push approach, also known as 'necessity' entrepreneurship, individuals are moved to create a firm in order to escape an unsatisfactory situation. Among the push factors, unemployment is typically the most important (Storey 1991; Ritsilä and Tervo 2002). Vismara and Meoli (2016) find that a lack of academic job positions at regional level results in a higher propensity to spin-offs. Accordingly, they argue that academics sometimes become entrepreneurs as a second-best solution, because of shortcomings in the market for knowledge. Civera, Meoli, and Vismara (2020) found that that that necessity-oriented academic spinoffs are associated with higher survival profiles, while opportunity-oriented spinoffs exhibit higher post-entry growth rates.

2.2. Institutional factors

Another stream of literature addresses a further enabling factor for spinoff creation, identified in institutional university system (Clarysse and Moray 2004; Clarysse et al. 2005; Di Gregorio and Shane 2003; Lockett, Wright, and Franklin 2003; Degroof and Roberts 2004; Stuart and Dingle, 2006). Stuart and Ding (2006) examined the conditions prompting university-employed life scientists to become entrepreneurs, focusing on biotechnology. The orientation towards entrepreneurship is stronger when academics work in university departments that have employed other scientists who had ventured into the commercial sector and when these scientists are prestigious. Kenney and Patton (2011) contributed to the literature by investigating the role of inventor ownership in generating spinoffs instead of the probability of becoming an entrepreneur. They show that eminent institutions have a greater propensity to generate spinoffs at the technological field level. However, low-status universities may be able to increase their performance by stimulating entrepreneurship since inventor ownership seems to be a powerful intervening variable that can mitigate the role of status. More recently, Avnimelech and Feldman (2015) confirmed that the founder-spawning rate is positively affected by the quality of the institutions and their departments, besides R&D expenditure and the strength of local clusters. As far as reputation is concerned, Civera and Meoli (2018) argue that prestigious universities are likely to provide crucial information, resources and contacts to affiliated firms, enhancing the performance of academic spin-offs. Moreover, since the university's reputation is at stake, there is an incentive for prestigious institutions to scrutinise the quality of spin-offs before allowing them to hit the market. From a different perspective, Meoli and Vismara (2016) argue that academics may also choose to launch an independent company by pursuing alternative business engagement activities when their university provides inadequate support. A recent stream of literature also highlights the importance of governance structure and features in determining institutional orientation for innovation. Meoli, Paleari, and Vismara (2019) relate the governance structure of universities to their capacity to foster the establishment of academic spin-offs. In this same stream of research, Civera, Donina and Meoli (2020) study the impact of the academic leadership on the university's innovative and entrepreneurial orientation, finding that the mobility of university leaders positively affects innovative and entrepreneurial orientation. These positive externalities are larger in internationalised universities as well as in international-oriented regions.

Some scholars argue that university features may shape the success profile of newly established ventures in terms of survival rates, performance, and reputation (Audretsch 2014; Di Gregorio and Shane 2003; Degroof and Roberts 2004; Clarysse et al. 2005; Harrison and Leitch 2005). Affiliation with a university is beneficial for academic spinoffs because it signals that a firm has access to specific resources and contacts, enhancing the valuation of the firms in the eyes of investors (Meoli, Paleari, and Vismara 2013; Cattaneo, Meoli, and Vismara 2015). The signal can be stronger for more eminent universities because the affiliation with a prestigious institution provides a connection to more qualified resources (Colombo, Meoli, and Vismara 2019). Prominent higher education institutions are expected to possess the best faculties, instruments, and equipment and to provide high-quality research that may result in leading-edge innovations (Wang and Shapira 2012).

At the same time, other scholars underline the negative consequences of strong ties with parent universities, such as dependency, non-beneficial reputation effects, and delayed graduation from incubators (Rothaermel and Thursby 2005)

2.3. Context

Extant literature also highlights the role of context conditions in fostering the creation of academic spinoffs, particularly high-tech spinoffs. Bekkers, Gilsing, and Van Der Steen

(2006) analyse the role and relevance of a variety of factors concerning national, sectoral, regional, and managerial institutions and how they interrelate. These authors show that the combination of national and sectoral institutions is the key influence on the probability of establishing an academic spinoff whereas managerial institution conditions determine the chances of success.

The characteristics of the universities can also contribute to the social and economic developments of regions and countries in their role of fostering entrepreneurial attitudes. Braunerhjelm (2008) detects whether and to what extent universities influence regional productivity, focusing on the age of higher education institutions. The results of this paper suggest the existence of a correspondence in specialisation between universities and regions, as well as a positive effect in terms of productivity created by the universities.

2.4. Interaction among the factors

The existence of a complementary role between individual and institutional factors has been addressed since Landry, Amara, and Rherrad (2006). Investigating the determinants of the creation of university spinoffs, they find that a complementary set of resources needs to be mobilised by researchers to launch university spinoffs. The probability of establishing spinoffs increases as researchers gain access to financial resources from operating grants and university–industry partnership programmes. Besides mere financial resources, more intellectual property assets, knowledge assets in the fields of computer science and engineering, knowledge expertise in consulting, higher social capital assets, the resources of large research universities, the resources of large laboratories, and many years of experience in research are enablers of spinoff creation. In these respects, it is known that academic entrepreneurs show a lack of commercial experience (Zahra, Van De Velde, and Larraneta 2007). As far as the complementary role of institutions is concerned; however, Ensley and Hmieleski (2005) show that university support tends to focus on technology and marketing instead of spending adequate time developing the human capital of the academics engaged in the new ventures.

Indeed, both individual and institutional features play a different role depending on the reference context. Horta, Meoli, and Vismara (2015) have linked research on technology transfer to the literature on opportunity and necessity entrepreneurship by showing that the rate of creation of academic spinoffs is higher when the regional skilled unemployment rate is higher. Patton and Kenney (2010) underline the importance of universities in fostering regional development by arguing that the external environment makes a difference. Analysing different university clusters, the authors conclude that higher education institutions plant seeds that fructify only if planted in a dynamic entrepreneurial context.

3. Overview of the papers included in this special issue

Applying and integrating theories, methodologies, and conceptions borrowed from multiple stream of research, this special issue has called both qualitative and quantitative research to investigate the new trends in how individual and institutional incentives play a major role in the creation of innovative knowledge in higher education institutions, and how such knowledge is translated to a technological advantage for the surrounding environment. This volume is therefore diversified, characterised by contributions from different perspectives, though as a whole, these papers contribute to a better understanding of today's research in innovation and entrepreneurship in higher education institutions.

In these respects, the five contributions of this special issue contribute to the literature on individual and institutional perspectives, and they do so by considering interaction between factors and different contexts, with reference to a variety of units of analysis. The papers can be broadly classified into two groups, depending on the main perspective: three papers mainly focus on individual behaviours and their role in innovation creation and transfer; two papers look at institutional conditions. An overview is provided in Table 1.

The first group of papers analysed policies affecting individual behaviours, either academics or students. The first paper, by Martinez and Sterzi (2020), focuses on individual incentives generated by different policy regimes across Europe. The authors examine how intellectual property regimes governing university inventions were quite diverse in Europe at the end of the 1990s. Several European countries maintained the so-called professor's privilege, an exception to employment law whereby university researchers could retain the ownership of academic inventions. The 2000s were characterised by convergence towards a more homogeneous system, in which university administration took control of IP management. The authors investigate the impact of the reform and observe a decline in the technological importance and the value of the patents owned and managed by universities in the countries abolishing the professor's privilege. However, by differentiating the academic patents by type of ownership, they find that the technological importance of academic patents owned by companies has instead increased. Their study produced some new results that may alert policymakers to the possible unintended consequences of the university ownership model.

Table 1. Papers in this Special Issue.

Authors	Title	Context of analysis	Focus
C. Martinez and V. Sterzi	The impact of the abolishment of the professor's privilege on European university-owned patents	Patents and university patenting in a selection of European countries (Austria, Belgium, Denmark, France, Germany, Norway, Portugal, Spain, Sweden, Switzerland, United Kingdom)	Individual behaviours (academics)
S. Schweitzer and J. Brendel	A Burden of Knowledge Creation in Academic Research: Evidence from Publication Data	Publications by researchers who published in the field of Economics	Individual behaviours (academics)
C. Bock, D. Dilmez and B. Selznick	How the university ecosystem shapes the innovation capacities of undergraduate students – Evidence from Germany	345 students of a German university	Individual behaviours (students)
J. Cunningham and M. Menter	Transformative Change in Higher Education: Entrepreneurial Universities and High-Technology Entrepreneurship	102 German universities	Institutional features
M. Guerrero and D. Urbano	Looking inside the determinants and the effects of entrepreneurial innovations projects in an emerging economy	514 Mexican enterprises	Institutional features

Schweitzer and Brendel (2020) also focus on individual behaviours, by contributing to the literature on the vital role of academic research for innovation and industrial growth. In fact, a potential burden of processing ever more knowledge could be affecting research output and researchers' careers. The authors look at a dataset of researchers who have been published in journals in the field of economics during a period of 45 years. For a subset of these researchers, they amass data from journals listed in the EconLit database, supplemented with years of birth from public sources. Their results show an increase in the age of researchers at their first publication, in the number of articles referenced in debut articles and in the number of co-authors. Simultaneously, they observe a decline in the probability of researchers changing research fields. Their findings extend earlier findings on patents and hint at a burden of knowledge pervading different areas of human progress. Moreover, these results indicate that researchers develop strategies of specialisation to deal with this challenge.

Third, one paper analyses individual behaviour with a focus on students as agents for innovation. Bock et al. (2020) focus on how universities should fulfil their so-called 'third mission' concerning knowledge and technology transfer for the society. However, extant knowledge on the impact of the university ecosystem on students' innovative output is still scarce. Their study sheds light on whether the university ecosystem stimulates students' innovation capacities or whether innovators are mainly determined by personality traits or family background. The results of two rounds of surveys, with a total of 345 students from a technical university in Germany, reveal that factors such as functional experiences (e.g. resources and physical spaces within the university) and connecting experiences (e.g. practical application of skills learned during courses) have significant impact on students' innovation capacities.

A second group of papers analyses institutional characteristics determining innovation and entrepreneurial orientation. Cunningham and Menter (2020) argue that, whereas the positive externalities of entrepreneurial universities in the context of regional development in general and entrepreneurship in specific are undisputed, the effectiveness of policy measures trying to accelerate these beneficial effects is much less clear. Public policies focusing on the higher education landscape often pursue a paradigm shift among universities that may ultimately lead to the transformation towards entrepreneurial universities. Set in the German context, the purpose of their paper is to examine whether a higher education policy-induced transformation significantly influenced regional high-technology entrepreneurship. They thereby focus on the German Excellence Initiative, a higher education policy intervention designed to foster and support the transformative change of German universities towards an entrepreneurial paradigm. Their results reveal that the German Excellence Initiative had a positive and significant impact on regional high-technology entrepreneurship. Further, they show that the higher the interaction with industry, the more conducive universities become for regional high-technology entrepreneurship. In addition, universities' overarching scientific focus decisively affects regional high-technology entrepreneurship. Based on these results, the authors conclude by outlining implications for policy-makers, high technology entrepreneurs and university managers as well as present future avenues for research.

A second paper in this group, by Guerrero and Urbano (2020), discusses the ongoing research agendas regarding the intersection between entrepreneurship and innovation in academia, which still demand analysis about the antecedents/consequences of enterprise-university collaborations. On one hand, little is known about how enterprise university collaborations manage their resources/capabilities to develop entrepreneurial innovation projects (antecedents), as well as how do enterprises-university collaborations capture economic benefits (consequences). On the other hand, regarding the context, there is also a gap concerning the effect of institutional voids on entrepreneurship/innovation strategies in emerging economies. This paper analyses the determinants and the consequences of entrepreneurial innovation projects within enterprise-university collaborations in an emerging economy. By using a sample of 514 Mexican enterprises, the proposed framework offers insights into the remarkable effect in the transformation of enterprises-universities' capabilities and state funds into the generation of economic value from entrepreneurial innovation projects. This paper contributes to a thought-provoking discussion about future research agendas and implications for triple-helix actors in emerging economies.

4. Conclusions and avenues for future research

Taken together, the five papers in this special issue offer a showcase of the current discussion on the role of individual and institutional incentives for innovation and entrepreneurship in the Higher Education framework, allowing a better understanding of how the policies supporting the development of entrepreneurial ecosystem may play a role at the different levels of analysis, and how an overwhelming approach is required for the control of a complex system. The integration of both qualitative and quantitative approaches, as well as the multidisciplinary approach characterising this special issue, makes it possible to provide an in-depth understanding of today's dynamics.

However, we need to be aware that the COVID-19 pandemic has transformed human relationships at multiple levels and across a wide range of contexts. In these respects, all activities in higher education institutions have been dramatically affected, involving teaching and research activities, as well as financial and sustainability concerns (Sá and Serpa 2020). We strongly believe that the contributions in this special issue provide a valuable overview of what have been the most relevant debates in research on innovation and knowledge transfer up to now, and provide a good starting point to address the future challenges of innovation and entrepreneurship in the academic context. How will the pandemic change the way individuals look at entrepreneurial opportunities in the academic context? How have institutional features played a role in how new ventures reacted to the pandemic? And how do different contexts, characterised by different impacts and reactions to the pandemic play a role in these challenges? The near future will be featured by a lively research activity nurtured by the pandemic experience faced worldwide, and we hope that the content of this special issue will be a good starting point for these reflections. We leave this to future research.

Moreover, following Owen-Smith (2018), documenting rising scepticism towards experts all over the world, we argue that communication towards a broader audience is needed. The two examples of academic spin-offs discovering the first vaccine against Covid-19 demonstrate the societal benefits of academic research and academic entrepreneurship. This requires a call for action, possibly involving academics, public authorities, and sensitive components of our societies, for the promotion of applied academic research and a strong defence of academic entrepreneurship.

Disclosure statement

No potential conflict of interest was reported by the authors.

References

Audretsch, D. B. 2014. "From the Entrepreneurial University to the University for the Entrepreneurial Society." *The Journal of Technology Transfer* 39 (3): 313–321. doi:10.1007/s10961-012-9288-1.

Audretsch, D. B., E. E. Lehmann, and M. Wright. 2014. "Technology Transfer in a Global Economy." *The Journal of Technology Transfer* 39 (3): 301–312. doi:10.1007/s10961-012-9283-6.

Audretsch, D. B., E. E. Lehmann, and S. Warning. 2005. "University Spillovers and New Firm Location." *Research Policy* 34 (7): 1113–1122. doi:10.1016/j.respol.2005.05.009.

Audretsch, D. B., M. Hülsbeck, and E. E. Lehmann. 2011. "Regional Competitiveness, University Spillovers, and Entrepreneurial Activity." *Small Business Economics* 39 (3): 587–601. doi:10.1007/s11187-011-9332-9.

Avnimelech, G., and M. P. Feldman. 2015. "The Stickiness of University Spin–offs: A Study of Formal and Informal Spin–offs and Their Location from 124 US Academic Institutions." *International Journal of Technology Management* 68 (1–2): 122–149. doi:10.1504/IJTM.2015.068755.

Baumol, W. J. 1990. "Entrepreneurship: Productive, Unproductive, and Destructive." *Journal of Political Economy* 98 (5): 893–921. doi:10.1086/261712.

Bekkers, R., V. Gilsing, and M. Van Der Steen. 2006. "Determining Factors of the Effectiveness of IP-based Spin-offs: Comparing the Netherlands and the US." *The Journal of Technology Transfer* 31 (5): 545–546. doi:10.1007/s10961-006-9058-z.

Bock, C., D. Dilmez, B. Selznick, L. Zhang, and M. J. Mayhew. 2020. "How the University Ecosystem Shapes the Innovation Capacities of Undergraduate Students – Evidence from Germany." *Industry and Innovation*. this issue. doi:10.1080/13662716.2020.1784710.

Braunerhjelm, P. 2008. "Specialization of Regions and Universities: The New versus the Old." *Industry and Innovation* 15 (3): 253–275. doi:10.1080/13662710802040853.

Cattaneo, M., M. Meoli, and S. Vismara. 2015. "Cross-border M&As of Biotech Firms Affiliated with Internationalized Universities." *Journal of Technology Transfer* 40: 409–433. doi:10.1007/s10961-014-9349-8.

Civera, A., Donina, D., Meoli, M. (2020), Fostering the creation of academic spinoffs: does the international mobility of the academic leader matter?. Int Entrep Manag J, 16, 439–465 (2020). https://doi.org/10.1007/s11365-019-00559-8

Civera, A., and M. Meoli. 2018. "Does University Prestige Foster the Initial Growth of Academic Spin-offs?" *Economia e Politica Industriale* 45 (2): 111–142. doi:10.1007/s40812-017-0072-y.

Civera, A., M. Meoli, and S. Vismara. 2020. "Engagement of Academics in University Technology Transfer: Opportunity and Necessity Academic Entrepreneurship." *European Economic Review* 123: 103376. doi:10.1016/j.euroecorev.2020.103376.

Clarysse, B., M. Wright, A. Lockett, E. Van De Velde, and A. Vohora. 2005. "Spinning Out New Ventures: A Typology of Incubation Strategies from European Research Institutions." *Journal of Business Venturing* 20 (2): 183–216. doi:10.1016/j.jbusvent.2003.12.004.

Clarysse, B., and N. Moray. 2004. "A Process Study of Entrepreneurial Team Formation: The Case of A Research-based Spin-off." *Journal of Business Venturing* 19 (1): 55–79. doi:10.1016/S0883-9026(02)00113-1.

Colombo, M. G., M. Meoli, and S. Vismara. 2019. "Signaling in Science-based IPOs: The Combined Effect of Affiliation with Prestigious Universities, Underwriters, and Venture

Capitalists." *Journal of Business Venturing* 34 (1): 141–177. doi:10.1016/j.jbusvent.2018.04.009.

Cunningham, J., and M. Menter. 2020. "Transformative Change in Higher Education: Entrepreneurial Universities and High-Technology Entrepreneurship." *Industry and Innovation* 1–22. this issue. doi:10.1080/13662716.2020.1763263.

D'este, P., and M. Perkmann. 2011. "Why Do Academics Engage with Industry? The Entrepreneurial University and Individual Motivations." *The Journal of Technology Transfer* 36 (3): 316–339. doi:10.1007/s10961-010-9153-z.

Degroof, J. J., and E. B. Roberts. 2004. "Overcoming Weak Entrepreneurial Infrastructures for Academic Spin-off Ventures." *The Journal of Technology Transfer* 29 (3–4): 327–352. doi:10.1023/B:JOTT.0000034126.23592.23.

Di Gregorio, D., and S. Shane. 2003. "Why Do Some Universities Generate More Start-ups than Others?" *Research Policy* 32 (2): 209–227. doi:10.1016/S0048-7333(02)00097-5.

Ensley, M. D., and K. M. Hmieleski. 2005. "A Comparative Study of New Venture Top Management Team Composition, Dynamics and Performance between University-based and Independent Start-ups." *Research Policy* 34 (7): 1091–1105. doi:10.1016/j.respol.2005.05.008.

Etzkowitz, H., A. Webster, C. Gebhardt, and B. R. C. Terra. 2000. "The Future of the University and the University of the Future: Evolution of Ivory Tower to Entrepreneurial Paradigm." *Research Policy* 29 (2): 313–330. doi:10.1016/S0048-7333(99)00069-4.

Fini, R., R. Grimaldi, and M. Sobrero. 2009. "Factors Fostering Academics to Start up New Ventures: An Assessment of Italian Founders' Incentives." *The Journal of Technology Transfer* 34 (4): 380–402. doi:10.1007/s10961-008-9093-z.

Fritsch, M., and C. Schwirten. 1999. "Enterprise-University Co-operation and the Role of Public Research Institutions in Regional Innovation Systems." *Industry and Innovation* 6 (1): 69–83. doi:10.1080/13662719900000005.

Goel, R. K., D. Göktepe-Hultén, and C. Grimpe. 2017. "Who Instigates University–industry Collaborations? University Scientists versus Firm Employees." *Smalll Business Economics* 48 (3): 503–524. doi:10.1007/s11187-016-9795-9.

Grimpe, C., and K. Hussinger. 2013. "Formal and Informal Knowledge and Technology Transfer from Academia to Industry: Complementarity Effects and Innovation Performance." *Industry and Innovation* 20 (8): 683–700. doi:10.1080/13662716.2013.856620.

Guerrero, M., and D. Urbano. 2020. "Looking inside the Determinants and the Effects of Entrepreneurial Innovations Projects in an Emerging Economy." *Industry and Innovation* 1–29. this issue. doi:10.1080/13662716.2020.1753021.

Harrison, R. T., and C. M. Leitch. 2005. "Entrepreneurial Learning: Researching the Interface between Learning and the Entrepreneurial Context." *Entrepreneurship Theory and Practice* 29 (4): 351–371. doi:10.1111/j.1540-6520.2005.00089.x.

Horta, H., Meoli, M. & Vismara, S. Skilled unemployment and the creation of academic spin-offs: a recession-push hypothesis. *J Technol Transf 41*, 798–817 (2016). https://doi.org/10.1007/s10961-015-9405-z

Kenney, M., and D. Patton. 2011. "Does Inventor Ownership Encourage University Research-derived Entrepreneurship? A Six University Comparison." *Research Policy* 40 (8): 1100–1112. doi:10.1016/j.respol.2011.05.012.

Ketchen, D. J., and C. W. Craighead. 2020. "Research at the Intersection of Entrepreneurship, Supply Chain Management, and Strategic Management: Opportunities Highlighted by COVID-19." *Journal of Management* 46 (8): 1330–1341. doi:10.1177/0149206320945028.

Landry, R., N. Amara, and I. Rherrad. 2006. "Why are Some University Researchers More Likely to Create Spin-offs than Others? Evidence from Canadian Universities." *Research Policy* 35 (10): 1599–1615. doi:10.1016/j.respol.2006.09.020.

Lehmann, E. E. 2015. "The Role of Universities in Local and Regional Competitiveness." In *The Oxford Handbook of Local Competitiveness*, edited by D. B. Audretsch, A. N. Link, and M. L. Walshok, 211–236. Oxford/New York: Oxford University Press.

Lockett, A., M. Wright, and S. Franklin. 2003. "Technology Transfer and Universities' Spin-out Strategies." *Small Business Economics* 20 (2): 185–200. doi:10.1023/A:1022220216972.

Martinez, C., and V. Sterzi. 2020. "The Impact of the Abolishment of the Professor's Privilege on European University-owned Patents." *Industry and Innovation* 1–36. this issue. doi:10.1080/13662716.2019.1709421.

McKelvey, M., and O. Zaring. 2017. "Co-delivery of Social Innovations: Exploring the University's Role in Academic Engagement with Society." *Industry and Innovation* 25 (6): 594–611. doi:10.1080/13662716.2017.1295364.

Meoli, M., S. Paleari, and S. Vismara. 2013. "Completing the Technology Transfer Process: M&As of Science-based IPOs." *Small Business Economics* 40 (2): 227–248. doi:10.1007/s11187-012-9416-1.

Meoli, M., S. Paleari, and S. Vismara. 2019. "The Governance of Universities and the Establishment of Academic Spin-offs." *Small Business Economics* 52 (2): 485–504. doi:10.1007/s11187-017-9956-5.

Meoli, M., and S. Vismara. 2016. "University Support and the Creation of Technology and Non-technology Academic Spin-offs." *Small Business Economics* 47 (2): 345–362. doi:10.1007/s11187-016-9721-1.

Owen-Smith, J. 2018. *Research Universities and the Public Good: Discovery for an Uncertain Future.* Stanford: Stanford University Press.

D. Patton, M. Kenney. 2010. The role of the university in the genesis and evolution of research-based clusters. In D. Fornahl, S. Henn, M.-P. Menzel (Eds.), Emerging Clusters, Edward Elgar, Cheltenham, Northampton (2010), pp. 239-264.

Ritsilä, J., and H. Tervo. 2002. "Effects of Unemployment on New Firm Formation: Micro-level Panel Data Evidence from Finland." *Small Business Economics* 19 (1): 31–40. doi:10.1023/A:1015734424259.

Rothaermel, F. T., and M. Thursby. 2005. "University–incubator Firm Knowledge Flows: Assessing Their Impact on Incubator Firm Performance." *Research Policy* 34 (3): 305–320. doi:10.1016/j.respol.2004.11.006.

Sá, M. J., and S. Serpa. 2020. "The COVID-19 Pandemic as an Opportunity to Foster the Sustainable Development of Teaching in Higher Education." *Sustainability* 12 (20): 8525. doi:10.3390/su12208525.

Schweitzer, S., and J. Brendel. 2020. "A Burden of Knowledge Creation in Academic Research: Evidence from Publication Data." *Industry and Innovation.* this issue. doi:10.1080/13662716.2020.1716693.

Smith, H. L., and S. Bagchi-Sen. 2006. "University–industry Interactions: The Case of the UK Biotech Industry." *Industry and Innovation* 13 (4): 371–392. doi:10.1080/13662710601032697.

Storey, D. J. 1991. "The Birth of New Firms – does Unemployment Matter? A Review of the Evidence." *Small Business Economics* 3 (3): 167–178. doi:10.1007/BF00400022.

Stuart, T. E., & Ding, W. W. (2006). When do scientists become entrepreneurs? The social structural antecedents of commercial activity in the academic life sciences. *American journal of sociology, 112*(1), 97–144.

Stuart, T. E., and W. W. Ding. 2006. "When Do Scientists Become Entrepreneurs? The Social Structural Antecedents of Commercial Activity in the Academic Life Sciences1." *American Journal of Sociology* 112 (1): 97–144. doi:10.1086/502691.

V.J. Thomas, Martin Bliemel, Cynthia Shippam, Elicia Maine. 2020. Endowing university spin-offs pre-formation: Entrepreneurial capabilities for scientist-entrepreneurs, Technovation, 96–97, 2020, 102153

Vismara, S., and M. Meoli. 2016. "Poor Opportunities in the Academic Labor Market as a Cause of Spin-offs." In *Academic Entrepreneurship*, edited by P. Phan, 39–62. Translating discoveries to the marketplace, Cheltenham: Edward Elgar Publishing.

Wang, J., and P. Shapira. 2012. "Partnering with Universities: A Good Choice for Nanotechnology Start-up Firms?" *Small Business Economics* 38 (2): 197–215. doi:10.1007/s11187-009-9248-9.

Zahra, S. A., E. Van De Velde, and B. Larraneta. 2007. "Knowledge Conversion Capability and the Performance of Corporate and University Spin-offs." *Industrial and Corporate Change* 16 (4): 569–608. doi:10.1093/icc/dtm018.

Zhang, J. 2009. "The Performance of University Spin-offs: An Exploratory Analysis Using Venture Capital Data." *The Journal of Technology Transfer* 34 (3): 255–285. doi:10.1007/s10961-008-9088-9.

The impact of the abolishment of the professor's privilege on European university-owned patents

Catalina Martínez and Valerio Sterzi

ABSTRACT

Intellectual property regimes governing university inventions were quite diverse in Europe at the end of the 1990s. Several European countries maintained the so-called professor's privilege, an exception to employment law whereby university researchers were allowed to retain the ownership of academic inventions. The 2000s were characterised by convergence towards a more homogeneous system, in which university administrations took control of IP management. We investigate the impact of the reform and we observe a decline in the technological importance and the value of the patents owned and managed by universities in the countries abolishing the professor's privilege. On the contrary, by differentiating the academic patents by type of ownership, we find that the technological importance of academic patents owned by companies has instead increased. Our study produces some new results that may alert policymakers to the possible unintended consequences of the university ownership model.

1. Introduction

University research is nowadays widely recognised to be an engine for the economic growth of national and regional economies. Firms can benefit from such research indirectly or directly in many ways. Indirectly, they can profit from the spillovers generated by university research and the networks built upon university-industry collaboration. Directly, they can hire university graduates and researchers to undertake business projects in-house or via contract research or consulting; they undertake projects jointly with university researchers and they can also exploit university research results by acquiring or licencing university-owned patents.

Analysts often claim that one of the key reforms facilitating the recent technological success of university research commercialisation in United States is the Bayh-Dole Act, introduced in 1980. Since this reform, American universities have the right to own patents on inventions funded by federal public funds and to provide exclusive licences to third parties. Many other countries have adopted initiatives to emulate the success of the US model and as a result universities have gradually taken a more aggressive stance towards IP appropriation.

Focusing on Europe, this paper exploits the heterogeneity characterising university IP regimes within and across European countries, to investigate whether major shifts towards the institutional ownership of university inventions, and specifically the abolishment of the professor's privilege in some of them, have affected the technological importance of the inventions disclosed to university administrations and the effective exploitation of their value, relative to patents unaffected by such changes.

Changes to the IP regime in universities are expected to impact on the incentive structure of two types of agents involved in the production and commercialisation of academic research, namely researchers and university administrators. Following Arqué-Castells et al. (2016), Hvide and Jones (2018) and Sterzi, Pezzoni, and Lissoni (2019) we consider the commercialisation of university-owned patents to be the result of the effort of academic researchers and the investment of university administrations in facilitating the protection and exploitation of inventions resulting from university research. That is to say, the effectiveness of commercialisation is taken to be the result of the combination of the technological importance (quality) of the invention and the effectiveness of IP management in exploiting the invention.

To our knowledge, we are the first to address the question of the impact of the abolishment of the professor's privilege on the technological importance and the efficiency of the management of university-owned patents. Using a multidimensional approach to the measurement of the quality and value of inventions, our findings are in line with previous results for individual countries (Hvide and Jones 2018 for Norway, Czarnitzki et al. 2015 for Germany, Ejermo and Toivanen 2018 for Finland). We observe a relative decline in the average technological importance and effective exploitation of the value of university-owned patents in the countries abolishing the professor's privilege.

Moreover, we also provide new evidence of a shift of ownership of the academic-invented patents of lower quality from companies to universities. When we consider in the analysis also patents invented by academics but applied for by companies, we observe a rise in the average technological importance.

The paper is organised as follows. The next section describes the principal laws governing IP ownership in universities in different countries, and the changes some of them have experienced in recent years. The related literature is discussed in Section 3. The background and the principal hypotheses guiding our empirical analysis is presented in Section 4. Section 5 introduces our empirical strategy and offers some descriptive statistics of the novel international database with information on university and company-owned patents we have constructed for the project. The principal results of the econometric analysis are offered in Section 6. Section 7 provides additional evidence including in the analysis academic-invented patents owned by companies for a selection of countries. Section 8 concludes.

2. University ip regimes

The emphasis on the linear model of innovation and technology transfer[1] and the pressure on universities and their TTOs to file patents on faculty inventions (hoping to obtain

[1]According to the linear model of technology transfer, the process begins with a discovery by the university researcher (laboratory) and follows a linear path from disclosure to the university administration (possibly to the TTO) overseeing the patenting process and, finally, to licences to an existing firm for further development and commercialisation (see Bradley, Hayter, and Link 2013 for reviews of the literature on technology transfer).

millions in royalty fees by licencing them to industry) is usually traced back to the Bayh-Dole Act, enacted in 1980 in the United States. International emulations of the Act began to proliferate in the following years, notably in Europe (Mowery and Sampat 2005).[2]

2.1. The Bayh-Dole Act

Supporters of the Bayh-Dole Act believed that university contributions to innovation were limited by difficulties in patenting the outputs of federally funded research and in licencing the patents exclusively to industry, although such arguments generally lacked empirical evidence (Mowery and Sampat 2005). In fact, it has been claimed that the debate was mainly ideological. As argued in Eisenberg (1996, 1664), the passing of the Bayh-Dole Act meant that the US Congress endorsed a new vision of how best to exploit publicly sponsored research results: 'In this new vision, public ownership of research results was equivalent to "dead-hand" control, and the public domain was a treacherous quicksand pit in which discoveries sink beyond reach of the private sector. If the results of federally-sponsored research were to be rescued from oblivion and successfully developed into commercial products, they would have to be patented and offered up for private appropriation.' The Act permitted universities to file patents on the results of government-sponsored research and to provide exclusive licences to third parties, and enabled the government to retain march-in rights in their regard.[3] As summarised by Loise and Stevens (2010), the Act stated that inventions produced with federal funding could be owned by the institutions in receipt of such funds. These institutions should also: i) grant licences rather than transfer ownership; ii) disclose the government's interest in patent applications and notify the government before abandoning any patent applications; iii) share the income received with the inventors (how much to share was left up to individual institutions); iv) use any residual income retained by the institution for research and education; v) grant a royalty-free non-exclusive licence to the US government for its own use; v) require licensees to manufacture products in the US that were to be sold in the US; vi) give preference to small businesses. Moreover, according to Henderson, Jaffe, and Trajtenberg (1998), the 1984 approval of Public Law 98–620 expanded the rights of universities still further by removing certain restrictions contained in the Bayh-Dole Act regarding the kinds of inventions that universities could own and the rights of universities to assign their property rights to other parties. In addition to universities, the Act gave permission to small businesses to retain the ownership of patents of government-sponsored research, and in 1984 this provision was extended to large enterprises (Eisenberg 1996). For the top US research universities with patenting experience, the change introduced by the Act simply accelerated and facilitated the way things were already done: 'First, it replaced a web of Institutional Patent Agreements (IPAs) that had been negotiated between individual universities and federal agencies with a uniform policy. Second, the Act's provisions expressed Congressional support for the negotiation of exclusive licences between universities and industrial firms for the results of federally funded research' (Mowery and Sampat 2005, 119). For the

[2]The influence of the Act has also extended to other parts of the world, in addition to Europe, both in developed countries such as Japan (Takenaka 2005) and in emerging countries such as Malaysia, South Africa or the Philippines (Zuniga 2011).

[3]These march-in rights have not been exercised at the time of writing.

remaining universities it represented a more radical change, as it made patents a potential source of additional revenue. New TTOs were created and new patent policies and incentives for academics established.

The expansion of university patenting had begun prior to 1980, from when on it increased more markedly due to a combination of factors, in which the Bayh-Dole Act was just one among many. Other factors included the increasing importance of the biotechnology and software sectors, which were emerging at that time, the rise of industry applications based on biomedical research and a general trend towards strengthening the intellectual property rights in the United States. The latter included the establishment of the US Court of Appeals for the Federal Circuit and was reflected in several pro-patent decisions expanding the patent subject matter to cover more inventions in biotechnology and software (Martínez and Bares 2018). Nevertheless, the changes brought about by the Bayh-Dole Act were mainly seen outside the United States as a way of increasing the attractiveness of European university inventions to industry and raise university revenues in a context of increasing funding constraints (with block grant funding being replaced by project funding).

2.2. Changes to IP regimes in europe

The legislation governing patent ownership of publicly funded inventions was quite heterogeneous in Europe in the 1980s and 1990s but began to converge to more homogenous IP regimes in the early 2000s.[4] Five European countries (Denmark in 2000, Germany and Austria in 2002, Norway in 2003 and Finland in 2007) abolished the professor's privilege regarding IP ownership, allowing university researchers to retain the ownership of inventions developed at universities. New IP regulations were enacted to grant universities the right to own and manage university inventions, following the US model. At the same time, countries which had never established the professor's privilege gradually strengthened institutional ownership controls and made commercialisation and technology transfer one of their principal missions, a stance reflected in a number of laws, policy changes, university statutes and guidelines. The apparent outliers were Italy and Sweden. Italy introduced the professor's privilege in 2001, but the measure was counterbalanced by other legal changes granting universities tighter control over their faculties' activities regarding inventions, rendering the professor's privilege ineffective. A change introduced in 2005, narrowing this privilege to results fully funded by intramural university resources, reduced the influence of the professor's privilege in Italy still further. In contrast, Sweden maintained and maintains today the professor's privilege. Table 1 describes the IP regimes and the principal policy and legal changes affecting university patenting in recent decades in a selection of European countries.

3. Related literature

Several econometric studies have analysed the impact of changes to IP regimes derived from the abolishment of the professor's privilege in a number of European countries.

[4]Damsgaard and Thursby (2013), Greenbaum and Scott (2010), Grimaldi et al. (2011), Kenney and Patton (2011), Mowery and Sampat (2005), Schacht (2012), Valentin and Jensen (2007), Von Proff, Buenstorf, and Hummel (2012).

Table 1. Changes in IP regimes for university patenting in Europe.

Policy and legal changes	Country	Change	Trend
Abolishment of the professor's privilege, to increase scientists' incentives to disclose inventions to university managers	Denmark Germany Austria Norway Finland	2000 2002 2002 2003 2007	Universities assign a share of the patent licencing revenue to the inventor and pay all the costs associated with the patent application
Stronger enforcement of institutional ownership system already in place	United Kingdom Spain France Switzerland Belgium Portugal	1977 1986 1999 1991 1997 1998	Harmonisation, measures to encourage intellectual property awareness, commercialisation and creation of technology transfer offices
Mixed changes: Introduction of professor's privilege (from institutional ownership to inventor ownership) + Introduction of managerial and financial autonomy for universities	Italy	2001	Only applies to inventions fully funded by the university employing the inventor since 2005
Continuation of the professor's privilege	Sweden	1949	Recurrent national debate about IP regimes. The conclusion is always that there is no need for legislative change

Source: Based on information from Geuna and Rossi (2011) for most countries; Chardonnens (2010) for Switzerland; Della Malva, Lissoni, and Llerena (2013) for France; Lissoni et al. (2013) for Italy; Martinez *et al.* (2013) for Spain; Mejer (2011) for Belgium (the change applied in 1997 in the Flemish region and in 1998 in the French); for Portugal, Arqué-Castells et al. (2016). See also Martinez and Sterzi (2019).

For Norway, Hvide and Jones (2018) find a decline of approximately 50% in the aggregate rate of new venture creation and patenting by university researchers following the reform, as well as a decline in the quality of university start-ups and patents. They do so by using multiple difference-in-difference regressions to compare patents and start-ups by university researchers and researchers working outside universities (public research institutes, companies, etc.).[5]

For Denmark, Valentin and Jensen (2007) take advantage of the fact that Sweden has maintained the professor's privilege, whereas Denmark abolished it in 2000; they perform difference-in-difference regressions to compare biotech patenting involving Danish and Swedish domestic academic inventors.[6] They find significant reductions in contributions from Danish researchers, combined with a simultaneous substitutive increase of non-Danish ones and a moderate increase in academic inventions channelled into university-owned patents following the policy change. They argue that the reduction in Danish academic patenting can be attributed, at least in part, to the reform. In their own

[5]Two previous descriptive studies, using data from Norway, find less drastic decreases. Iversen, Gulbrandsen, and Klitkou (2007) distinguish between patents with inventors affiliated to Norwegian universities and patents with inventors affiliated to public research institutes and filed between 1998 and 2003. They observe a decrease in 2003, but argue that this is temporary and attribute it to a lack of experience and uncertainty in face of the change. They further note that 'the conception of "professor privilege" patents as predominantly single-inventor patents held by the researcher himself tends to be inaccurate in most sectors. Individual public sector research inventor patents are in fact relatively limited.' Using a larger sample, Spilling et al. (2015) show that the share of patent filings having inventors affiliated to the Norwegian public sector fell slightly (about 1%) between 1999–2003 and 2004–2008, but they warn against attributing it to the policy change, as the overall economic context changed greatly during this period in Norway.

[6]Valentin and Jensen (2007) use data from the Scanbit Database from the Research Centre on Biotech Business at Copenhagen Business School, which includes patent information and other indicators of pharmaceutical discovery by firms dedicated to biotechnology in Denmark, Sweden and Norway.

words, 'the larger part of the inventive potential of academia, previously mobilized into company-owned patents, seems to have been rendered inactive as a result of the reform' (Valentin and Jensen 2007, p.251). They claim that the ex-ante allocation of intellectual property rights to universities required by the reform harmed exploratory collaborative research, for which the results are still uncertain at the time when contracts must be signed and the allocation of potential future outputs must be discussed.

Two studies provide diverse results for Germany.[7] On the one hand, Von Proff, Buenstorf, and Hummel (2012) find no impact of the abolishment of the professor's privilege on the number of patents with academic inventors. Instead, they observe an increase in university-owned patents, leading them to conclude that the reform has principally caused a shift in ownership rights to universities. On the other hand, Czarnitzki et al. (2015) use patents with inventors from Public Research Organisations (PROs) as a control group in a difference-in-difference estimation of the impact of the change on patents with inventors from universities, by consolidating German and EPO filings at the family level, and excluding patents filed by researchers with dual affiliation, PRO and university. They find that academic-invented patents decreased following the change, in line with Hvide and Jones (2018) for Norway. When they distinguish between different types of university researchers they find that patenting by researchers with previous connections to industry fell after the change and patenting by researchers without such connections rose; consequently, they conclude that the latter benefited more from the institutionalisation of technology transfer, as the absence of support from their universities made patenting relatively more costly. Also on Germany, but focused on entrepreneurship, Cunningham et al. (2019) find that the policy change also had an initial positive effect on the number of start-ups measured by business registrations, although the effect declined over time.

For Finland, where the professor's privilege was abolished more recently (in 2007), Ejermo and Toivanen (2018) estimate the effect of the policy change on the number of patents with inventors from universities, compared to those with inventors from research institutes and firms. They find a decrease in patenting of almost 30% after the change became effective, and an even sharper fall three years earlier, following the announcement of the forthcoming policy change.[8]

Finally, and for Italy, Lissoni et al. (2013) and Sterzi, Pezzoni, and Lissoni (2019) find that the 2001 introduction of the professor's privilege was irrelevant to the ownership of academic patents. However, as highlighted by these authors, the change was anticipated and followed by several national legislative changes that granted universities full managerial and financial autonomy regarding patents. This autonomy allowed Italian universities to exert a degree of control over their faculties' inventions and render the professor's privilege virtually ineffective.

[7] In descriptive analyses for Germany, Schmoch (2007) observes no evidence of a change in the numbers of academic-invented patents before and after the abolishment of the privilege, while Dornbusch et al. (2012) point to a different trend in patent filings made at EPO and the German Patent Office by German academics. However, EPO filings, which are likely to be considered of a higher expected value by applicants, increased after the change, whereas filings to the German patent office decreased.

[8] As we will see later, we exclude Finland from our econometric analysis because it abolished the professor's privilege in 2007, some years later than the other IP reform countries we consider.

4. Theoretical arguments

The abolishment of the professor's privilege in several European countries in the early 2000s led to a shift in the allocation of rights, modifying incentives for the two types of agents involved in the inventive and commercialisation activity of universities. Individual researchers (or teams) are the source of new ideas, and university TTO managers or, more generally, university administrators, have the tasks of commercialising university knowledge and managing their intellectual property rights. In what follows we present theoretical arguments in support of the empirical strategy described later.

4.1. The value of university-owned patents: a combination of technological importance and effective exploitation

Both individual inventors and TTO managers contribute to the value of university-owned patents. In line with Bessen (2008), we distinguish the technological importance of inventions from the ability to exploit them. In greater detail, we follow Sterzi, Pezzoni, and Lissoni (2019), considering patent value to be the result of two components (determined at different points in time, before and after the patent filing), namely the technological importance of the invention and the exploitation process. Technological importance is an attribute of the invention which emerges during research. The exploitation process begins when the patent application is filed and depends on the commercialisation resources and experience of the university TTO managers.

4.2. The effect of IP reforms on incentives to university researchers and TTO managers

IP reforms may affect the incentives of university researchers at the origin of the invention and of TTO managers, who decide whether to file a patent at their universities. Hvide and Jones (2018) argue that the abolishment of the professor's privilege in Norway could be interpreted as an increase in the expected tax rate for the faculty. Prior to the reform, researchers were able to perceive 100% of the revenue from patent royalties; following the reform, they were required to share such revenue with the university administration. In terms of expectations, academic inventors see their predicted income reduced and may therefore have fewer incentives to produce high quality inventions (Lach and Shankerman 2008).[9] Nevertheless, this argument is incomplete if it is not taken into account that abolishment means that universities are not only expected to receive a share of the potential income from commercialisation but are also required to invest in the process of innovation and lower the cost of protection and exploitation for researchers. If this is the case, as Hvide and Jones (2018) also highlight, strengthening the university share of income might also lead researchers to invest more. This occurs when, in the case of complementary investments, the university's investment which

[9]We may also expect changes to the IP regime to have little or no effect on researchers' inventive efforts. This would be the case if university researchers abide by Mertonian norms of science rather than financial rewards (Stephan 1996; Evans and Leighton 1989; Hamilton 2000; Shane, Locke, and Collins 2003).

follows the new IP regime increases the marginal product of the researcher's investment.[10]

On the other hand, IP reforms can also affect the institutional evaluation and career prospects of TTO managers. Since university patent counts and rankings are often part of the evaluation indicators used by funding agencies, TTO managers may obtain rewards or promotions based on the number of initial patent filings, before the technological importance of the patents is revealed, leading to a possible decrease in the average quality of the patents filed.

4.3. The effect of IP reforms on the effectiveness of IP exploitation and resulting value of university-owned patents

Given the double-edged composition of patent value and the expected effect of IP reforms on the incentives of university researchers and TTO managers, there are several forces at play that make it difficult to determine the expected sign of the effect of reforms on patent value.

Firstly, and conditional on technological importance, the exploitation process should improve following the abolishment of the professor's privilege, as university administrators and TTOs then receive a greater share of revenue when ownership is institutional. However, average patent value may decrease if the increase in the effectiveness of IP exploitation does not compensate for a reduction of technological importance overall, eventually deriving from lower incentives for university researchers.

Secondly, it may be that universities reduce the average investment per patent (and, in turn, the average effectiveness of the IP exploitation) when the increase in the number of patents filed by universities is unaccompanied by an increase in (public) investment. In such a case, TTO managers would manage more patents than before with the same resources (as they would add to their portfolio those that were managed directly by faculty or simply undisclosed), consequently dividing the time and budget available among a greater number of patents.

Thirdly, it may be also possible that the IP reform does attract mainly inexperienced universities in the patenting field, which had never been in the IP business and lack the IP management to exploit effectively the academic inventions.

5. Empirical model and variables

5.1. Estimation

We estimate the consequences of abolishment on the technological importance and overall value of university-owned patents. We therefore propose a model in which the unit of analysis is the patent, and we use its priority filing year to distinguish between patents filed before or after the change to the IP regime. Our approach is similar to Rosell and Agrawal (2009), in which the authors study the change in the concentration of knowledge flows over time of university-owned patents by employing a difference-in-difference estimation to compare university and corporate patents in two periods.

[10]From this point of view, the abolition of the professor's privilege may also induce inventors to begin patenting.

In the group of countries characterised by abolishment we consider Denmark, Germany, Austria and Norway. This is our *treated* group of countries. In the group of countries that are not characterised by abolishment (our *control* group) we include the United Kingdom, Spain, France, Switzerland, Belgium, Sweden and Portugal.

The year of abolition of the professor's privilege is different among the countries included in the *treated* group. As Table 1 shows, the year of change in the IP regime for Denmark is 2000, for Germany and Austria it is 2002 and for Norway it is 2003. We thus identified two periods for each country. The first extends from 1990 to the year before the change in the IP regime; the second period spans its respective IP regime change year to 2008.

We define *university patents* as those in which a university appears as the priority applicant in the European patent family (see Section 5.2 for further information). We classify patents according to the owner at the priority date, with the aim of identifying the institution where the decision to file the patent was made and the first decisive steps of IP management were taken.

In our econometric approach, we compare university patents in *treated* countries (before and after the policy change), with corporate patents in the *treated* countries and with university patents in the *control* group of countries. Thus, we consider four classes of patents, which are defined in two categories: i) university versus company patents, and ii) patents applied for by institutions of countries which abolished the professor's privilege versus patents applied for by institutions in countries without such a change in IP law. The change in IP policy only applies to one category, the treated group of patents is composed by university-owned patents in the group of countries that experienced the abolishment of the professor's privilege.

We thus estimate the following general model:

$$y_p = \beta_0 + \beta_1 Post_t + \beta_2 University_p + \beta_3 Treat_p + \beta_4 Post_t Treat_p + \beta_5 Post_t University_p + \beta_6 Treat_p University_p + \beta_7 Post_t Treat_p University_p + X_p \gamma + \varepsilon_p \quad (1).$$

In our framework, the dependent variable $y_p$may represent both the technological importance of the invention, which we call for the sake of simplicity *Invention Quality* (IQ), and the *Patent Value* (PV), since we expect the change in the IP regime to impact upon both. $Post_t$ identifies patents issued in the year of the IP reform and subsequent years. For the countries in the control group the policy change (which does not affect them) has been identified as occurring in 2002, so that the variable takes the value of one in 2002 and subsequent years. $University_p$ identifies patents originally applied for by universities.$Treat_p$ is a dummy that takes a value of one if p is assigned to applicants with addresses in countries affected by abolishment (*treated* group of countries).ε_p is a mean zero random error.X_p is a set of covariates that control for patent characteristics which may affect the dependent variables. In particular, depending on the models, we control for technological dummies, year dummies, common trend and country-specific trend. Finally, ε_p is a mean zero random error. The variables are presented in Section 5.3.

Potentially, this model can account for unobserved trends in the dependent variable in both groups of countries (*treated* and *control* groups) and for both types of patents (university and company).

The effect of the policy is captured by β_7. This parameter measures, in countries abolishing the professor's privilege, its effect on the IQ and PV of university patents.

We estimate two versions of Equation 1. Firstly, we investigate the impact of abolishment on the quality (IQ) of university researchers' inventions retained and successively applied by their universities. In order to do so, we simply replace $y_p$with $IQ_p$and estimate the following model:

$$IQ_p = \beta_0 + \beta_1 Post_t + \beta_2 University_p + \beta_3 Treat_p + \beta_4 Post_t Treat_p + \beta_5 Post_t University_p + \beta_6 Treat_p University_p + \beta_7 Post_t Treat_p University_p + X_p \gamma + \varepsilon_p \tag{2a}$$

Secondly, we investigate the impact of abolishment on patent value (PV). To measure the impact of the change in the IP regime on the management of patent quality, we estimate the following equation:

$$PV_p = \beta_0 + \beta_1 Post_t + \beta_2 University_p + \beta_3 Treat_p + \beta_4 Post_t Treat_p + \beta_5 Post_t University_p + \beta_6 Treat_p University_p + \beta_7 Post_t Treat_p University_p + X_p \gamma + \varepsilon_p \tag{2b}$$

Building upon Hvide and Jones (2018) and Arqué-Castells et al. (2016), and following Sterzi, Pezzoni, and Lissoni (2019), we assume that the patent value (PV) is a function of two components: the *technological importance* of the invention or invention quality (IQ) – which is related to researchers' ability and effort in conducting applied research – and the IP *exploitation effectiveness*, which is related to the ability of patent holders to commercialise and exploit inventions. By inserting IQ in the list of control variables (X) we are speculating that a residual part of the patent value is principally explained by the exploitation effectiveness of IP, and thus the parameter β_7 captures the impact of abolishment on the average IP management in universities.

5.2. Data

We focus on EPO-granted patents with priority filing years between 1990 and 2008 from the EPO Worldwide Patent Statistics Database, PATSTAT (April 2016 version).[11] We rely on the so-called DOCDB families, a type of families available in PATSTAT, where only direct priority links and relations added by EPO examiners are considered to define the patent family (Martinez 2011). To distinguish university-owned patents[12] from other types of patents we examine all the members of the DOCDB family of the sampled EPO patents,

[11]We do not consider in the analysis patents filed after 2008 in order to have enough years of observation for collecting data on forward citations that we use to proxy the technological importance of the inventions.

[12]We use the terms 'university-owned patents' or 'university patents' to refer to patent applications originally owned by universities at the time of the priority filing. Patents are thus classified by first ownership. Alternatively, patents can be classified by the affiliation of inventors, and distinguish between patents invented by academics but owned by companies and patents invented by academics and owned by universities, the latter are the university-owned patents we focus for the most part of the present paper, but for completeness, we also include an analysis of academic-invented patents, comparing company-owned and university-owned in Section 7 later.

in order to distinguish EPO patent filings with priorities filed by universities from EPO patent filings with priorities filed by companies.

We begin with a sample of EPO patents with priority applicants from the thirteen European countries presented in Table 1 and priority applications filed either at the EPO or at their national patent offices, but in the empirical model we restrict the sample to eleven countries, excluding Italy and Finland. We exclude Italy because the country experienced both the introduction of the professor's privilege and an increased autonomy of universities in the 2000s. We also exclude Finland because it abolished the professor's privilege in 2007, and for which we do not have enough years for studying the impact of the IP reform.

5.3. Variables and descriptive statistics

We assign each patent to a country, based on the address reported by the applicant. We thereby define two groups of countries in our sample: countries abolishing the professor's privilege in the early 2000s and countries that did not experience such a change in the IP regime. In the former group we consider Denmark, Germany, Austria and Norway. In the latter group we include the UK, Spain, France, Switzerland, Belgium, Sweden, and Portugal.

We omit 3,074 patents with co-applicants both in countries that had experienced abolishment and in countries that had not experienced it. Table 2 reports the total number of patents and the number of university patents in the selected countries. What does it emerge from Table 2 is that, as expected, the average percentage of university-owned patents over the total number of patents filed is high for those countries that had already implement the university-ownership model (the 'Other' countries, with the exclusion of Sweden).

For the classification of applicants we rely on KUL-Eurostat applicant harmonisation (Callaert et al. 2011) and use their institutional sector allocation (university, company,

Table 2. Patents and university patenting in a selection of European countries. (Priority years: 1990–2008).

	Number of patents (a)	Number of university patents (b)	Number of university patents (c)	(b)/(a)	(c)/(a)
		Countries abolishing the professor's privilege			
Denmark	6655	67	88	1.0%	1.3%
Germany	192,495	842	1138	0.4%	0.6%
Austria	8183	51	63	0.6%	0.8%
Norway	2496	9	12	0.4%	0.5%
		Other countries			
United Kingdom	35,421	1767	1991	5.0%	5.6%
Spain	4395	209	229	4.8%	5.2%
France	69,668	354	882	0.5%	1.3%
Switzerland	30,993	235	297	0.8%	1.0%
Belgium	7806	472	574	6.0%	7.4%
Sweden	20,524	31	43	0.2%	0.2%
Portugal	244	22	31	9.0%	12.7%

Two definitions of university patents are considered: (b) EPO patents with 'university' as the only type of priority applicant in the DOCDB family; and (c) EPO patents having at least one 'university' among the priority applicants in the DOCDB family. A patent may be counted more than once in case of co-applicants residing in more than one country.

Table 3. Breakdown of patents by applicant type.

Applicant type	# of patents	*Percent*
1. Company	**359682**	*95.3*
2. Company-other	1204	*0.3*
3. Other	11108	*2.9*
4. University	**4047**	*1.1*
5. University-company	579	*0.2*
6. University-company-other	132	*0.0*
7. University-other	504	*0.1*
Total	377256	*100.00*

The category 'Other' refers to the following cases: hospital, government non-profit, company government non-profit, company university, and company hospital. Individual patents are excluded. EPO-granted patents with priority dates 1990–2008.

private-non-profit, hospital, etc.).[13] The tabulation of patents by applicant type is given in Table 3.

We further select patents having either only university applicants or company applicants (categories #1 and #4 in Table 3).[14] A patent is thus defined as a 'university patent' if it has only university applicants in its priority filing (university-owned). Likewise, a patent is defined as a 'company patent' if it has only company applicants in its priority filing (company-owned).

The final sample is thus composed of 363,729 patents, either *university* patents (4,047 patents, corresponding to 1.11% of the sample) or *company* patents (359,682 patents, 98.89%). Our units of analysis are thus EPO patents deriving from inventions owned by universities at the priority filing from a selection of eleven European countries. If one of our patents was originally owned by a European university when filed at a national patent office, and was acquired by a company during the priority year so that by the time of the EPO filing the university was not among its applicants, we take such change of ownership as evidence of technology transfer and consider it in the construction of the commercialisation variables used in the analysis.

Figure 1 reports the percentage of university patents over total patent activity (defined here as the sum of the categories of university patents and of company patents) for the two groups of countries; the *Treated* group is composed of countries that experienced abolishment and the *Control* group comprises the remaining countries. The figure illustrates how countries in the former group saw the contribution of university patents increase gradually between 1990 and 2008, in response to the institutional and policy changes described in section 2; this is particularly true for pharmaceuticals and biotechnology, sectors in which university patenting has traditionally played an important role. This pattern can be explained both by an increasing patenting activity of universities and, at the same time, by a trend towards strengthened control over ownership of patents invented at universities and formerly assigned to individuals or companies.

[13]As included in Table tls906_person of PATSTAT April 2016.

[14]University-company co-applications (categories #5 and #6) are excluded from the analysis as they represent only a small share of patents with at least one university as applicant and the origin and management of the inventions is unclear. However, they represent an increasing share of patents in all countries and the results do not change when co-applications are include.

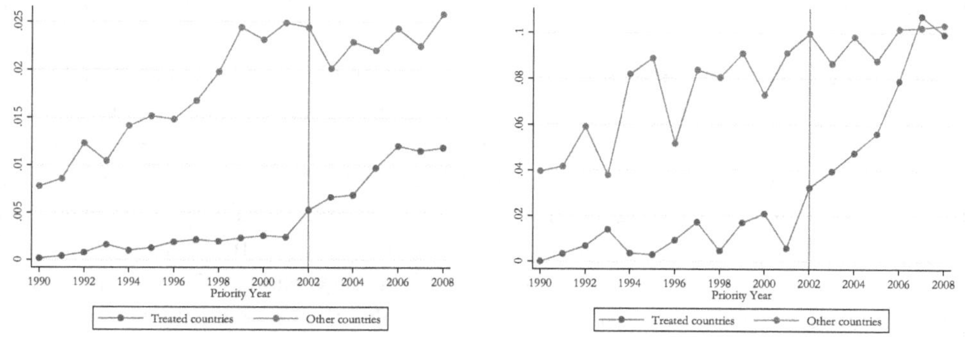

Figure 1. University patenting intensity in countries with IP regime changes (treated) and without (other countries): All Sectors vs Pharma and Biotechnology.
Countries in the treated group are Denmark, Germany, Austria and Norway. Countries in the control group are the UK, Spain, France, Switzerland, Belgium, Sweden and Portugal. University-granted patents are defined as EPO patents having only university applicants in the priority patent document. Company-granted patents are defined as EPO patents having only company applicants in the priority patent document. The shares of the figures are the ratio between the number of university patents and the sum of university and company patents.

5.3.1. Dependent variables

In Equation (2a) the dependent variable is the technological importance, or quality, of the invention (IQ). As the principal indicator of technological importance, scholars use forward citations, since they relate first and foremost to the inventive step and the non-obviousness of the invention (for a recent survey, see Jaffe and De Rassenfosse 2017). This measurement captures both the capacity to generate spillovers and to contribute to the advancement of scientific and technological knowledge. However, forward citations are also often used by scholars as a proxy for the economic value of the invention. Harhoff et al. (1999) find forward citations to be strongly correlated with the payment of renewal fees and, for this reason, they may also be related to patent management. To mitigate this problem and help to interpret forward citations as a proxy for technological importance, we exclude early citations[15], received in the years immediately following publication, as they may be more strongly affected by the commercialisation activity of the applicant than citations made later in time (Lanjouw and Schankerman 2004). Long-term citations are more likely to be more dependent on the quality of the underlying technology. Moreover, Sampat, Mowery, and Ziedonis (2003), Czarnitzki, Hussinger, and Schneider (2012) and Sterzi (2013) find that citations to university patents tend to occur later than citations of other patents. In the empirical analysis, our dependent variable (*Long-term Citations*) therefore excludes from the computation the citations received in the first three years since the first application. Data on citations is taken from the OECD citations database (Webb et al. 2005, OECD database version 2017).

We further refine this measurement by examining the origin of the citations to exclude those originating in other university patents, in order to track the knowledge transfer across institutional boundaries and focus on those originating in companies (*Long-term*

[15]However, the inclusion of early citations does not change the main results of the paper.

Citations from Companies), as university patents are more relevant when they are used and put into practice by companies.[16]

Regarding Patent Value (PV), the dependent variable in Equation (2b), we define it broadly as the overall revenue generated by the patent, which results from the combination of the characteristics of the invention and the effectiveness of the exploitation of the patent protecting it. As we have no data for such revenue, we rely principally upon one proxy widely used in the literature: *Patent Renewals*, defined as the number of years of validity of the patent since the date of filing at the EPO. The number of renewals is taken from the OECD Patent Quality Dataset (Squicciarini, Dernis, and Criscuolo 2013, database version 2017). Since maintaining patent protection over time is costly, we may assume that the value of patents covers at least the costs related to their renewal and that, conditional on technology-specific differences in knowledge obsolescence, more valuable patents are expected to be renewed for longer.

As an alternative proxy for patent value we also use *Family Size*, defined as the number of patent offices at which a given invention has been protected (Martinez 2011), which is also taken from the OECD Patent Quality Dataset (Squicciarini, Dernis, and Criscuolo 2013, database version 2017). Since extending patent protection to several countries is costly (in terms of application and examination fees), patents granted in more than one country are expected to be those of higher value, and in the case of university patents those that are extended internationally are more likely to have been commercialised (Martínez and Bares 2018).

5.3.2. Independent variables

The variable $Post_t$ identifies patents issued in the year of the IP reform and subsequent years.[17] In some models we also replace this variable with year dummies that capture time-specific fixed effects for all the groups of patents (in the treated and control groups). $University_p$ identifies patents originally applied for only by universities. The reference group is formed by patents applied for only by companies.$Treat_p$ is a dummy that takes a value of one if the patent p is assigned to applicants with addresses in countries affected by the end of the professor's privilege. In the group of countries abolishing the professor's privilege we include Denmark, Germany, Austria and Norway. In the list of countries with no IP reform in the period considered we include the UK, Spain, France, Switzerland, Belgium, Sweden, and Portugal. As stated above, we omit from the analysis patents that have been (co)applied for by institutions residing in countries in both the *treated* and *control* groups.

[16] As an alternative measure of the technological importance of the invention we use *Patent Originality*. This variable is taken from the OECD Patent Quality Dataset (Squicciarini, Dernis, and Criscuolo 2013, database version 2017) and refers 'to the breadth of the technology fields on which a patent relies' (Squicciarini, Dernis, and Criscuolo 2013). This indicator, proposed by Henderson, Jaffe, and Trajtenberg (1998) and refined by Hall, Jaffe, and Trajtenberg (2005), is based on the dispersion of the technological classifications of the backward citations and varies between zero and one, with higher values for more original patents. We acknowledge that the concept of patent originality is closer to technological diversity than to technological importance (Jaffe and De Rassenfosse 2017). Our data do however corroborate this intuition; the correlation between the two indicators is only 10%. Consequently, the results of using patent originality as the dependent variable (see Table A2) are quite different from those shown in Table 7. Firstly, university patents do not differ from company patents in terms of originality. The dummy *University* is positive but not significantly different from zero in almost all the models. Secondly, we observe no difference between university patents in countries abolishing the professor's privilege and the control group, neither before nor after the reform.

[17] The dummy POST takes the value one in year 2002 and following years for all the countries in the data (treated and controls), with the exception of Denmark (for which the 'post' variable identifies the IP regime change in 2000) and Norway (2003).

5.3.3. Control variables

Together with the principal independent variables, which emerge from the empirical strategy described in Section 5.1 and aim to quantify the impact of abolition, we control for the following variables, in addition to technology fields, priority year and priority country:

- *Backward citations*: references to patented prior art are sometimes used as a complementary proxy for patent value (Harhoff, Scherer, and Vopel 2003; Harhoff and Reitzig 2004), but they also signal the incremental nature of the underlying technology (Lanjouw and Schankerman, 2004). They are an expression of the possible invalidity of the patent, since patents citing many other patents are more likely to be highly controversial, challenged and found invalid (Hovenkamp et al. 2013). The number of backward citations is taken from the OECD Patent Quality Dataset (Squicciarini, Dernis, and Criscuolo 2013, database version 2017).

- *Number of applicants*: the number of (co)applicants listed in the priority document of the patent family controls for the fact that patents co-applied for by more than one organisation may be of higher value or may be better exploited. Since we have excluded patents co-applied for by different types of applicant, having more than one applicant in the group of university patents means having more than one university as the priority applicant.

- *Team size*: refers to the number of inventors listed in the priority document of the patent family and controls for the fact that patents applied for by larger teams may be of higher value or may be better exploited.

Country-fixed effects do control for time invariant unobserved differences among countries in the treated and control groups. In addition, country-specific trend are intended to capture the country-specific dynamic of specialisation and industry composition.

Table 4 provide descriptive statistics of the main variables.

6. Results

In the following sections we present the principal results of the paper regarding the impact of abolishment on the *Technological Importance* and on the overall *Patent Value* of university inventions. The coefficient of greatest interest is the interaction *Post*Treat*University*, whereby we estimate β_7 in Equation (2a) from the invention quality regressions and β_7 in Equation (2b) from the patent value regressions, respectively. We firstly present the results based on the aggregate analysis; this averages values at the sector and year level (Section 6.1). We then provide evidence based on patent level (Section 6.2 and 6.3).

6.1. Aggregate results

Table 5 presents an aggregate analysis examining the change in our preferred measurements of technological importance and patent value: *Long-term Citations* and *Renewals*. In this analysis averages are constructed per technology field, country and year. The regressions implement the econometric model (2a) and (2b).[18]

[18]Given that there are 35 technology fields, we should have 35*18*11 = 6930 observations, but we miss data points because not all countries, fields and years have patents granted at EPO.

Table 4. Descriptive statistics.

	# Obs.	Mean	Std. Dev.	Min	Max
Dependent variables					
Long-term citations	363 729	3.07	5.09	0	230
Long-term citations (from companies)	363 729	2.01	3.20	0	112
Renewals	363 729	11.07	4.15	1	20
Family size	363 729	6.55	4.57	1	56
Independent variables					
Post	363 729	0.41	0.49	0	1
University	363 729	0.01	0.10	0	1
Treated	363 729	0.56	0.50	0	1
Control variables					
Backward citations	363 729	4.03	2.15	0	36
Number of applicants	363 729	1.03	0.18	1	8
Team size	363 729	2.39	1.65	1	31

Among the control variables, not shown in this table, we include dummies for application year, country of the applicant and technological field (Schmoch (2008)) 35-Sector classification). Patents granted by the EPO with priority dates 1990–2008.

The *Post*Treat*University* coefficients show that the reductions in the average technological importance and patent value are statistically significant when controlling for changes in the dependent variables for university patents in the control group and for company patents in the treated group.

Interestingly, concerning technological importance (Column 1), these results also show a premium for university patents. These are on average more technologically relevant than company patents (they receive on average 1.2 more long-term citations than company patents, as shown by the coefficient of *University*). We observe no differences between university patents in the treatment group and the control group before the change in the IP regime (the coefficient for *Treat*University* is positive, but not significant).

As regards renewals (Columns 2 and 3), we observe that even though university patents are on average of greater technological importance, they are renewed less often than patents applied for by companies (*University* coefficient). As with technological importance, we observe no difference between company and university patents before the change to the IP regime (*Treat*University* coefficient); but following abolishment university patents are renewed even less often than company patents, as shown by the negative and significant coefficients of *Post*Treat*University*. These results also hold true when controlling for the technological importance of inventions, measured by long-term citations (Column 3).

6.2. Patent level results: invention quality (IQ)

Table 6 presents results from the regression at the patent level, based on econometric model 2a. The dependent variable is the number of long-term citations (*Long-term Citations*) as a proxy of the technological importance of the invention (IQ). We use count models (Poisson pseudo-maximum likelihood estimation, PPML) with standard errors clustered at the country level.

Table 5. IQ and PV models: aggregate level analysis. OLS estimates.

	(1)	(2)	(3)
	Long-term citations	Renewals	Renewals
Post	−1.745***	−3.773***	−3.550***
	(0.108)	(0.0785)	(0.137)
University	1.207***	−0.869***	−1.023***
	(0.146)	(0.219)	(0.224)
Treat	−1.033***	0.0163	0.148**
	(0.0972)	(0.0461)	(0.0652)
Post*Treat	0.605***	0.00279	−0.0744
	(0.110)	(0.0836)	(0.0858)
Post*University	−0.502**	0.422	0.486*
	(0.175)	(0.237)	(0.235)
Treat*University	2.074	0.581	0.316
	(1.281)	(0.383)	(0.392)
Post*Treat*University	**−2.338***	**−0.924****	**−0.626***
	(1.097)	(0.317)	(0.324)
Long-term citations			0.128*
			(0.0644)
Constant	4.236***	10.93***	10.39***
	(0.431)	(1.660)	(1.661)
Technological field dummies	Yes	Yes	Yes
R2	0.161	0.485	0.514
Observations	2,140	2,140	2,140

Errors clustered at the country level in parentheses. The dependent variable is the average of the long-term citations in column (1) and the mean of renewals in column (2). EPO- granted patents with priority dates 1990–2008.

Column (1) in Table 6 presents a simplified analysis of the invention quality model. Column (2) adds fixed effects for technological fields; column (3) augments the model by considering the number of backward citations and the number of (co)applicants as controls; column (4) adds a trend to control for the changes in the dependent variables affecting all patents in the analysis; column (5) includes yearly fixed effects and column (6) adds country fixed effects. Finally, our preferred specification is that shown in column (7), where we control for several country-trend fixed effects. We observe little variation in the *Post*Treat*University* coefficient. In all models the triple interaction coefficient is negative and significant.

The variable *University* is positive and significant in all the models. In line with the results for the aggregate case, university patents receive on average more citations than company patents in the long term (the coefficient for university is always positive and significant). In particular, in column (7), the coefficient for *University* is 0.158, corresponding to an incidence ratio of 1.17. Comparing university patents to company patents, while holding the other variables constant in the model, these are expected to have a rate 1.17 times greater for long-term citations.

The variable *Post* has, as expected, a negative sign. At least in part, this reflects the fact that more recent patents have had less time for citation. However, the interaction term *Post*University* appears to suggest that, on average and in both groups of countries, university patents are of lower technological importance in the most recent years: the coefficient of *Post*University* is negative and significant in our preferred specification

Table 6. IQ model: Abolishment of the professor's privilege and long-term citations. PPML estimates.

	(1)	(2)	(3)	(4)	(5)	(6)	(7)
Post	−0.481***	−0.489***	−0.533***	−0.290***			−0.297***
	(0.0515)	(0.0384)	(0.0328)	(0.0334)			(0.0269)
University	0.441***	0.178**	0.195***	0.227***	0.209***	0.144***	0.158***
	(0.0888)	(0.0755)	(0.0735)	(0.0722)	(0.0726)	(0.0528)	(0.0518)
Treat	−0.267*	−0.209	−0.244*	−0.239*	−0.245*	0.132***	0.137**
	(0.146)	(0.130)	(0.132)	(0.133)	(0.132)	(0.0482)	(0.0621)
Post*Treat	0.0796	0.102*	0.112**	0.106**	0.106*	0.0518	0.0841***
	(0.0697)	(0.0574)	(0.0526)	(0.0526)	(0.0541)	(0.0431)	(0.0270)
Post*University	−0.0888	−0.0946	−0.111	−0.140*	−0.109	−0.0954	−0.128**
	(0.0877)	(0.0765)	(0.0762)	(0.0793)	(0.0754)	(0.0649)	(0.0615)
Treat*University	0.207*	0.198*	0.170	0.175	0.170	0.305**	0.315**
	(0.118)	(0.119)	(0.115)	(0.117)	(0.116)	(0.129)	(0.131)
Post*Treat*University	**−0.390*** **	**−0.413*** **	**−0.322*** **	**−0.313*** **	**−0.260*** **	**−0.330*** **	**−0.393*** **
	(0.0965)	(0.0851)	(0.0865)	(0.0885)	(0.0848)	(0.0958)	(0.120)
Backward citations			0.0587***	0.0603***	0.0601***	0.0581***	0.0585***
			(0.00220)	(0.00221)	(0.00191)	(0.000977)	(0.00101)
Number of applicants			0.266***	0.257***	0.263***	0.250***	0.247***
			(0.0265)	(0.0225)	(0.0262)	(0.0171)	(0.0165)
Team size			0.0820***	0.0845***	0.0835***	0.0866***	0.0873***
			(0.00445)	(0.00453)	(0.00446)	(0.00351)	(0.00339)
Trend				−0.0273***			
				(0.00248)			
Constant	1.415***	1.054***	0.392***	54.79***	−0.587***	−0.701***	0.157***
	(0.138)	(0.131)	(0.150)	(5.025)	(0.139)	(0.0559)	(0.0551)
Technological field dummies	NO	YES	YES	YES	YES	YES	YES
Year dummies	NO	NO	NO	NO	YES	YES	NO
Country dummies	NO	NO	NO	NO	NO	YES	YES
Country*Trend	NO	NO	NO	NO	NO	NO	YES
Observations	363,729	363,729	363,729	363,729	363,729	363,729	363,729

Standard errors clustered at the country level are reported in parentheses. *** p < 0.01, ** p < 0.05, * p < 0.1.

(eq.7) although it is not significant in almost all other models. In addition, university patents in the treated group of countries appear to be of higher technological value than those in the control group *before* abolishment (at least for models which control for country-specific fixed effects): the coefficient of *Treat*University* is positive and (weakly) significant, suggesting that university patents in the group of countries that experienced abolishment were of greater technological importance before the IP reform, with respect to university patents in countries in the control group in the same years. However, following the reform, we observe a reduction in the number of long-term citations (the *Post*Treat*University* coefficient is always negative and significant, showing an approximate 33% (*exp*(−0.393)-1) decline in citations received according to the estimates in model 7). This suggests that the increase in the number of patents observed in the group of countries that abolished the professor's privilege has been at the expense of technological quality. Results considering only long-term citations made by companies, as an alternative measurement of invention quality, are in line with these and available in Table A1 in the Appendix A1.

6.3. Patent level results: the patent value (PV)

Table 7 considers regression evidence at the patent level, where the dependent variable is the number of renewals, taken as a proxy of the patent value (Equation 2b).

As for the IQ model, we control for different observable patent characteristics which, if omitted, may affect the results. In particular, we control for the *invention quality* (*IQ*) of the invention, as proxied by *Long-term Citations*. By inserting *IQ* into the list of control variables (Columns 2–8) we speculate that the residual part of patent value is mainly explained by the effectiveness of the IP exploitation. The results change only marginally when adding controls and fixed effects to the model. Our preferred model is Column 8, where we control for technological field dummies, country dummies and country-trend fixed effects.

Column 8 shows that university patents are on average renewed least often. The coefficient for *University* is −0.0264, corresponding to an incidence ratio of 0.97, meaning that university patents receive 3% fewer renewals than company patents, if the other variables in the model are held constant. We observe no difference between the two groups of countries in the years before the IP reform (the dummy *Treat*University* is not significant). However, in countries experiencing abolishment we observe a further fall in the number of expected renewals following the IP reform (the dummy *Post*Treat*University* is always negative and significant). In particular, the effect of the reform on Patent Value is also negative when we control for *Technological Importance*, meaning that TTO managers and university administrators in countries which have witnessed abolishment have not only seen a reduction in the average technological importance of the invention disclosed by the faculty, but have also diminished the effectiveness of the average IP exploitation. For robustness, we also applied matching techniques (Propensity Score Matching) to further control for the characteristics of the patents used in the analysis. The analysis, presented in Appendix A2, shows results which are in line with those presented in Table 7.

Results for family size (Table A3 in the Appendix) are very similar to those based on renewals; in all the models we observe a negative coefficient for the triple interaction '*Post*Treat*University*' which captures the impact of the policy on the patent value of university patents in the treated countries.

Before concluding, however, it is worth mentioning that these negative results appear to be driven by Germany. The average effect of the abolishment of the professors' privilege on the patent value conditional on invention quality for other countries (Austria, Norway, Denmark) is positive, when we exclude Germany from the regressions.[19] This may reflect that on average IP exploitation in German universities has been particularly inefficient, which is probably related to the much larger number of university patents entering the system, and the fact that these were likely to be managed by universities which did not have extensive patenting experience. This is in line with Cunningham et al. (2019) who argue that the abolishment of the professor's privilege was not sufficient to trigger the desired effects on regional entrepreneurship and business innovation, which are two aspects indirectly related to effective university IP exploitation via licencing, transfer and cooperations with business that would lead to keeping the university patent active (renewed) for longer.

[19]Results available upon request.

Table 7. PV model: Abolishment of the professor's privilege and renewals. PPML estimates.

	(1)	(2)	(3)	(4)	(5)	(6)	(7)	(8)
Post	−0.349***	−0.334***	−0.339***	−0.340***	−0.204***			−0.200***
	(0.00288)	(0.00416)	(0.00464)	(0.00474)	(0.00685)			(0.0107)
University	−0.0348**	−0.0571***	−0.0652***	−0.0650***	−0.0470***	−0.0558***	−0.0383***	−0.0264**
	(0.0151)	(0.0154)	(0.0131)	(0.0130)	(0.0142)	(0.0134)	(0.0110)	(0.0128)
Treat	−0.0118	−0.00214	−0.000248	−0.00141	0.00171	−0.00159	−0.0507**	−0.0210
	(0.0107)	(0.0101)	(0.00958)	(0.00962)	(0.0106)	(0.00965)	(0.0249)	(0.0325)
Post*Treat	0.0142***	0.00878*	0.0109**	0.0114**	0.00743	0.00508	0.00601*	−0.00359
	(0.00463)	(0.00528)	(0.00541)	(0.00546)	(0.00610)	(0.00344)	(0.00345)	(0.0127)
Post*University	0.00760	0.0202***	0.0224***	0.0220**	0.00594	0.0197**	0.0169*	−0.00441
	(0.00675)	(0.00769)	(0.00854)	(0.00872)	(0.00808)	(0.00796)	(0.00871)	(0.00873)
Treat*University	0.0321	0.0243	0.0249	0.0246	0.0296	0.0233	0.00679	0.00978
	(0.0243)	(0.0294)	(0.0278)	(0.0275)	(0.0277)	(0.0279)	(0.0258)	(0.0251)
Post*Treat*University	**−0.104*** **	**−0.0896*** **	**−0.0965*** **	**−0.0949*** **	**−0.0925*** **	**−0.0535** **	**−0.0516** **	**−0.0832*** **
	(0.0119)	(0.0140)	(0.0146)	(0.0147)	(0.0157)	(0.0241)	(0.0238)	(0.0138)
Long-term citations		0.00901***	0.00911***	0.00897***	0.00863***	0.00784***	0.00780***	0.00853***
		(0.000916)	(0.000978)	(0.000943)	(0.000931)	(0.000835)	(0.000874)	(0.000999)
Backward citations				0.00149***	0.00241***	0.00249***	0.00259***	0.00264***
				(0.000525)	(0.000458)	(0.000358)	(0.000337)	(0.000420)
Number of applicants				0.00563	0.00117	0.00971**	0.0112***	0.00358
				(0.00578)	(0.00706)	(0.00386)	(0.00410)	(0.00694)
Team size				0.00293***	0.00464***	0.00432***	0.00430***	0.00469***
				(0.000875)	(0.000686)	(0.000674)	(0.000727)	(0.000735)
Trend					−0.0152***			
					(0.000779)			
Constant	2.538***	2.499***	2.506***	2.490***	32.80***	2.462***	2.488***	2.432***
	(0.0104)	(0.0109)	(0.0123)	(0.0145)	(1.558)	(0.0102)	(0.0135)	(0.0270)
Technological field Dummies	NO	NO	YES	YES	YES	YES	YES	YES
Year dummies	NO	NO	NO	NO	NO	YES	YES	NO
Country dummies	NO	NO	NO	NO	NO	NO	YES	YES
Country*Trend	NO	NO	NO	NO	NO	NO	NO	YES
Observations	363,729	363,729	363,729	363,729	363,729	363,729	363,729	363,729

Standard errors clustered at the country level are reported in parentheses. *** $p < 0.01$, ** $p < 0.05$, * $p < 0.1$.

7. The ownership of academic patents

Throughout the paper we have focused on university-owned patents and defined them as those in which a university appears as the priority applicant in the European patent family protecting the invention. Academic inventions owned by companies have thus been confounded with other company-owned patents, as our interest has mainly lied on whether the abolishment of the professor's privilege had affected the quality and effective exploitation of university-owned patents.

We may thus question whether the abolishment of the professor's privilege have also had an impact on academic inventions in general, regardless of their owner. First of all, these IP reforms might have made more difficult for professors and companies to retain the property of academic inventions, leading to a transformation of the ownership structure of academic-invented patents. Secondly, IP reforms may have also had an impact on the technological quality of academic inventions that remained outside the control of universities.

To address these issues, we have collected data on academic patents on two countries that experienced the professor's privilege abolishment (Austria and Germany) and compared it with data on academic patents from two countries included in the group of controls in previous sections (France and Spain). For our collection of patents invented by university professors in Germany and Austria we rely on a method used by other scholars before (Czarnitzki et al. 2015). We identify patents invented by university professors by searching for the title 'Prof. Dr.' in the text field of the inventors' names in EPO granted patents from PATSTAT.[20] Since the German language convention to include titles next to names also applies to Austria, we apply the same method to both countries. This method has some limitations however, as shown by von Proff *et al.* (2012). One limitation is that researchers below the professor rank are excluded when this method is used, leading to underestimations, another is that titles may not be used consistently across patent applications.[21]

As regards academic patenting data on countries not affected by the policy change, we focus on Spain and France. For Spain we use the data described in Maraut and Martinez (2014). The benchmark used by Maraut and Martinez is the list of authors with affiliations to Spanish public universities listed in scientific articles published in journals indexed in Elsevier's Scopus database and published in the years 2003–2008. For France we rely on a newly built dataset on academic invented patents which matches

[20]A better method to identify academic patents relies on matching inventors and academic staff lists, but that is fraught with problems and requires an enormous effort beyond the scope of this paper (e.g. difficulty in obtaining staff lists, problems of homonymy, imperfect disambiguation strategies, lack of large scale golden standards to estimate precision and recall rates and overall reliability of resulting datasets). To our knowledge, there have only been two important paneuropean collective efforts in the past to gather data on academic patenting based on matching academic staff lists. The first one, excluding Germany, is the KEINS project in the early 2000s (Lissoni et al. 2008). The second one is the APE-INV project in the late 2000s (Lissoni 2012), to which the authors of this paper have made significant contributions, with studies of academic patenting in the UK, Italy and Spain. German data is available in the APE-INV public datasets but the time range available is limited to 2006–2007 and thus not useful for pour purposes (Schoen, Heinisch, and Buenstorf 2014). Austria is also included, but for a different time period 1997–2009 (Backs, Günther, and Stummer 2019). With the aim to keep a sample as homogenous as possible in the data sampling and identification strategy, we use the 'Prof.Dr.' title technique for both Germany and Austria for this new section whose main purpose is to provide some robustness tests.

[21]Another limitation put forward by von Proff et al (2012) is that top-level R&D employees of R&D intensive firms may hold honorary professorships at universities, but that is a limitation that could also affect other methods to identify academic patents, such as those based on matching names of university professors to names of academic inventors.

academic staff lists to inventor names, where university employees are those active between 2005 and 2012, to inventor names (Carayol and Carpentier 2019).[22]

Table 8, Figure 2 and Figure 3 show the main statistics and trend related to academic patenting activities and patent quality in these countries.

What is evident from Figure 2 is that the allocation of rights over academic inventions has significantly changed in the years following the abolishment of the professor's privilege.

Moreover, if the abolishment of the professor's privilege has gradually led to a shift of IP rights over academic inventions to universities, what Figure 3 suggests is that the average technological quality of academic inventions in those countries has not been immune to that change. The average technological importance of university-owned academic patents was much higher than that of company-owned academic invented patents before the policy change in the treated countries (and much higher than university-owned patents in the control group – see Figure 3(b)), but converged after the passage of the law. On the contrary, we do not observe the same strong reduction in the average technological importance before and after the professor's privilege abolishment for the group of patents applied by France and Spain who did not experienced the IP reform.

To further investigate this issue, we focus on the two countries that experienced the professor's privilege abolishment (Austria and Germany) and we compare the technological quality of *Academic Patents* (before and after the policy change), with company patents (before and after the policy change), controlling for the ownership of the academic patents.[23] Although the method used for identifying academic inventors in Germany and Austria might be subject to criticism, it does not affect the econometric results, as the errors in the identification should be uniformly distributed over time (before and after the abolishment of the professor's privilege).

In the specification, we include the variable (*University Ownership*) that identifies academic patents assigned to universities. We thus estimate the following general model:

$$\begin{aligned} y_p = \beta_0 &+ \beta_1 Post_t + \beta_2 AcademicPatent_p + \beta_3 AcademicPatent_p * UniversityOwnership_p \\ &+ \beta_4 Post_t * AcademicPatent_p + \beta_5 Post_t * AcademicPatent_p * UniversityOwnership_p \\ &+ X_p \gamma + \varepsilon_p \end{aligned} \quad (3).$$

As for the previous models, the dependent variable $y_p$represents the *Invention Quality* (IQ), while $Post_t$ identifies patents issued in the year of the IP reform and subsequent years. $AcademicPatent_p$ Identifies patents invented by university professors, irrespective of whether they have been applied by for universities or companies.$UniversityOwnership_p$ is a dummy that takes a value of one if p is assigned to university.ε_p is a mean zero random error.X_p is a set of covariates that control for patent characteristics which may affect the dependent variables. Depending on the models, we do control for technological field effects, year fixed effects, country fixed effects, trend and country-specific effects.

Results presented in Table 9 show that the average quality of academic inventions assigned to companies has increased after the reform. The coefficient is highly significant

[22]We thank Nicolas Carayol and Elodie Carpentier for the data.

[23]We also run models by adding as further controls corporate and academic (university- and company-owned) French and Spanish patents. Results do not substantially differ and are available upon request from the authors.

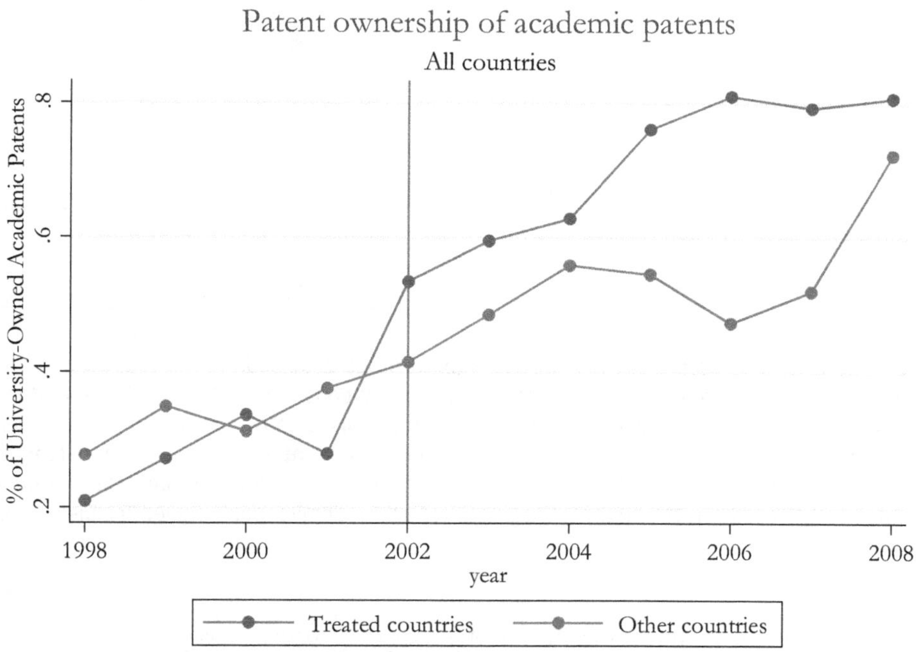

Figure 2. Ownership of *Academic patents.*
Countries in the treated group are Austria and Germany. Countries in the control group are France and Spain. *Academic patents* are those where academics appear as inventors in the patent document irrespective of whether they have been applied for by universities. Only patents assigned to domestic universities or domestic companies are considered in the analysis. *University-Owned academic patents* are those in which universities appear as the unique applicant in the European patent family protecting the invention (these figures include patents co-applied with non-university institutions). *Company-owned academic patents* are those invented by academics and assigned to solely domestic companies.

at 1% level in all models and implies that the technological importance of company-owned patents invented by university professors increased by about 26% (*exp*(.234)-1, Column 7), on average. However, in line with findings previously shown in the paper (Table 6), a negative and strong impact is found for university-owned academic patents, with an estimated reduction of invention quality of about 35% (*exp*(−.426)-1, Column 7).

The negative impact of the professor's privilege abolishment on the average technological importance of the academic inventions assigned to universities is thus in line with the findings of Table 7 and may be due to the higher number of lower quality patents that inexperienced German and Austrian universities had to manage during and after the abolishment of the professor's privilege (Martinez and Sterzi 2019).

In turn, the positive impact of the IP reform on the average technological importance of the academic inventions assigned to companies may be due to a mix of factors. First of all, given that the changed environment made more difficult for companies to retain the ownership of academic patents, it is reasonable

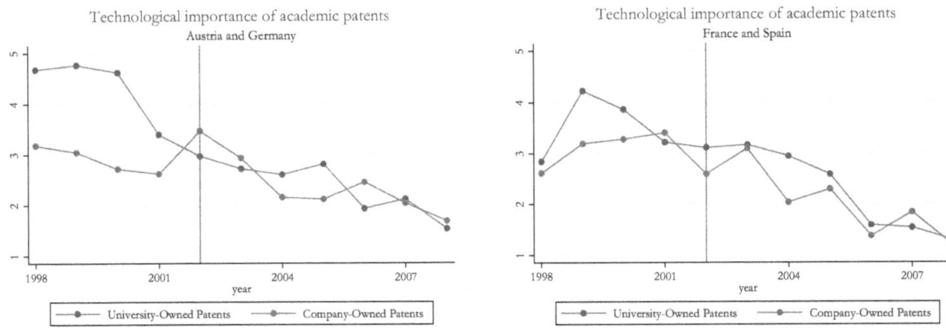

Figure 3. Quality of *Academic patents*: university- and company-owned.
Technological importance is measured by the long-term citations. Only patents assigned to domestic universities or domestic companies are considered in the analysis. *University-Owned academic patents* are those in which universities appear as the unique applicant in the European patent family protecting the invention (these figures include patents co-applied with non-university institutions). *Company-owned academic patents* are those invented by academics and assigned to solely domestic companies.

Table 8. Academic patenting activity, by type of first assignee (patent families).

	Number of *University-owned patents*	Number of *University-owned patents*	Number of *Company-owned Patents*	Number of *Academic patents*	Percentage of university-owned patents	Percentage of university-owned patents
	(a)	**(b)**	**(c)**	**(d)**	**[(a)/(d)]**	**[(b)/(d)]**
Germany	774	1092	1187	1863	41.5%	58.6%
Austria	51	63	30	93	54.8%	67.7%
Spain	179	202	304	506	35.4%	39.9%
France	265	728	666	1394	19.0%	52.2%

Only patents with a domestic university or domestic company as assignee are considered: patents assigned solely to individuals, public research organisations and foreign organisations are excluded. Only granted patents with priority years: 1998–2008. *University-owned patents* (Column a) are those in which a university appears as the priority applicant in the European patent family protecting the invention (these figures exclude patents co-applied with non-university institutions); In column (b) figures do include also co-applications with other types of assignees; (c) *Company-owned patents* are those where university researchers are listed as inventors in the patent document and the patent has been assigned solely to a company; (d) *Academic patents* are those in which university researchers appear as inventors, regardless the patent ownership.

to expect that exceptions only happened when the inventions were of sufficient quality to be worth the hassle. Secondly, an academic patent may be assigned to a company because it was the main funder of the academic research leading to the patented invention. The abolishment of the professor's privilege might have made clearer the legal IP environment, making more attractive for private companies the financing of university research. Finally, an academic patent may be owned by a company also when professors may have bypassed the university administration; and this may be more likely to happen when professors believe they have a high-valuable invention at hand (Carayol and Sterzi 2019).

Table 9. Academic inventions: Abolishment of the professor's privilege and long-term citations. PPML estimates.

	(1)	(2)	(3)	(4)	(5)	(6)	(7)
Post	−0.404***	−0.380***	−0.402***	0.147***			0.146***
	(0.00941)	(0.00238)	(0.00132)	(0.00726)			(0.00993)
Academic Patent	−0.0537	−0.197***	−0.275***	−0.289***	−0.274***	−0.274***	−0.288***
	(0.0759)	(0.0279)	(0.0201)	(0.0203)	(0.0205)	(0.0192)	(0.0198)
Academic Patent * University Ownership	0.463***	0.354***	0.446***	0.458***	0.448***	0.451***	0.461***
	(0.127)	(0.0653)	(0.0533)	(0.0544)	(0.0541)	(0.0467)	(0.0482)
Post * Academic Patent	0.256**	0.217***	0.238***	0.227***	0.205***	0.210***	0.234***
	(0.111)	(0.0542)	(0.0414)	(0.0362)	(0.0350)	(0.0285)	(0.0278)
Post* Academic Patent * University Ownership	**−0.518*** **	**−0.525*** **	**−0.479*** **	**−0.410*** **	**−0.378*** **	**−0.389*** **	**−0.426*** **
	(0.160)	**(0.0933)**	**(0.0788)**	**(0.0851)**	**(0.0868)**	**(0.0707)**	**(0.0645)**
Backward Citations			0.0535***	0.0554***	0.0554***	0.0553***	0.0554***
			(0.000765)	(0.000939)	(0.000836)	(0.000936)	(0.00107)
Number of Applicants			0.224***	0.223***	0.222***	0.227***	0.228***
			(0.0399)	(0.0353)	(0.0345)	(0.0327)	(0.0347)
Team Size			0.0834***	0.0840***	0.0836***	0.0842***	0.0846***
			(0.000660)	(0.000695)	(0.000722)	(0.00126)	(0.00116)
Trend				−0.105***			
				(0.00165)			
Constant	1.078***	0.738***	0.125***	211.1***	−0.735***	−0.493***	0.107***
	(0.00701)	(0.0146)	(0.0238)	(3.308)	(0.0183)	(0.0242)	(0.0282)
Observations	124,540	124,540	124,540	124,540	124,540	124,540	124,540
R-squared	0.015	0.057	0.083	0.092	0.095	0.096	0.093

Standard errors clustered at the country level are reported in parentheses. *** $p < 0.01$, ** $p < 0.05$, * $p < 0.1$.

8. Conclusions

As long as policymakers impose a single legal pathway for technology transfer, there is an increasing risk of placing obstacles in the way of formal (and informal) relationships between faculty and industry. The university ownership model is built upon a linear model of technology transfer that underestimates the importance of interactions between the inventor and licensee and, by contrast, overestimates the brokerage role played by the TTO.

This paper distinguishes between the technological importance of a patented invention and the exploitation of the related IP rights, which both contribute to generating the patent value.

We use long-term forward citations as a proxy for the technological importance of the invention, as they reflect the relevance of the patented knowledge in the technological domain and the extent to which it stimulates and facilitates further inventions. As our preferred proxy of the overall patent value we use the number of times a patent has been renewed; patent holders maintain their protection over time only if the value of the patent covers at least the cost of its renewal.

We exploit the heterogeneity characterising IP regimes for university inventions within and across countries in Europe, to estimate the impact of the change towards the predominant institutional ownership model on the technological importance of university-owned inventions and their value. We find a significant decrease in the technological importance of university inventions and their overall value in countries abolishing the professor's privilege; we control for changes in the dependent variables for university patents in the remaining countries and for company patents in their own countries. The negative effect on long-term citations, our preferred proxy for technological importance, is strongly significant and robust to different specifications.

As regards our estimates of the impact of change in the IP regime on patent value, we find strongly significant negative effects on renewals. Following the reform, university patents are on average renewed less often. The results are robust to the inclusion of technological importance as a determinant of patent value, suggesting that part of the lower number of renewals of university patents is due to inefficient IP exploitation strategies by TTO managers and university administrators.

Our findings are consistent with previous studies (Czarnitzki et al. 2015; Hvide and Jones 2018; Ejermo and Toivanen 2018) which have also found negative effects of abolishment on university patenting activity and entrepreneurship. They add a broad international dimension previously absent in the literature and show that econometric results are robust to different specifications and numerous controls.

Furthermore, by including in the analysis also academic patents, that is, patents in which university researchers appear as inventors regardless the patent ownership, we also provide additional evidence of an increase in the average technological quality of academic inventions owned by companies in countries abolishing the professor's privilege, consistent with a shift of ownership of the academic-invented patents of lower quality from professors and companies to universities.

Nevertheless, our study is not exempt from limitations. Further quantifiable information on technological importance, IP exploitation and patent value would be needed to ascertain the impact of change in the IP regime in the countries considered.

Qualitative information from interviews with university inventors and TTOs would also be useful, as well as case studies of university patent management before and after changes to the IP regime in a variety of countries, including information on academic entrepreneurship. The average negative effect on (long-term) citations and renewals (which remains even after controlling for country and sectoral differences) may be more noteworthy for some countries than others, or for some sectors than others. More research, to better understand the mechanisms driving the results is still required, but overall the evidence available indicates the need to consider alternative or complementary approaches to the model of university patent ownership and licencing through the TTOs. Bradley, Hayter, and Link (2013) argue that 'a linear model of technology transfer is no longer sufficient or perhaps even no longer relevant'. One of the drawbacks of this approach is that it has placed excessive emphasis on the importance of patents as the primary output in the technology transfer process, overlooking other mechanisms for commercialisation. These include joint laboratories between academia and industry, spinoffs, research contracts, sponsored research, researcher mobility, joint publications, conferences, expositions and specialised media, informal contacts with professional networks, the flow of graduates from university to industry or simply serendipity (Bercovitz and Feldman 2006; Heinzl et al. 2008).

Acknowledgments

We gratefully acknowledge funding from the French Agence Nationale de la Recherche (UTTO Project ANR-15-CE26-0005 and NPEIE Project ANR-17-CE26-0014-01), the Spanish Ministry of Economy and Competitiveness (CSO2016-79045-C2-1-R), the Regional Government of Madrid (PRODECON-CM, S2015/HUM-3491) and the CNRS-CSIC 2018 IRP ALLIES - Associated Laboratory on Linkages between Innovation and Environmental Sustainability. We wish to thank Nicolas Carayol, Elodie Carpentier, Chirantan Chatterjee, Alberto Galasso, Marco Giarratana, Francesco Lissoni, Gerard Llobet, Manuel Mira-Goudinho, Michele Pezzoni and seminar participants at the 2017 EPIP Conference, Bordeaux, at the 2017 PRODECON-CM Conference on Innovation and Industrial Organization, Madrid, at the 2019 Collegio Carlo Alberto Seminar in Turin, at the 2019 Catedra per al Foment de la Innovació Empresarial Seminar at Universitat Rovira I Virgili in Reus and at the 2019 University of Insubria, Economics Department Seminar, in Varese for helpful comments.

Disclosure statement

No potential conflict of interest was reported by the authors.

ORCID

Catalina Martínez http://orcid.org/0000-0003-1010-8384

References

Arqué-Castells, P., R. M. Cartaxo, J. García-Quevedo, and M. M. Godinho. 2016. "Royalty Sharing, Effort and Invention in Universities: Evidence from Portugal and Spain." *Research Policy* 45 (9): 1858–1872. doi:10.1016/j.respol.2016.06.006.

Backs, S., M. Günther, and C. Stummer. 2019. "Stimulating Academic Patenting in a University Ecosystem: An Agent-based Simulation Approach." *The Journal of Technology Transfer* 44 (2): 434–461. doi:10.1007/s10961-018-9697-x.

Bercovitz, J., and M. Feldman. 2006. "Entrepreneurial Universities and Technology Transfer: A Conceptual Framework for Understanding Knowledge-Based Economic Development." *Journal of Technology Transfer* 31: 175–188. doi:10.1007/s10961-005-5029-z.

Bessen J. 2008. The Value of US Patents by Owner and Patent Characteristics. *Research Policy* 5, 932–945.

Bradley, S., C. Hayter, and A. Link. 2013. "Models and Methods of University Technology Transfer." *Foundations and Trends in Entrepreneurship* 9 (6): 571–650. doi:10.1561/0300000048.

Callaert, J., M. Du Plessis, J. Grouwels, C. Lecocq, T. Magerman, B. Peeters, X. Song, B. Van Looy, and C. Vereyen 2011. "Patent Statistics at Eurostat: Methods for Regionalisation, Sector Allocation and Name Harmonisation." *Eurostat Methodologies and Working Papers*, 72 pp. Luxembourg: European Union.

Carayol, N., and E. Carpentier. 2019. "Two Decades of Academic Inventions in France." *Mimeo.*

Carayol, N., and V. Sterzi. 2019. *The Transfer and Value of Academic Inventions When The TTO is one option.* Mimeo.

Chardonnens, F. 2010. "Legislation and Technology Transfer in Switzerland." *Les Nouvelles, Licensing Executives Society International Journal.* December.

Cunningham, J. A., E. E. Lehmann, M. Menter, and N. Seitz. 2019. "The Impact of University Focused Technology Transfer Policies on Regional Innovation and Entrepreneurship." *The Journal of Technology Transfer* 44(5): 1451–1475.

Czarnitzki, D., D. Thorsten, K. Hussinger, P. Schliessler, and A. A. Toole. 2015. "Individual versus Institutional Ownership of University-discovered Inventions." *ZEW Discussion paper*, no. 15-007.

Czarnitzki, D., K. Hussinger, and C. Schneider. 2012. "The Nexus between Science and Industry: Evidence from Faculty Inventions." *The Journal of Technology Transfer* 37 (5): 755–776. doi:10.1007/s10961-011-9214-y.

Damsgaard, E. F., and M. C. Thursby. 2013. "University Entrepreneurship and Professor Privilege." *Industrial and Corporate Change* 22 (1): 183–218. doi:10.1093/icc/dts047.

Della Malva, A., F. Lissoni, and P. Llerena. 2013. "Institutional Change and Academic Patenting: French Universities and the Innovation Act of 1999." *Journal of Evolutionary Economics* 23 (1): 211–239. doi:10.1007/s00191-011-0243-3.

Dornbusch, F., U. Schmoch, N. Schulze, and N. Bethke. 2012. "Identification of University-based Patents: A New Large-scale Approach." *Research Evaluation* 22 (1): 52–63. doi:10.1093/reseval/rvs033.

Eisenberg, R. S. 1996. "Public Research and Private Development: Patents and Technology Transfer in Government-sponsored Research." *Virginia Law Review* 1663–1727. doi:10.2307/1073686.

Ejermo, O., and H. Toivanen. 2018. "University Invention and the Abolishment of the Professor's Privilege in Finland." *Research Policy* 47 (4): 814–825. doi:10.1016/j.respol.2018.03.001.

Evans, D., and L. S. Leighton. 1989. "Some Empirical Aspects of Entrepreneurship." *American Economic Review* 79 (3): 519–535.

Geuna, A., and F. Rossi. 2011. "Changes to University IPR Regulations in Europe and the Impact on Academic Patenting." *Research Policy* 40 (8): 1068–1076. doi:10.1016/j.respol.2011.05.008.

Greenbaum, D., and C. Scott. 2010. "Hochschullehrerprivileg - Modern Incarnation of the Professor's Privilege to Promote University to Industry Technology Transfer." *Science, Technology and Society* 15: 55–76. doi:10.1177/097172180901500103.

Grimaldi, R., M. Kenney, D. Siegel, and M. Wright. 2011. "30 Years after Bayh–Dole: Reassessing Academic Entrepreneurship." *Research Policy* 40: 1045–1057. doi:10.1016/j.respol.2011.04.005.

Hall, B. H., A. Jaffe, and M. Trajtenberg. 2005. "Market Value and Patent Citations." *Rand Journal of Economics* 36(1): 16–38.

Hamilton, B. H. 2000. "Does Entrepreneurship Pay? an Empirical Analysis of the Returns to Self-Employment." *Journal of Political Economy* 108 (3): 604–631. doi:10.1086/262131.

Harhoff, D., F. Narin, F. M. Scherer, and K. Vopel. 1999. "Citation frequency and the value of patented inventions." *Review of Economics and Statistics* 81 (3): 511–515.

Harhoff, D., F. M. Scherer, and K. Vopel. 2003. "Citations, Family Size, Opposition and the Value of Patent Rights." *Research Policy* 32 (8): 1343–1363. doi:10.1016/S0048-7333(02)00124-5.

Harhoff, D., and M. Reitzig. 2004. "Determinants of Opposition against EPO Patent Grants - the Case of Biotechnology and Pharmaceuticals." *International Journal of Industrial Organization* 22 (4): 443–480. doi:10.1016/j.ijindorg.2004.01.001.

Heinzl, J., A. Kor, G. Orange, and H. Kaufmann, 2008. "Technology Transfer Model for Austrian Higher Education Institutions." paper presented at the European and Mediterranean Conference on Information Systems, Dubai (UAE), May 25-26.

Henderson, R., A. B. Jaffe, and M. Trajtenberg. 1998. "Universities as a Source of Commercial Technology: A Detailed Analysis of University Patenting, 1965–1988." *Review of Economics and Statistics* 80 (1): 119–127. doi:10.1162/003465398557221.

Hovenkamp, H., M. Janis, M. Lemley, and C. Leslie. 2013. *IP and Antitrust: An Analysis of Antitrust Principles Applied to Intellectual Property Law.* Austin: Aspen Publishers.

Hvide, H. K., and B. F. Jones. 2018. "University Innovation and the Professor's Privilege." *American Economic Review* 108 (7): 1860–1898. doi:10.1257/aer.20160284.

Iversen, E., M. Gulbrandsen, and A. Klitkou. 2007. "A Baseline for the Impact of Academic Patenting Legislation in Norway." *Scientometrics* 70: 393–414. doi:10.1007/s11192-007-0209-2.

Jaffe, A., and G. De Rassenfosse. 2017. "Patent Citation Data in Social Science Research: Overview and Best Practices." *Journal of the Association for Information Science and Technology* 68 (6): 1360–1374. doi:10.1002/asi.2017.68.issue-6.

Kenney, M., and D. Patton. 2011. "Does Inventor Ownership Encourage University Research-derived Entrepreneurship? A Six University Comparison." *Research Policy* 40: 1100–1112. doi:10.1016/j.respol.2011.05.012.

Lach, S., and M. Schankerman. 2008. "Incentives and invention in Universities." *RAND Journal of Economics* 39 (2): 403–433.

Lanjouw, J. O., and M. Schankerman. 2004. "Patent Quality and Research Productivity: Measuring Innovation with Multiple Indicators." *The Economic Journal* 114 (495): 441–465. doi:10.1111/j.1468-0297.2004.00216.x.

Lissoni, F. 2012. "Academic Patenting in Europe: An Overview of Recent Research and New Perspectives." *World Patent Information* 34 (3): 197–205. doi:10.1016/j.wpi.2012.03.002.

Lissoni, F., M. Pezzoni, B. Poti, and S. Romagnosi. 2013. "University Autonomy, the Professor's Privilege and Academic Patenting: Italy, 1996–2007." *Industry and Innovation* 20 (5): 399–421. doi:10.1080/13662716.2013.824192.

Lissoni, F., P. Llerena, M. Mckelvey, and B. Sanditov. 2008. "Academic Patenting in Europe: newevidence from the KENIS database." *Research Evaluation* 17 (2): 87–102.

Loise, V., and A. J. Stevens. 2010. "The Bayh-Dole Act Turns 30." *Science translational medicine* (52): 52.

Maraut, S., and C. Martínez. 2014. "Identifying author–inventors from Spain: Methods and a firstinsight into Results." *Scientometrics* 101 (1): 445–476.

Martinez, C. 2011. "Patent Families: When Do Different Definitions Really Matter?" *Scientometrics* 86 (1): 39–63. doi:10.1007/s11192-010-0251-3.

Martinez, C., and V. Sterzi. 2019. "University Patenting and the Quest for Technology Transfer Policy Models in Europe." In *Handbook of Universities and Regional Development*, Chapter 8, edited by A. Varga and K. Erdos (pp. 111–150). Edward Elgar, Cheltenham, UK.

Martínez, C., J. M. Azagra-Caro, and S. Maraut. 2013. "Academic inventors, scientific impact and the institutionalisation of Pasteur's Quadrant in Spain." *Industry and Innovation* 20 (5): 438–455.

Martínez, C., and L. Bares. 2018. "The Link between Technology Transfer and International Extension of University Patents: Evidence from Spain." *Science and Public Policy* 45 (6): 827–842. doi:10.1093/scipol/scy008.

Mejer, M. 2011. "Entrepreneurial Scientists and Their Publication Performance. An Insight from Belgium. ECARES Working Paper 2011-017." European Center for Advanced Research in Economics and Statistics. Université Libre de Bruxelles. Brussels.

Mowery, D., and B. Sampat. 2005. "The Bayh-Dole Act of 1980 and University-Industry Technology Transfer: A Model for Other OECD Governments?" *Journal of Technology Transfer* 30: 115–127. doi:10.1007/s10961-004-4361-z.

Rosell, C., and A. Agrawal. 2009. "Have University Knowledge Flows Narrowed? Evidence from Patent Data." *Research Policy* 38: 1–13. doi:10.1016/j.respol.2008.07.014.

Rosenbaum, P. R., and D.B. Rubin. 1983. "The Central Role Of The Propensity Score in Observational Studies for Causal Effects." *Biometrika* 70 (1): 41–55.

Sampat, B. N., D. C. Mowery, and A. A. Ziedonis. 2003. "Changes in University Patent Quality after the Bayh-Dole Act: A Re-examination." *International Journal of Industrial Organization* 21 (9): 1371–1390. doi:10.1016/S0167-7187(03)00087-0.

Schacht, W. 2012. "The Bayh-Dole Act: Selected Issues in Patent Policy and the Commercialization of Technology." *CRS Report for Congress*. https://fas.org/sgp/crs/misc/RL32076.pdf

Schmoch, U. 2007. "Patentanmeldungen Aus Deutschen Hochschulen." Studien zum deutschen Innovationssystem no. 10-2007. doi:10.1094/PDIS-91-4-0467B.

Schmoch, U. 2008. "Concept of a Technology Classification for Country Comparisons." Final report to the World Intellectual Property Office (WIPO). Karlsruhe: Fraunhofer ISI.

Schoen, A., D. Heinisch, and G. Buenstorf. 2014. "Playing the 'name Game'to Identify Academic Patents in Germany." *Scientometrics* 101 (1): 527–545. doi:10.1007/s11192-014-1400-x.

Shane, S., E. A. Locke, and C. J. Collins. 2003. "Entrepreneurial Motivation." *Human Resource Management Review* 13 (2): 257–279. doi:10.1016/S1053-4822(03)00017-2.

Spilling, O. R., S. B. Brorstad, E. J. Iversen, E. Rasmussen, and E. Solberg. 2015. "Virkemiddelapparatet for Kommersialisering Av Forskning – Status Og Utfordringer (Kap 2: Patentering) Rapport 18/2015."

Squicciarini, M., H. Dernis, and C. Criscuolo 2013. "Measuring Patent Quality: Indicators of Technological and Economic Value." OECD Science, Technology and Industry Working Papers, 3.

Stephan, P. 1996. "The Economics of Science." *Journal of Economic Literature* 34 (3): 1199–1235.

Sterzi, V. 2013. "Patent Quality and Ownership: An Analysis of UK Faculty Patenting." *Research Policy* 42 (2): 564–576. doi:10.1016/j.respol.2012.07.010.

Sterzi, V., M. Pezzoni, and F. Lissoni. 2019. "Patent Management by Universities: Evidence from Italian Academic Inventions." *Industrial and Corporate Change* 28 (2): 309–330. doi:10.1093/icc/dty070.

Takenaka, T. 2005. "Technology Licensing and University Research in Japan." *International Journal of Intellectual Property Law, Economy and Management* 1 (1): 27–36. doi:10.2321/ijip.1.27.

Valentin, F., and R. L. Jensen. 2007. "Effects on Academia-industry Collaboration of Extending University Property Rights." *The Journal of Technology Transfer* 32 (3): 251–276. doi:10.1007/s10961-006-9015-x.

Von Proff, S., G. Buenstorf, and M. Hummel. 2012. "University Patenting in Germany before and after 2002: What Role Did the Professors' Privilege Play?" *Industry and Innovation* 19: 23–44. doi:10.1080/13662716.2012.649060.

Webb, C., H. Dernis, D. Harhoff, and K. Hoisl. 2005. "Analysing European and International Patent Citations: A Set of EPO Patent Database Building Blocks." OECD STI Working Paper 2005/9.

Zuniga, P. 2011. "The State of Patenting at Research Institutions in Developing Countries: Policy Approaches and Practices." *WIPO Economic Research Working Papers*, 4.

APPENDIX

APPENDIX A1. Further results

Table A1. IQ model: The abolishment of the professor's privilege and long-term citations from companies. PPML estimates.

	(1)	(2)	(3)	(4)	(5)	(6)	(7)
Post	−0.562***	−0.570***	−0.608***	−0.208***			−0.206***
	(0.0417)	(0.0330)	(0.0266)	(0.0283)			(0.0333)
University	−0.0204	−0.148***	−0.137***	−0.0845**	−0.0976**	−0.136***	−0.123***
	(0.0479)	(0.0417)	(0.0413)	(0.0388)	(0.0397)	(0.0397)	(0.0400)
Treat	−0.168**	−0.141**	−0.170**	−0.161**	−0.165**	0.0484	0.119
	(0.0796)	(0.0711)	(0.0719)	(0.0734)	(0.0729)	(0.134)	(0.150)
Post*Treat	0.0519	0.0667	0.0757*	0.0638	0.0643	0.0337	0.0244
	(0.0546)	(0.0485)	(0.0433)	(0.0424)	(0.0432)	(0.0320)	(0.0328)
Post*University	−0.0483	−0.0518	−0.0650	−0.112*	−0.0884	−0.0827	−0.113**
	(0.0622)	(0.0584)	(0.0569)	(0.0610)	(0.0601)	(0.0536)	(0.0533)
Treat*University	0.279***	0.267***	0.244***	0.254***	0.249***	0.324***	0.326***
	(0.0821)	(0.0835)	(0.0805)	(0.0818)	(0.0818)	(0.0981)	(0.0970)
Post*Treat*University	**−0.572*** **	**−0.571*** **	**−0.495*** **	**−0.481*** **	**−0.440*** **	**−0.478*** **	**−0.523*** **
	(0.0631)	(0.0611)	(0.0590)	(0.0633)	(0.0642)	(0.0589)	(0.0711)
Backward citations			0.0543***	0.0569***	0.0567***	0.0556***	0.0558***
			(0.00233)	(0.00247)	(0.00234)	(0.00174)	(0.00180)
Number of applicants			0.249***	0.234***	0.240***	0.230***	0.228***
			(0.0397)	(0.0322)	(0.0343)	(0.0310)	(0.0312)
Team size			0.0709***	0.0752***	0.0744***	0.0764***	0.0770***
			(0.00349)	(0.00405)	(0.00406)	(0.00423)	(0.00405)
Trend				−0.0443***			
				(0.00214)			
Constant	0.977***	0.714***	0.106	88.56***	−0.969***	−1.049***	−0.172**
	(0.0765)	(0.0660)	(0.0962)	(4.270)	(0.112)	(0.0818)	(0.0843)
Technological field dummies	NO	YES	YES	YES	YES	YES	YES
Year dummies	NO	NO	NO	NO	YES	YES	NO
Country dummies	NO	NO	NO	NO	NO	YES	YES
Country*Trend	NO	NO	NO	NO	NO	NO	YES
Observations	363,729	363,729	363,729	363,729	363,729	363,729	363,729

Standard errors clustered at the country level are reported in parentheses. *** $p < 0.01$, ** $p < 0.05$, * $p < 0.1$.

Table A2. IQ model: the abolishment of the professor's privilege and originality. OLS estimates.

	(1)	(2)	(3)	(4)	(5)	(6)	(7)
Post	0.0350***	0.0422***	0.0321***	−0.0124***			−0.00573***
	(0.00410)	(0.00298)	(0.00170)	(0.00320)			(0.000750)
University	0.0275**	0.00152	0.0141**	0.00835	0.00798	0.00254	0.00368
	(0.00927)	(0.00656)	(0.00542)	(0.00522)	(0.00530)	(0.00591)	(0.00596)
Treat	0.00118	0.00294	0.00242	0.00129	0.00119	0.0172**	0.0107
	(0.00965)	(0.00616)	(0.00545)	(0.00538)	(0.00538)	(0.00701)	(0.0101)
Post*Treat	0.00259	0.00381	0.00379*	0.00520**	0.00506**	0.00398**	−0.00516***
	(0.00424)	(0.00306)	(0.00173)	(0.00169)	(0.00170)	(0.00144)	(0.00107)
Post*University	−0.0158	−0.0246**	−0.0193	−0.0142	−0.0138	−0.0119	−0.0134
	(0.00939)	(0.00947)	(0.0109)	(0.0113)	(0.0113)	(0.0105)	(0.0103)
Treat*University	−0.00798	0.00179	−0.00703	−0.00843*	−0.00856*	−0.00199	−0.00316
	(0.00936)	(0.00613)	(0.00456)	(0.00428)	(0.00427)	(0.00513)	(0.00530)
Post*Treat*University	**−0.0151**	**−0.0179***	**−0.00162**	**−0.00266**	**−0.00142**	**−0.00388**	**−0.00333**
	(0.00951)	(0.00926)	(0.0108)	(0.0113)	(0.0110)	(0.0105)	(0.0104)
Backward citations			0.0309***	0.0307***	0.0307***	0.0306***	0.0306***
			(0.000951)	(0.000958)	(0.000967)	(0.000933)	(0.000924)
Number of applicants			0.0105***	0.0118***	0.0120***	0.0109***	0.0102***
			(0.00278)	(0.00223)	(0.00227)	(0.00276)	(0.00291)
Team size			0.00669***	0.00623***	0.00622***	0.00627***	0.00631***
			(0.000634)	(0.000612)	(0.000609)	(0.000607)	(0.000617)
Trend				0.00497***			
				(0.000311)			
Constant	0.619***	0.554***	0.400***	−9.514***	0.372***	0.362***	0.415***
	(0.00955)	(0.00770)	(0.00655)	(0.617)	(0.00590)	(0.00649)	(0.0109)
Technological field dummies	NO	YES	YES	YES	YES	YES	YES
Year dummies	NO	NO	NO	NO	YES	YES	NO
Country dummies	NO	NO	NO	NO	NO	YES	YES
Country*Trend	NO	NO	NO	NO	NO	NO	YES
Observations	358,695	358,695	358,695	358,695	358,695	358,695	358,695

Standard errors clustered at the country level are reported in parentheses. *** $p < 0.01$, ** $p < 0.05$, * $p < 0.1$. Descriptive statistics of the sample are given in Table 5.

Table A3. PV model: the abolishment of the professor's privilege and family size. PPML estimates.

	(1)	(2)	(3)	(4)	(5)	(6)	(7)	(8)
Post	−0.128***	−0.0890***	−0.0715***	−0.0836***	−0.0722***			−0.0615***
	(0.0336)	(0.0331)	(0.0271)	(0.0269)	(0.0206)			(0.0117)
University	−0.0245	−0.0854***	−0.246***	−0.248***	−0.247***	−0.252***	−0.255***	−0.250***
	(0.0300)	(0.0238)	(0.0401)	(0.0444)	(0.0442)	(0.0445)	(0.0349)	(0.0332)
Treat	−0.315***	−0.287***	−0.251***	−0.267***	−0.267***	−0.270***	−0.157***	−0.167***
	(0.0582)	(0.0441)	(0.0345)	(0.0362)	(0.0362)	(0.0359)	(0.0508)	(0.0426)
Post*Treat	0.0573	0.0424	0.0467*	0.0530*	0.0527*	0.0534*	0.0436	0.0258**
	(0.0351)	(0.0322)	(0.0281)	(0.0278)	(0.0278)	(0.0285)	(0.0282)	(0.0109)
Post*University	−0.0577	−0.0182	−0.0526	−0.0597*	−0.0610*	−0.0521*	−0.0490*	−0.0531***
	(0.0465)	(0.0392)	(0.0329)	(0.0324)	(0.0319)	(0.0305)	(0.0288)	(0.0169)
Treat*University	0.123***	0.0851	0.114**	0.115**	0.116**	0.115**	0.140***	0.141***
	(0.0464)	(0.0875)	(0.0563)	(0.0550)	(0.0549)	(0.0537)	(0.0362)	(0.0324)
Post*Treat*University	**−0.152*** **	**−0.101**	**−0.121***	**−0.111***	**−0.110***	**−0.0976**	**−0.126*** **	**−0.139*** **
	(0.0590)	(0.0968)	(0.0711)	(0.0658)	(0.0662)	(0.0654)	(0.0507)	(0.0419)
Long-term citations		0.0213***	0.0163***	0.0154***	0.0154***	0.0151***	0.0143***	0.0144***
		(0.00232)	(0.00135)	(0.00123)	(0.00125)	(0.00124)	(0.00140)	(0.00146)
Backward citations				0.000125	0.000201	0.000172	−0.000126	0.000468
				(0.00144)	(0.00146)	(0.00143)	(0.00135)	(0.00134)
Number of applicants				0.0478***	0.0475***	0.0503***	0.0427***	0.0379***
				(0.0118)	(0.0116)	(0.0110)	(0.0110)	(0.0108)
Team size				0.0316***	0.0317***	0.0316***	0.0336***	0.0339***
				(0.00194)	(0.00185)	(0.00183)	(0.00125)	(0.00123)
Trend					−0.00128			
					(0.00168)			
Constant	2.085***	1.984***	1.843***	1.752***	4.310	1.733***	1.665***	1.684***
	(0.0473)	(0.0392)	(0.0434)	(0.0362)	(3.375)	(0.0348)	(0.0454)	(0.0375)
Technological field dummies	NO	NO	YES	YES	YES	YES	YES	YES
Year dummies	NO	NO	NO	NO	NO	YES	YES	NO
Country dummies	NO	NO	NO	NO	NO	NO	YES	YES
Country*Trend	NO	NO	NO	NO	NO	NO	NO	YES
Observations	363,729	363,729	363,729	363,729	363,729	363,729	363,729	363,729

Standard errors clustered at the country level are reported in parentheses. *** $p < 0.01$, ** $p < 0.05$, * $p < 0.1$. Descriptive statistics of the sample are shown in Table 4.

APPENDIX A2. Propensity score matching (patent management model)

The sample used in the main analysis of the paper (Sections 5 and 6) consists of 363,729 granted patents, of which only 4,047 patents are university patents, representing 1.1% of the sample. In order to reduce heterogeneity and to construct a more balanced sample of patents applied for by companies and universities of similar characteristics (with the exception of the number of renewals and family size), we apply propensity score matching (PSM); we calculate the predicted probability of each patent being applied for by a university (university patent) or a company (company patent) according to its characteristics, as they appear in the list of independent variables in Model (2b). Subsequently, for each university patent we select from the pool of company patents that having the closest propensity score.[24] Our final sample is thus composed of 4,043[25] university patents and 4,043 company patents of similar characteristics, with the exception of the number of renewals, our dependent variable. With regard to the quality of the match, Figure A1 below displays the Kernel distribution for the two groups of patents (university and company patents) before and after the matching, when the nearest-neighbour algorithm is implemented. Prior to the matching, the shape of the distribution differs and there is only a partial overlap between the distributions of the propensity score of the two groups. After the matching, the two shapes are almost identical, suggesting that the PSM has been successful in correcting for the selection bias. Table A4 presents descriptive statistics.

Due to the PSM, we are now comparing university patents and company patents of similar characteristics allowing us to speculate that the difference in the number of renewals is linked principally to the difference in the effectiveness of the IP *exploitation*.

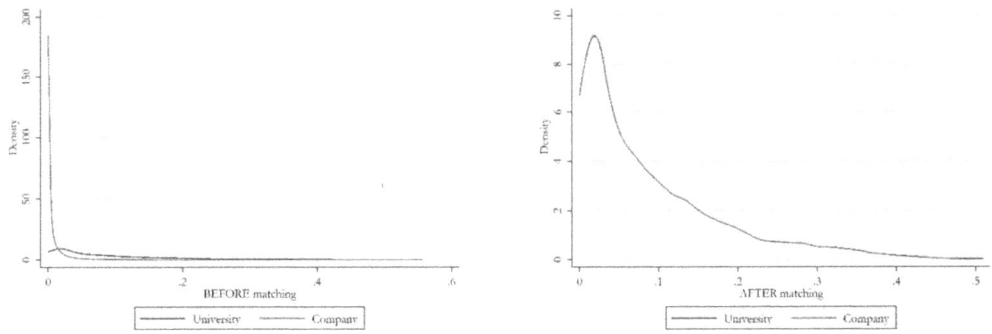

Figure A1. Distributions of the propensity score for university and company patents before and after matching.

Table A4. Descriptive statistics for the principal variables in the unmatched and matched sample.

	Unmatched				Matched			
	University	Company	%Bias	T-test	University	Company	%Bias	T-test
Long-term citations	4.62	3.05	25.4	19.45	4.62	4.74	−2.0	−0.73
Backward citations	3.31	4.11	−34.5	−22.95	3.31	3.37	−2.6	−1.21
Number of applicants	1.06	1.03	12.8	9.84	1.06	1.04	5.0	2.05
Team size	2.94	2.39	33.1	21.28	2.94	3.01	−4.4	−1.67

Other variables included in the PSM and not reported in Table A4 are dummies for the country of the applicant, the priority year and the technological field.

[24]The STATA module *psmatch2* has been used for matching. We adopt the nearest-neighbour algorithm (Rosenbaum and Rubin 1983) and we match each university patent to a company patent.

[25]Three university patents have not been matched to any company patent.

The PPML results based on the PSM are depicted in Table A5. The results are very similar to those produced when all patents are used. Conditional on the observed technological importance (IQ) of the invention[26], as proxied by the number of long-term citations, university patents receive fewer renewals, suggesting that TTO managers exploit patents less effectively. University patents, compared to company patents, have similar observable characteristics, but are expected to be renewed less often. Moreover, in the years following abolishment, the average patent management quality declines still further.

[26]After matching (as shown in Table A4), the averages of invention quality (IQ, long-term citations) are not statistically different in the group of university patents and company patents, confirming that the balance of covariates has been successfully achieved; prior to PSM, universities receive 4.62 (long-term) citations and company patents only 3.05. After matching, the difference between the two groups disappears (t-test of 0.73).

Table A5. PV model: the abolishment of the professor's privilege and renewals. Conditional PPML.

	(1)	(2)	(3)	(4)	(5)	(6)	(7)	(8)
Post	−0.377***	−0.356***	−0.357***	−0.357***	−0.102***			−0.120***
	(0.00500)	(0.00714)	(0.00746)	(0.00731)	(0.0295)			(0.0213)
University	−0.0305**	−0.0279**	−0.0315***	−0.0302***	−0.0296**	−0.0278**	−0.0293**	−0.0317**
	(0.0128)	(0.0116)	(0.0108)	(0.0105)	(0.0140)	(0.0129)	(0.0127)	(0.0132)
Treat	−0.00432	0.0109	0.00705	0.00734	0.0159	0.0112	−0.210***	87.85***
	(0.0133)	(0.0129)	(0.0113)	(0.0111)	(0.0100)	(0.0113)	(0.0709)	(2.957)
Post*Treat	0.0169***	0.0105	0.00927	0.00946	0.00288	0.00692	0.0107	0.106***
	(0.00605)	(0.00853)	(0.00899)	(0.00884)	(0.00619)	(0.00710)	(0.00882)	(0.0231)
Post*University	0.0357***	0.0360***	0.0361***	0.0329***	0.0278**	0.0195*	0.0192*	0.0291**
	(0.00956)	(0.00982)	(0.0110)	(0.0109)	(0.0121)	(0.0112)	(0.0113)	(0.0115)
Treat*University	0.0247	0.0112	0.0191	0.0186	0.0281	0.0176	0.0165	0.0298
	(0.0287)	(0.0313)	(0.0285)	(0.0290)	(0.0281)	(0.0307)	(0.0322)	(0.0302)
Post*Treat*University	**−0.107*** **	**−0.0939*** **	**−0.0946*** **	**−0.0915*** **	**−0.0885*** **	**−0.0618** **	**−0.0596** **	**−0.0871*** **
	(0.0145)	(0.0168)	(0.0162)	(0.0164)	(0.0187)	(0.0263)	(0.0276)	(0.0213)
Long-term citations		0.00708***	0.00714***	0.00702***	0.00625***	0.00594***	0.00602***	0.00625***
		(0.000527)	(0.000554)	(0.000555)	(0.000552)	(0.000477)	(0.000442)	(0.000459)
Backward citations				0.00312**	0.00491***	0.00428***	0.00420***	0.00481***
				(0.00138)	(0.00160)	(0.00127)	(0.00134)	(0.00164)
Number of applicants				0.0377	0.0405*	0.0425**	0.0397**	0.0395*
				(0.0281)	(0.0216)	(0.0183)	(0.0196)	(0.0239)
Team size					0.00223	0.00204	0.00154	0.00172
					(0.00240)	(0.00255)	(0.00263)	(0.00230)
Trend					−0.0317***			
					(0.00357)			
Constant	2.534***	2.484***	2.449***	2.398***	65.61***	2.408***	2.548***	2.371***
	(0.00733)	(0.0103)	(0.0318)	(0.0352)	(7.130)	(0.0326)	(0.0772)	(0.0666)
Technological field dummies	NO	NO	YES	YES	YES	YES	YES	YES
Year dummies	NO	NO	NO	NO	NO	YES	YES	NO
Country dummies	NO	NO	NO	NO	NO	NO	YES	YES
Country*Trend	NO	NO	NO	NO	NO	NO	NO	YES
Observations	8,086	8,086	8,086	8,086	8,086	8,086	8,086	8,086

Standard errors clustered at the country level are reported in parentheses. *** $p < 0.01$, ** $p < 0.05$, * $p < 0.1$. The sample is composed of 4,043 university patents matched to 4,043 company patents in the same technological field and having the same priority

A burden of knowledge creation in academic research: evidence from publication data

Sascha Schweitzer and Jan Brendel

ABSTRACT

Academic research is vital for innovation and industrial growth. However, a potential burden of processing ever more knowledge could be affecting research output and researchers' careers. We look at a dataset of researchers who have published in journals in the field of economics during a period of 45 years. For a subset of these researchers, we amass data from journals listed in the EconLit database, supplemented with years of birth from public sources. Our results show an increase in the age of researchers at their first publication, in the number of articles referenced in debut articles, and in the number of co-authors. Simultaneously, we observe a decline in the probability of researchers changing research fields. Our findings extend earlier findings on patents and hint at a burden of knowledge pervading different areas of human progress. Moreover, our results indicate that researchers develop strategies of specialisation to deal with this challenge.

1. Introduction

The impact of science as a source of industrial growth is indisputable (Solow 1962; Stephan 1996). Therefore, the production of scientific knowledge is a vital policy goal and diverse attempts have been made at its scholarly investigation and measurement. In his seminal work, Price (1963) reports a doubling of scientific knowledge every 10 to 15 years. Bibliometric studies such as Tague, Beheshti, and Rees-Potter (1981), Archibald and Line (1991), or Fernández-Cano, Torralbo, and Vallejo (2004) confirm the continuation of scientific growth over the recent decades. However, as noted by Jones (2009) and Bloom et al. (2017), this growth is enabled by an increasing number of researchers who operate, like all humans, within the natural limits of their cognitive abilities (Miller 1955; Kotovsky, Hayes, and Simon 1985; Marois and Ivanoff 2005). Researchers spend a significant time in school, in Ph.D. programmes, and in research positions, studying the prerequisite knowledge that will enable them to contribute to their field. Each of their contributions further adds to the body of knowledge that future researchers study before they contribute new insights themselves. The question of this paper is whether climbing the growing mountain of scientific knowledge is taking more and more time and effort.

Jones (2009) introduced the term burden of knowledge to describe a potential slowdown of innovation due to an accumulation of pre-existing knowledge. He examines a sample of US data on patents and inventors. For this sample, he obtains the age of inventors at their first invention, the amount of preceding knowledge measured by the references given in the corresponding patents, the size of inventor teams, and the probability of switching between technological fields from one patent to the next (measuring the degree of an inventor's specialisation). He reports increasing age at first invention and increasing specialisation. These results are in line with a general slowdown of productivity in knowledge creation reported by previous literature (Schankerman and Pakes 1986; Evenson 1993; Arbesman 2011; also cf. literature section).

Our study bridges the gap between research on the burden of knowledge in patenting and scientometric research on academic publishing. In contrast to patent research such as Jones (2009) and Melero and Palomeras (2015), we empirically test the burden of knowledge hypothesis in academic research. We adopt methods used previously for patent data, since the data structures of documents and meta information such as author names and citations are similar (cf. the literature section for a more elaborate comparison of incentives in industrial vs. academic publishing). In contrast to scientometric studies on life-cycle productivity in economics (e.g. Oster and Hamermesh 1998; McDowell and Singell 2000; Conley and Önder 2014), our measurement approach focuses on the beginning of an academic researcher's life-cycle, which is the threshold when a researcher first transitions from mere knowledge absorption to new knowledge creation. For this purpose, we modify measures established in patent research such as the number of references and team size. Moreover, we employ novel measures such as authors' field jumps and age at first publication that characterise how individuals can be affected by the burden of knowledge mechanism.

For our analysis, we compile a sample of economists and their careers over the 45 year-period from 1970 to 2014. To construct the sample, age data was collected from publicly available resources and combined with a dataset of scientific publications from *EconLit*. The field of economics affords us two main advantages as a subject of investigation: First, the Journal of Economic Literature (JEL) has established a consistent classification system that is applied by most economics journals. This allows us to consistently examine subfields within economics that individuals contribute to over time and across journals. Second, we are interested in the effect of the burden of knowledge on individuals rather than organisations. An author-centred research field such as economics makes it relatively easy to attribute research outcomes to individual researchers. Laboratory-centred fields such as some areas of natural sciences make this attribution less clear-cut, because up to thousands of researchers can be included as co-authors of a single article (Castelvecchi 2015). Four indicators serve as proxies for measuring the burden of knowledge: The *age* of researchers at their first article in a journal covered by *EconLit* indicates how long it takes researchers to process the base knowledge they will eventually contribute to. The number of *references* in single-author debut articles serves as a proxy for the quantity of prerequisite knowledge processed by the author. The *specialisation* of innovators indicates how broadly they can cover different fields. We measure specialisation by computing how likely researchers jump from one JEL field to another between successive publications. According to the model of Jones (2009), researchers should compensate for their increasing specialisation by dividing labour among multiple contributors. Thus, team size measured by the number of co-authors is the fourth proxy for this analysis. A detailed description of how the four proxies are computed from the data is given in the third section 'Data'.

We define our main hypotheses based on the assumption that the newly developed proxies for the burden of knowledge in academic research behave consistently with the burden of knowledge model by Jones (2009). The hypotheses thus expect the following time trends:

H1: The age of researchers at their first article increases.

H2: The number of references in single-author debut articles increases.

H3: The likelihood of field jumps between successive publications decreases.

H4: The number of co-authors of an article increases.

In the following section, we provide an overview of how our hypotheses and findings relate to the existing literature. In the later sections of this paper, we present the data and results with respect to the hypotheses. Note that rather than establishing causality, our research provides data and examines its consistency with the burden of knowledge hypothesis. Similarly to related studies that focus on time as an independent variable such as Jones (2009) and Hamermesh (2013), we likewise consider several additional individual and institutional factors and their consistency with the empirical results. Given the scope of our dataset, the findings of this study are limited to academic publishing in economics and do not necessarily extend to other domains. Nevertheless, the more evidence can be gathered from different areas of knowledge creation, the more complete our understanding of the burden of knowledge mechanism will become.

2. Related literature

There is a large body of literature on the nature and determinants of *knowledge growth*. During the past decades, there have been several indications for a slowdown of knowledge growth. For example, for scientific discovery, Arbesman (2011) finds that the discovery of mammalian species, chemical elements, and minor planets is becoming increasingly difficult. For economics research, Ellison (2002) observes that the review process has become more cumbersome. For technological Evenson (1984, 1993) reports decreasing per capita returns from research and development expenditures; Kortum (1993) finds decreasing patent to research and development ratios; and Schankerman and Pakes (1986, 1072, Table 6) report decreasing patent applications and patent values per inventor.

We contribute to this literature by investigating a fundamental limitation of knowledge growth that is predicted by the burden of knowledge model by Jones (2009). According to Jones, human capital differs from other stock variables in that it cannot be transferred easily: 'The vessel of human capital – the individual – is born with little knowledge and absorbs information at a limited rate' (p. 283). Jones argues that this limitation makes human capital vulnerable to a *burden of knowledge* that consists of two aspects: Firstly, new knowledge usually builds on existing knowledge, which implies that existing knowledge must be processed before moving beyond the existing limits. As the knowledge available to researchers in books, databases, and from other sources increases over the course of history, scientists and inventors need to assimilate a growing body of knowledge before they can create new knowledge. Secondly, the open problems that remain to be solved might be increasingly difficult. This is because, given a set of problems to choose from, a rational researcher would first tackle those problems with the highest expected return for the expected effort.[1]

To understand the context in which the burden of knowledge affects research output, consider the following three aspects: First, *individual life-cycle productivity* has been identified as a key ingredient as well as limitation of knowledge growth. Second, it is well known that individual researchers make their career decisions in the respective *incentive structures* of academia and industry. Third, researchers have developed various *strategies to deal with* the burden of knowledge such as the collaboration with co-authors. We will briefly discuss each of these aspects in the following.

2.1. Individual life-cycle productivity

The earliest research on individual life-cycle productivity that influenced the present study dates back to the 1950s. Lehman (1953, 1962) studies personal vitae of scientists and people in leading positions such as statesmen or college presidents, and finds that for most areas the 'rate for creative work of the highest quality' grows until an individual's thirties and declines thereafter. Similar observations of an inverse U-shaped pattern such as those by Levin and Stephan (1991) for physics and earth sciences lend support to the universal relevance of Lehman's original results. Our study borrows from Lehman's tradition by placing individual researchers at the centre of the analysis. Individuals are at the core of knowledge growth.

Generally, humans are restricted by natural limits that, for instance, affect their cognitive performance (Miller 1955; Kotovsky, Hayes, and Simon 1985; Sweller 1994, p. 310; Marois and Ivanoff 2005). Combined together, the growth of information and the limitation of humans as knowledge workers might lead to an increase in the age of great achievement. There are several studies, including the present one, supporting this conjecture. For physics and earth sciences, Levin and Stephan (1991) express surprise to find that the latest educated researchers do not appear to be more productive than their earlier-born colleagues. Gonzalez-Brambila and Veloso (2007) replicate this result for a data set of researchers in Mexico in various areas of knowledge ranging from biology to engineering and the social sciences. Jones (2010) finds great scientific achievement increasingly being attained at more senior ages and argues that this might be due to longer training phases in the early life cycle. Similar results are reported by Jones and Weinberg (2011) for the peak of scientific creativity.

The data of the present study is collected from the field of economics. For this field, there are first hints at a potential upwards shift in the age of academic achievement. Conley et al. (2013) report that per capita productivity of economists in the first six years after obtaining their Ph.D. is about 60% higher for those who graduated in 1987 compared to

[1]This is also argued by Segerstrom (1998). An assumption in this context is that problems are independent. The effect in the case of problems with sequential dependencies is unclear, since there is no obvious reason to expect later problems to be easier (or harder) to solve than earlier problems.

those that graduated in 1999.[2] In an interesting twist, the authors argue that lowering requirements for tenurable records could be a policy to address this issue. Further evidence is provided by Hamermesh (2013) who finds that the fraction of authors who publish in top general economics journals at the age of 35 or younger has decreased from its height of 61.5% in 1973 to 33.0% in 2011. Hamermesh reviews and dismisses a number of possible explanations. Neither do people start their Ph.D. careers later, nor can the increase of age be explained by the publishing process, an inflow of older international researchers, the growth of consulting opportunities, or improved health. Hamermesh wonders whether increased complexity that results in longer 'incubation times' of new researchers might be an alternative explanation (this question is not resolved within the scope of his study, though). The studies by Conley et al. and by Hamermesh both look at the total life-cycle research output. By contrast, the present study seeks to identify the first substantial output of a researcher to approximate the efforts processing the accumulated knowledge that led to the threshold to create new knowledge.

2.2. Research institutions and incentives

To fully understand individual research productivity, we need to understand what motivates individual humans to engage in research, publish their work, and cite others. For example, Becker (1962) and Schultz (1963) contribute important work to the theoretical understanding of the possible mechanisms that determine human life-cycle productivity. Their respective investment models postulate that an inverse U-shape pattern of productivity can arise from decisions on human capital. Again, by contrast, our analysis of the burden of knowledge isolates the effect of knowledge accumulation that precedes the later life cycle of researchers, the burden of knowledge model builds on the same assumption that researchers are motivated to maximise their knowledge gain given an available investment budget of time and effort.

Franzoni, Scellato, and Stephan (2011) provide evidence that only career incentives, result in a significant increase of accepted publications and, interestingly, the acceptance rate of articles is correlated negatively with cash incentives. The substantial impact of career incentives on publishing activity is also illustrated by Önder and Schweitzer (2017) at the example of German economists. The authors report that the share of publishing Ph.D.'s increased from 18% in 1991 to 46% in 2008 after a reform of the previous mentoring system to a system with individual career incentives for publishing.

Incentives in academic research are sometimes not straight-forward. This can be illustrated at the question of why citations are made. At the example of a frequently cited paper on the case study methodology in accountancy research, Massaro, Dumay, and Bagnoli (2019) argue that citations are routinely placed not only for supporting factual claims, but also for strategic reasons such as pleasing reviewers and editors. They describe how authors increasingly engage in shallow citation patterns due to new digital tools such as Google Scholar. In a pungent critique of citation incentives, Payson (2019) dissects selected examples from publications in economics, where he lays out that even in prominent articles a majority of citations are made for strategic reasons rather than

[2]It should be noted that Conley et al. (2013) correct for the number of authors and quality measured in AER equivalents. Absent those corrections, differences are less pronounced.

scientific necessity. He suggests a radical reform of the citation system that would require authors to mark their citations as either essential, relevant, or irrelevant fodder. Thus, with increased access to articles, we need to be aware that increases in the number of references might not merely be explained by an increase of the knowledge base of the citing article, but also by strategic aspects.

Another frequently discussed variable, that through individual incentives and institutional factors affects research productivity, is gender. Larivière et al. (2013) show gender disparities in academic research output, extent of collaboration, and impact in almost all countries globally. They identify a relative lack of collaboration as a reason of the gender gap in academic research and argue for programmes fostering international collaboration for female researchers to help level the playing field. Controlling for factors such as research funding, number of articles published by the researcher, and number of co-authors, Beaudry and Larivière (2016) find that researchers who collaborate with a higher proportion of female co-authors are cited less in science and medicine. These findings are surprising and indicate a fundamental bias, as gender differences in impact remain, even after controlling for most other gender specific differences that could explain them. Not only are female academics less visible in academic publishing, but they are also less likely to venture into patenting (Ding, Murray, and Stuart 2006; Azoulay, Ding, and Stuart 2007). A main reason for this could be that women tend to be more risk averse (Croson and Gneezy 2009). While there are also signs that, over time, the gender gap could narrow (Holden 2001; Bentley and Adamson 2003; Ding, Murray, and Stuart 2006), there is still a substantial gap that persists. The present study sheds light on how female researchers could be affected by a burden of knowledge in academic publishing.

As our study builds on previous research on patent data, it is interesting to compare the incentives in academic and industrial research. Both, patent and academic article publishing, can be interpreted as 'winner-takes-it-all' contests driving reputation and career success (Merton 1957; Stephan 1996; Xie 2014). While a patent grants a usage right to the first researcher claiming an invention, publishing a journal article establishes an academic researcher's priority on a new discovery. In addition to these similarities, there are certain differences between the two domains. Previous literature has described how academic and industrial research networks can differ in their structures (Murray 2002; Bonaccorsi and Thoma 2007). Typically, there is only little overlap in terms of cross-domain citations and exchange is driven by few key individuals who are active in both domains. Hence, when applying Jones's measurement approach the interpretation has to consider the different background of academic research.

2.3. Strategies for alleviating the burden of knowledge

To alleviate a potential burden of knowledge, researchers might resort to different solution strategies such as the increase of human effort, the reduction of research scopes, and the development of new technologies of knowledge processing. In the present study, we are mostly interested in the increase in sheer manpower and collaboration, which is a well-known phenomenon: Price (1963) states that the trend of increasing co-author numbers 'is one of the most violent transitions that can be measured in recent trends of scientific manpower and literature' (p. 79). McDowell and Melvin (1983) and Jones (2009) argue that if individuals cannot cover the same breadth of knowledge as in past times, a possible strategy to combat this might be to divide labour into larger teams, with each member specialising only in one part of the problem. Barnett, Ault, and Kaserman (1988) find strong support for this hypothesis, as well as for the hypothesis of 'increasing opportunity cost of time and the rising incentive to diversify against the uncertainty of the editorial review process.'

In general, from the 1950s onwards, there has been much evidence of a general long-term trend towards collaboration. Greene (2007) even speaks of the near extinction of single authorships. Several studies report increasing team sizes in economics (McDowell and Melvin 1983; Hudson 1996; Laband and Tollison 2000; Adams et al. 2005; Hamermesh 2015), medicine (Zuckerman 1977), biology (Laband and Tollison 2000), and for several social sciences (Henriksen 2016). Team sizes have especially increased in the natural sciences which leads Cronin (2001) to speak of 'hyperauthorship.' For instance, Castelvecchi (2015) reports physics and biology papers with several thousand authors. Finally, trends of increasing collaboration have also been reported for patents (e.g. Jones 2009; Singh and Fleming 2010). Note that, besides being a reaction to the burden of knowledge, the increase in collaboration and researchers' division of labour might be explained by additional factors such as increasing quantitative content of economic science (Hudson 1996), different research habits of scholars of different generations (Hamermesh 2015), and the advantage of heterogeneous teams that provide heterogeneous knowledge (Aral, Brynjolfsson, and Van Alstyne 2012; Melero and Palomeras 2015).

3. Data

We make use of the *EconLit* publication database. The database provides metadata on the majority of scientific articles in economic journals since 1886.[3] For the purpose of this study, we processed the publication year, the name of the journal, the names of the authors, and the number of references in articles. We supplemented this information with data from *JSTOR* and *Web of Science* (WOS). In addition, for reasons of data availability and comparability, we restrict our analysis to the years from 1970 to 2014. There are 762,826 articles and 381,964 researchers in the resulting dataset. Note that the number of observations differs between the different aspects of our analysis. This difference is due to varying availability of supplementary data, the requirements the different measures defined below imply, and different levels of analysis such as the author vs. team vs. article level. Hence, the number of observations varies between several hundred high-profile authors with full supplementary and a hundred thousand further authors with basic information.

The analysis is focused on authors who have published at least one article in journals that are covered by the *EconLit* database. For these authors, we divide our analysis into two tracks to deal with the challenge of a changing journal landscape, which could otherwise affect our results.[4] There are two opposing effects. On the one hand, digital publishing has arguably decreased the cost of initiating and running an academic journal (Odlyzko 1997; van Noorden 2013), which can make access for authors easier. On the other hand, the competition for

[3]The oldest professional journal of economics is the *Quarterly Journal of Economics* which appeared first in 1886.

[4]The dynamics of the journal landscape pose a difference to the field of patents where patent offices and categories stay more persistent over time.

publishing in top-ranking journals has become higher, as these journals represent a smaller fraction of a growing market (Mabe 2003). As Larsen and von Ins (2010) note, there is no perfect solution for accommodating both potential effects in one analysis.

Our analysis introduces a two-track approach that can accommodate the two opposing effects. The first track includes all journals and authors who have published in any journal covered by *EconLit*. The second track is restricted to a fixed set of nine long-established peer-reviewed top-ranking journals that have been available throughout the entire observation period. These journals are *American Economic Review, Econometrica, International Economic Review, Journal of Political Economy*, the *Economic Journal*, the *Journal of Finance*, the *Quarterly Journal of Economics*, the *Review of Economic Studies*, and the *Review of Economics and Statistics*.[5] As it turns out, the main results summarised above point to the same direction in both tracks and with or without controlling for journal-fixed effects. For brevity, we define the following two terms:

- *Top article*: An article that is published in one of the nine journals listed above.
- *Top author*: An author who has published at least one article in one of the nine journals listed above.

Using the data available, we define measures by which Hypotheses H1 to H4 can be tested. The first two measures are available directly from the dataset:

- *Team size*: The number of authors listed for each article.
- *Number of references*: The number of articles referenced in an author's first single-author article. This measure serves as a proxy for the immediate knowledge an author had to process before writing his/her first article. Note that we cannot separate between the breadth and the depth of knowledge represented by references, since we do not know if multiple references serve to cover multiple topics or deepen only one topic's understanding. The numbers of listed references were mainly drawn from *JSTOR* and *WOS*. This information is available for 55% of the articles in our database.

For the measure *number of references*, we identify authors by their first and last names. We employ a graph-based procedure for author disambiguation (cf. Appendix C).[6] This allows us to build detailed publication histories for each individual. We focus on authors whose first publication was a single-author article, in order to accurately attribute the knowledge processed to one author.

Further, we define the following proxy measure:

- *Specialisation*: The probability that an author jumps JEL fields between successive articles. The more specialised authors are, the less capable they are of jumping fields.

[5]We chose this list of top-ranking peer-reviewed journals after considering several different rankings, including Ritzberger (2008), Engemann and Wall (2009), Kodrzycki and Yu (2006), and www.journal-ranking.com. An overview of the journals and their numbers of articles, authors and time periods covered is provided in Table A1 in Appendix A (The Electronic Appendix is available at http://www.electronic-appendix.info/bok). Other studies have focused on similar samples of top-ranking journals, such as Kim, Morse, and Zingales (2006), Hamermesh (2013), or Card and DellaVigna (2013).

[6]The Electronic Appendix is available at http://www.electronic-appendix.info/bok.

> To deal with the 1991 reform of the JEL classification scheme, we convert old and new JEL codes, employing the mapping provided by Card and DellaVigna (2013). To emulate the binary nature of the field jumps defined by Jones (2009), we define jumps as complete changes of the JEL field profile. This means that we identify a jump, if there is no overlap between the JEL fields indicated between two successive articles. For instance, in 1992 as well as 1994 Susanne Lohmann published the articles 'Optimal Commitment in Monetary Policy: Credibility versus Flexibility' and 'Information Aggregation through Costly Political Action' in the *American Economic Review*. Lohmann assigned the JEL code 'Monetary Policy (E52)' to the first and 'Political Processes: Rent-seeking, Lobbying, Elections, Legislatures, and Voting Behavior (D72)' as well as 'Asymmetric and Private Information – Mechanism Design (D82)' to the second article. Following Card and DellaVigna we attributed these to the JEL fields 'Macroeconomics' and 'Microeconomics' respectively. Since these consecutive top articles have no JEL fields in common they constitute a field jump.

Since our *specialisation* measure is based on Jones (2009), it is subject to similar limitations. Deriving an author's probability of jumping between JEL fields is not straightforward for authors who publish in teams, since they might become more specialised and work in larger teams simultaneously, which makes them appear to jump as regularly as they did before. We therefore focus on single authors or rather single-author articles. However, the regressions for authors who work in teams show the same principle effects and speak for the robustness of these results.

To test for the effect of the burden of knowledge on authors' career lives, we investigate the *age* at their first major scientific contribution:

- *Age at first article*: Author's age at first publication in a listed journal.

The age at first publication marks an author's transition from the knowledge-processing phase to the active contribution phase. A first publication, in this context, can be a single- or a multiple-author article. Since authors' birth dates are not available in the publication databases, we resorted to publicly available external sources. These sources include an automated search of Wikipedia articles and a manual search of authors' CVs and online profiles on their private and work home pages, personal inquiries, and dedicated online search engines, such as prabook.com, intelius.com, and birthdatabase.com.[7] We manually searched for a randomly drawn sample of 20,000 authors out of the 381,964 authors in the dataset. Plausibility checks were performed for positive search results by matching metadata of publications and searches, such as the affiliation of the author as indicated in the journal article and the place of residence as indicated in the external source. By applying this procedure, we could confirm the birth dates of 2,656 authors. Note that the reduction of the sample size in the age data subsample compared to the original sample raises the issue of representation. In Appendix F, we address this issue and provide a calibrated version of our regression analysis.[8]

---

[7]We elaborate on the data sources used in this study in Appendix B (The Electronic Appendix is available at http://www.electronic-appendix.info/bok).

[8]The Electronic Appendix is available at http://www.electronic-appendix.info/bok.

In the regression analyses, specifications that control for individual and institutional variables are included. These variables are:

- Female: 1 for female authors and 0 for male authors. The gender information is guessed from the authors' forenames using the R package 'gender'. Mostly male forenames are classified as male and mostly female forenames are classified as female.
- Migrated: 1 for authors who have migrated from their country of birth and 0 otherwise. This individual variable is available only for the subset of authors that were manually researched.
- NonUS: 1 for authors who do not possess a US citizenship and 0 for US citizens. Again, this individual variable is available only for the subset of authors that were manually researched.
- NonAcad: 1 for non-academic author affiliations and 0 for academic author affiliations. The values are derived from author affiliations as indicated in research articles. Non-academic institutions are institutions whose primary focus is not on research. These include governmental, commercial and non-profit organisations such as commissions, councils, banks, corporations, funds, and foundations. Academic institutions include organisations primarily dedicated to research and education such as universities, research institutes, schools, and academies.
- TopInst: 1 for 50 top-ranking institutions and 0 for others. Again, the values are derived from author affiliations as indicated in research articles. A list of top-50 institutions was computed by combining the 2015/16 editions of the QS World University Rankings for Social Sciences and Management and the RePEc/IDEAS Ranking of Economics Institutions. The latter ranking was consulted because it includes non-academic institutions such as the International Monetary Fund and the World Bank along with academic institutions. Given that non-academic organisations include some of the most prolific contributors to our dataset, the combination of academic and non-academic institutions provides for a more complete picture.

4. Time series results

We consider the evolution over time of our five outcomes of interest. According to Hypotheses 1 to 4, we expect *team size, number of references*, and *age* to increase and *JEL field jump* to decrease over time. Figure 1 presents a graphical overview, while Table 1 through 3 explore the trends in more detail. Overall, the strong visual trends of the plots are confirmed in the regression analyses under various controls and in both the all articles as well as the top articles track of the analysis. Thus, the four hypotheses cannot be rejected.

First of all, consider H1, regarding the *age at first publication*. We define researchers' first publications as the first time they appear within our dataset as author of any article in the observation period from 1970 to 2014. By the same token, we define researchers' first *top* publications as the first time they appear as author of a top article. Since we would like to exclude those researchers whose first publication dates are prior to our observation period, we remove authors who appeared in the *EconLit* dataset between 1950 and 1969. Further, to eliminate outliers, we focus on the age window in which people tend to be most productive. Lehman (1953) reported the highest level of human productivity across a large range of professions and concluded that their most productive age is typically in

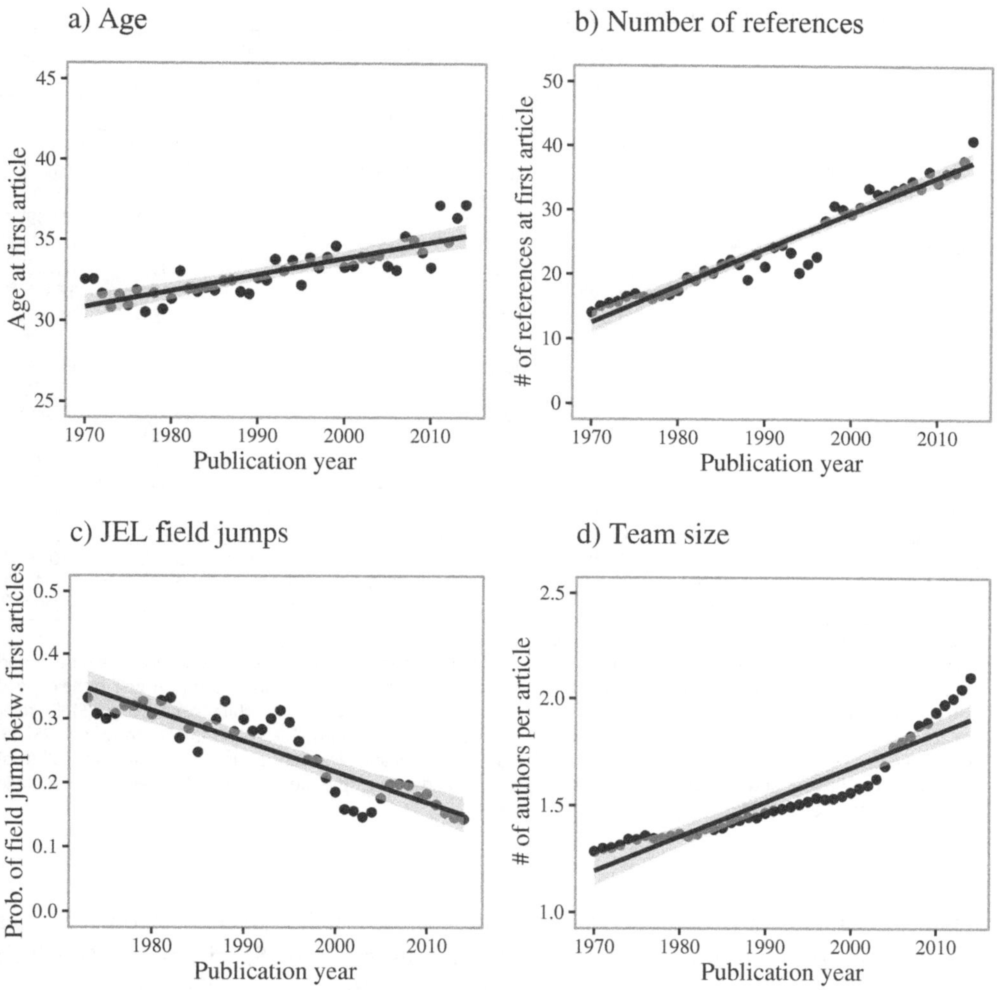

Figure 1. Basic time trends (yearly averages).

their thirties. This observation is consistent with our data and, correspondingly, we chose a window from 25 to 45 years. To check for the robustness of our results and to maintain comparability with preceding studies, in addition, we included in our analysis the window from 25 to 35 years as employed by Jones (2009).

The average age over time for authors' first articles is depicted in Figure 1(a). Despite there being much volatility, we see a strong upward trend. The average age of researchers at their first publication increased from 32.5 years in 1970 to 37.2 years in 2014 for the age window from 25 to 45 years. The regressions in Table 1 reveal a positive and significant time trend for top as well as for all journal articles. Moreover, those trends are confirmed under various controls and estimates for team size do not exhibit consistent effects when controlling for journals and fields, which are both significant. When analysing the trends within single top-ranking journals, the time estimates remain positive for each single journal and significant for all journals, except the *Review of Economic Studies*. The results are also similar when examining the shorter age window from 25 to 35 years. However,

Table 1. Trends in author's age at first article.

	Dependent variable: [age in years at first article]							
	(1)–(4): Top journals				(5)–(8): All journals			
	(1)	(2)	(3)	(4)	(5)	(6)	(7)	(8)
PubYear	0.098***	0.088***	0.101***	0.049***	0.084***	0.050***	0.055***	0.031***
	(0.010)	(0.011)	(0.012)	(0.008)	(0.008)	(0.012)	(0.013)	(0.009)
Team		0.311+	0.240	0.060		0.264+	0.177	−0.107
		(0.169)	(0.168)	(0.112)		(0.160)	(0.160)	(0.109)
Female			0.454	0.631***			0.425	0.417+
			(0.357)	(0.240)			(0.333)	(0.222)
TopInst			−1.568***	−0.967***			−1.313***	−0.631***
			(0.261)	(0.173)			(0.251)	(0.162)
NonAcad			1.108*	0.879*			1.590***	0.707*
			(0.501)	(0.367)			(0.413)	(0.294)
Migrated			−0.066	0.257			−0.546	−0.510
			(0.513)	(0.336)			(0.519)	(0.346)
NonUS			−0.018	0.165			0.201	0.138
			(0.272)	(0.181)			(0.262)	(0.173)
Journal	—	Yes	Yes	Yes	—	Yes	Yes	Yes
Field	—	Yes	Yes	Yes	—	Yes	Yes	Yes
AgeRange	25–45	25–45	25–45	25–35	25–45	25–45	25–45	25–35
Mean	33.46	33.46	33.45	30.86	32.59	32.59	32.58	30.09
	1,635	1,635	1,599	1,115	2,656	2,656	2,597	1,942
	0.055	0.097	0.124	0.101	0.037	0.339	0.359	0.308

Significance levels: *** $p < 0.001$; ** $p < 0.01$; *$p < 0.05$; + $p < 0.1$

(i) Regressions are ordinary least squares with standard errors in parentheses. (ii) All regressions observe the time period between 1970–2014 and include only those authors for whom age data is available and who appear first in the dataset in or after 1970. (iii) Specifications (1)–(4) observe author's ages at their first top article, while specifications (5)–(8) refer to articles from all journals from our dataset. (iv) Authors within specifications (1)–(3) and (5)–(7) are of age 25–45, while they are between 25–35 in specifications (4) and (8). (v) *Journal* and *Field* controls include dummies for all (top) journals in our dataset and the JEL fields, respectively. (vi) *Mean* describes the mean value of the dependent variable over the observation period.

the time estimates are reduced when examining all articles, instead of only articles published in top journals. For example, the time estimate for Specification (7), which includes all journals, is only 0.055, compared to 0.101 for Specification (3), which includes only top journals. This hints at a possible counter strategy of young (future) top authors. Instead of being resigned to the fact of prolonged waiting times for their first top article, researchers partly bridge the time by publishing in lower ranking journals.

Regarding other individual and institutional factors, we find a significant negative effect of *TopInst*. Authors who are affiliated with top-ranking institutions manage to begin publishing earlier in their lives. In contrast, to be affiliated with a non-academic institution has the opposite effect. One possible explanation is that employees at banks and corporations typically do not need to publish in order to obtain their position as other career incentives are in place. Instead, they might already be in senior positions when they obtain the resources and authority necessary to share knowledge with the public. It is also worth noting that estimates for *Female* are positive in all specifications, but the effect is only statistically significant in Specifications (4) and (8) which are restricted to authors of ages 25 to 35. To address concerns about multicollinearity when controlling for multiple variables, we provide regressions with variance inflation factors in Appendix E. Values are in a tolerable range between 1.005 and 1.254.

Next, we turn to H2, regarding *the number of references*. We consider this the most straightforward measure for the knowledge which a journal article builds on. Figure 1(b) shows the number of references of researchers' debut articles for the subset of those researchers whose first article is a single-author publication. The number of references sharply increases from 14.1 in 1970 to 40.9 in 2014. Again, the regressions in Table 2 show significant positive time trends in all specifications. The results appear very robust, as these trends are equally sharp for all specifications.[9] In every case, the number of references more than doubles over the observation period. Regarding the effects of individual and institutional factors, *TopInst* is positively and significantly related to the number of references, while *NonAcad* is negatively related, but significant only in some of the specifications. *Female* is related negatively and significantly for top journals but not for all journals.

Specifications (3) and (7) include publications by non-single authors. While there is no significant effect of team size for top journal publications, for all journals, team size is significant. The *Team* estimate indicates that each additional author leads to an increase in the number of references. The positive effect of *TopInst* and the negative effect of *NonAcad* are maintained in these specifications. Interestingly, the effect of *Female* becomes positive and significant in the all journals track. A possible explanation for this effect would be that female researchers are restrained in resources such as time but this effect is alleviated when working in a team. Specifications (4) and (8) shed light on this possibility by controlling for the interaction *Female x Team*. Both the interaction as well as the gender term turn out insignificant, while the team effect stays significant in the case of top journals and turns significant in the case of all journals.

Table 2. Trends in references at first article.

	Dependent variable: [number of references at first article]							
	(1)–(4): Top journals				(5)–(8): All journals			
	(1)	(2)	(3)	(4)	(5)	(6)	(7)	(8)
PubYear	0.028***	0.024***	0.024***	0.024***	0.023***	0.022***	0.024***	0.024***
	(0.001)	(0.001)	(0.001)	(0.001)	(0.000)	(0.001)	(0.000)	(0.000)
Team			0.019**	0.021**			0.022***	0.022***
			(0.007)	(0.008)			(0.002)	(0.003)
Female		0.072**	0.080***	0.050		0.001	0.012*	0.015
		(0.028)	(0.015)	(0.037)		(0.012)	(0.005)	(0.012)
TopInst		0.142***	0.084***	0.084***		0.093***	0.030***	0.030***
		(0.025)	(0.013)	(0.013)		(0.015)	(0.007)	(0.007)
NonAca		−0.026	−0.010	−0.010		−0.065***	−0.095***	−0.095***
		(0.045)	(0.020)	(0.020)		(0.020)	(0.008)	(0.008)
F x T				−0.015				−0.001
				(0.017)				(0.005)
Journal	–	Yes	Yes	Yes	–	Yes	Yes	Yes
Field	–	Yes	Yes	Yes	–	Yes	Yes	Yes
Mean	20.18	20.18	23.96	23.96	29.15	29.15	30.53	30.53
N	4,406	4,406	12,267	12,267	19,214	19,214	69,052	69,052

Significance levels: *** $p < 0.001$; ** $p < 0.01$; * $p < 0.05$; + $p < 0.1$

(i) Regressions are negative binomial regressions with standard errors in parentheses. (ii) All regressions observe the time period between 1970–2014. (iii) Specifications (1)–(4) include only author's first top articles, while specifications (5)–(8) include first articles for all journals in our dataset. (iv) Specifications (1), (2), (5), and (6) observe only single-author articles; (3), (4), (7), and (8) observe all team sizes. (v) *F x T* represents the interaction between female authors and team size. (vi) *Journal* and *Field* controls include dummies for all (top) journals in our dataset and the JEL fields, respectively. (vii) *Mean* describes the mean value of the dependent variable over the observation period.

[9]There are combinations of journals and years with no reference data available. To check for a potential bias of journals with higher numbers of references substituting those with lower numbers, we conducted separate regression analyses for each journal where data is available for at least 100 articles over at least 10 years. In 98.4% of the 124 journals that we detect a significant time trend for, the trend is positive.

Besides the quantity of knowledge to be processed prior to new contributions, the difficulty of the problems tackled might contribute to the age at first publication. We measure the difficulty of problems by examining the time lag between successive publications. For the lag between any successive articles of an author, we see a slight decrease from 0.93 in 1973 to 0.89 years in 2014. Also, for the lag between successive top articles of an author, we observe a slight increase from 1.21 in 1973 to 1.27 years in 2014. Both changes are confounded by much volatility and not statistically significant when controlling for journal and field fixed effects. For both tracks of the analysis, the total change of the average time lag over the observation period is less than half a year over the truncated 42-year observation period. Moreover, after adjusting for average time lags in the regressions of age at first publication in Table 1, effect directions and significance levels remain unchanged. Therefore, we deem the variation in time lags negligible in comparison to the pronounced changes in author age. In the big picture, the size of time lags appears to stagnate over the observation period.

Next we turn to H3, regarding *specialisation*. We measure specialisation by examining the probability of a researcher jumping from one set of JEL fields to another between successive publications. Since the time gap between two successive publications might influence the probability of JEL field jumps, we need to avoid biases that could arise from the construction of this measure. In the first year, the maximum time gap between two successive articles is zero, while it increases to 45 years in the final year. In order to avoid biasing the distribution of time gaps over the observation period, we look only at gaps of up to 3 years and truncate the first 3 years, since gaps in the beginning would be limited. Therefore, our observation period is reduced to the years from 1973 to 2014. In Table 3, we consider models with and without the truncation described. Note that while we restricted the JEL field jump analysis presented in this section to single-author articles, the principal trends are similar when admitting teams. Table 4 illustrates the development of author populations who published at least one single-author article compared to all authors over time. Despite an increase in absolute numbers, the relative frequency of single authors declined.

Figure 1(c) shows a robust downward trend for the probability of jumping between JEL field of top journal articles. Overall, the probability of changing from one top journal to another decreased from 33.2% in 1973 to 14.4% in 2014. The regression analyses in Table 3 confirm the principal downward trend under various controls, as well as with and without the truncation correction. In contrast to the results for all journals, when considering top-ranking journals, the probability of changing fields between two successive publications decreased more sharply from 28.3% in 1973 to 0% in 2014. To put this number into perspective, we need to note that the number of observations towards the end of the observation period is small due to the data selection and truncation described above.

Regarding individual and institutional factors, we find significant effects mostly in the specifications that include all journals. Authors affiliated to top institutions seem more likely to jump fields, while female authors seem less likely to jump fields. The latter finding is consistent with the results discussed in the literature section on academic entrepreneurship that show that female academics are less likely to venture into patenting due to higher levels of risk aversion. While our dataset does not provide a measure of risk preferences, risk aversion could offer a plausible explanation for why female authors tend to avoid jumps into new domains.

Table 3. Trends in probability of JEL field jump.

	Dependent variable: [probability of switching JEL field]							
	(1)–(4): Top journals				(5)–(8): All journals			
	(1)	(2)	(3)	(4)	(5)	(6)	(7)	(8)
PubYear	−0.020***	−0.012**	−0.013**	−0.014***	−0.021***	−0.011***	−0.011***	−0.015***
	(0.003)	(0.004)	(0.004)	(0.003)	(0.001)	(0.001)	(0.001)	(0.001)
TimeGap		0.003	0.001	0.041***		0.023***	0.023**	0.051***
		(0.035)	(0.035)	(0.007)		(0.007)	(0.007)	(0.001)
Female			−0.186	−0.241*			−0.065**	−0.059***
			(0.136)	(0.101)			(0.021)	(0.016)
TopInst			0.011	0.014			0.071**	0.064**
			(0.102)	(0.076)			(0.028)	(0.022)
NonAcad			0.393+	0.018			0.042	0.022
			(0.213)	(0.152)			(0.030)	(0.023)
Journal	–	Yes	Yes	Yes	–	Yes	Yes	Yes
Field	–	Yes	Yes	Yes	–	Yes	Yes	Yes
Mean	0.4	0.4	0.4	0.42	0.29	0.29	0.29	0.33
N	1,374	1,374	1,374	2,222	38,674	38,674	38,674	59,022

Significance levels: *** $p < 0.001$; ** $p < 0.01$; * $p < 0.05$; + $p < 0.1$

(i) Results are for probit regressions with standard errors in parentheses. (ii) All regressions observe the time period between 1973–2014. (iii) Specifications (1)–(4) include only top articles while specifications (5)–(8) include articles from all journals in our dataset. (iv) Specifications (1)–(3), and (5)–(7) include only articles where the time since the first top article is at most three years. (v) *Journal* and *Field* controls include dummies for each journal within the dataset and the JEL fields, respectively. (vi) *Mean* describes the mean value of the dependent variable over the observation period.

Table 4. Population of authors with single-author articles.

	1970–1984	1985–1999	2000–2014
1. # authors with single-author articles	29,463	52,906	104,437
2. # all authors	46,048	97,341	303,905
Relative frequency 1. vs. 2.	63.98%	54.35%	34.37%

Further, we do not observe a visible shift or systematic changes with the reform of the JEL classification scheme in 1991. The relative jump frequencies for all articles in the years before, during, and after the reform of the JEL classification scheme are 26.04% for 1989 old to 1990 old, 32.08% for 1990 old to 1991 new, and 30.80% for 1991 new to 1992 new. Thus, the immediate effect of the change in the JEL classification is opposed to the historical trend that we observe and cannot explain our results. Overall, it seems that the major fields of economics are covered accurately by the mapping by Card and DellaVigna (2013), which served to unify JEL codes for our study.

Finally, we turn to H4, regarding *team size*. Our results replicate the findings of the literature on team size discussed in the literature section. Likewise, we observe a growing number of co-authors (see Figure 1(d)). The number of co-authors, for example, increased steadily, from an average of 1.3 in 1970 to 2.1 in 2014. This is consistent with results reported by Card and DellaVigna (2013), who calculated an average of 1.3 authors in 1970 and 2.2 in 2011 for the five top economics journals investigated in their study. Table G1 in the appendix examines the consistent positive time trend in more detail, presenting multiple regressions relating team size to publication year.[10]

The composition of the sample might have changed over time, which could bias our results.[11] For example, the share of female researchers in the sample has increased from

[10]The Electronic Appendix is available at http://www.electronic-appendix.info/bok.

[11]We thank an anonymous referee for pointing this out.

6% in 1970 to 25% in 2014. Similar changes occurred with respect to the percentages of top-institution affiliations, non-academic institutions, and non-us researchers. As far as measures for these groups differ from the general population, changes might be affected by them. To address the robustness of the results against changes of the sample composition, we provide additional regressions in Appendix D. As it turns out, some of the subsamples show slightly stronger time trends, while others show slightly weaker time trends. Importantly, all effect directions remain consistent with those in the main part of the analysis. On the one hand, this strengthens the plausibility of the burden of knowledge hypothesis, while, on the other hand, it points to the relevance of other effects, which could be a rewarding subject for future research.

5. Discussion

The findings from the analysis of researchers' early careers provide new insights into the burden of knowledge in economics and help link various results from the literature on academic publishing. Regarding the age of authors in three economics top journals, Hamermesh (2013) established that the average age has increased over time. Our results conform to this finding for a larger set of economics journals. In addition, we establish that the age of authors is higher already at the very beginning of their careers when they publish their first articles. This result is consistent with findings on US researchers who receive their first grant from the *National Institutes of Health* (Gingras et al. 2008) and inventors who obtain their first patent (Jones 2009). The burden of knowledge hypothesis offers a plausible explanation: As the amount of knowledge increases, researchers need to process a greater number of previous findings. The more laborious learning process requires researchers to spend more time before their work reaches a quality level when it can appear in top journals. Additionally, our data shows that the effect is less severe in the sample of all journals compared to top journals. A possible explanation is that, faced with mounting career pressure to deliver at least intermediate or medium quality results, researchers settle for publishing in non-top journals and bridge the time until their high-end results are finalised.[12]

The amount of knowledge required for researchers to first contribute to the academic literature is reflected in the number of articles they cite in their debut articles. Results for biology (Cordero et al. 2016), engineering science (Ucar et al. 2013), finance (Esen, Tunahan, and Takil 2016), or psychology (Krampen 2010) indicate that the number of references in academic articles is increasing over time. Our findings replicate these trends for articles in economics. Additionally, the data show that the number of references is increasing already at the beginning of researchers' career life-cycles. Again, this finding is consistent with the burden of knowledge hypothesis (alternative explanations are discussed below).

To track the development of specialisation in early-career publishing in economics over time, we introduced the measure of JEL field jumps. We observe that authors are less likely to change fields between successive publications. Remaining in their debut fields

[12]To counter the inflation of quantity of research papers, potentially at the cost of quality, it has been proposed to focus on the citations per article, instead of focusing on the size of a researcher's list of publications when tenuring (e.g. Hirsch 2005; Egghe 2006; Marx 2011; Ellison 2013).

allows them to exploit their existing knowledge and working relationships with the people involved in the field's environment, such as editors, reviewers, and readers of relevant journals. Our results for academic publishing are consistent with the findings for patents by Jones (2009) who has employed an analogous measure and observes similar reductions in the likelihood of jumps between technological fields.

Specialisation is accompanied by the phenomenon of increasing team sizes. As laid out in the literature section, the trend of increasing team size is evident across scientific disciplines, including economics. If single authors' scope of expertise becomes more limited, they benefit from collaborating in larger teams in order to cover the sufficient scope to contribute to a given topic. In combination, co-authors can not only distribute the burden of acquiring the prerequisite knowledge, but also the effort of solving a problem. Note that, besides a horizontal division of the work on the various aspects of a research topic, contributors in a team can also take on tasks only indirectly related to the topic, such as acquiring funding, working on the text quality and presentation, or communicating with the community, editors, and reviewers. Our study establishes that, for the case of economics, an increase in team size affects researchers from the beginning of their career life-cycle.

5.1. Assumptions and limitations of the empirical approach

Of necessity, the measures in this study are based on specific assumptions and are not entirely complete. For example, for reasons of availability, we do not consider the impact of funding on academic careers. Funding might have substantial influence on the choices researchers make and the results they obtain. Regarding coauthorship, there is evidence that the criteria imposed by funding agencies can tilt decisions towards more and geographically more diversified collaboration (Adams et al. 2005). EU-funded research networks require researchers to collaborate across countries (Defazio, Lockett, and Wright 2009). Hence, even though we cannot control for trends in funding policies in our dataset, it seems plausible that part of increases in team size could be related to funding incentives. Regarding the time to arrive at a first publication, the number of references, and strategies of specialisation, the potential effect direction is less clear, though. For example, receiving funding and other resources can facilitate academic work, while the application for grants is competitive and time consuming.

Measuring specialisation by field jumps is convenient to operationalise and compare with previous work on economics publishing (Card and DellaVigna 2013; Angrist et al. 2017) and patenting (Jones 2009). However, there are potential caveats to this approach. The measure assumes that the cognitive distance between fields is comparable and stays the same over time. In reality, this is not always the case. The meaning of the JEL classification as well as the topics of articles themselves is evolving. When new topics arise or old topics fade away, some existing JEL classifications are hardly ever adopted. Thus, some new topics are disguised under either very generic or inappropriate JEL codes (Önder, Popov, and Schweitzer 2019). Alternative measures can address some of these issues. For example, Rafols et al. (2012) measure diversity across articles by their cognitive distance. This measure is computed from the mutual citations and the Web of Science categories of articles. Other approaches to capture research contents include keyword analysis (Mela, Roos, and Deng 2013) and topic analysis (Huber, Kamakura, and Mela 2014). To examine disciplines outside of economics, where a common classification scheme is not always available, these measures provide viable alternatives.

When we consider author age, we need to be aware that it might not only capture the time spent to acquire prerequisite knowledge. The relationship holds only if we assume that problem difficulty remains constant over time. This is important when we interpret the age of authors at their first publication as an indicator of how much effort it took them to reach the frontier of knowledge that constitutes the cutting edge of science. If the assumption on problem difficulty was wrong, there could be a second element, though: after researchers reach the frontier of their scientific field and before their first publication, they first need to solve an actual problem to create a new contribution. Hence, age is also an indicator of the difficulty of remaining border problems. While we cannot completely separate these two effects, our results regarding time lags between successive articles reveal no systematic change in the difficulty of border problems and adjusting for average time lags does not affect the principal results on author age. Therefore, the observed increase in age might be attributed to the growing quantity of knowledge rather than to changes in problem difficulty.

Besides an increase in knowledge, other factors could contribute to the increase in the number of references and cannot easily be separated. It seems plausible that the increased availability of lists of references in pre-existing papers and the incentive of authors to publish, cite, and get cited contribute to a certain inflation of references. Moreover, existing measures of impact rely on the number of citations (e.g. Garfield 1972; Hirsch 2005; Garfield 2006). Hence, authors and co-authors are increasingly incentivised to cite their own articles that they build on (e.g. Phelan 1999; Lawrence 2007; Bethard and Jurafsky 2010; Lin and Huang 2012; Teodorescu and Andrei 2014). Nevertheless, numerous previous studies relied on the analysis of references (e.g. Yitzhaki and Ben-Tamar 1991; Ucar et al. 2013; Bornmann and Mutz 2015; Cordero et al. 2016). Also, the increase in team size could be explained by lowered costs of geographically distant cooperations (Katz and Martin 1997). Furthermore, the cost of coordinating team members increases with team size (Hudson 1996; Cummings and Kiesler 2007; Bercovitz and Feldman 2011) and might increase teams even more by for instance making team leaders necessary. Hamermesh and Oster (2002) argue that distant coauthorships have increased due to advances in information and communication technology. Remarkably, at the same time, they provide evidence that the productivity of those coauthorships has actually decreased.

6. Conclusion and implications

Our results lend support to the existence of a burden of knowledge in economics. The quantity of knowledge that researchers process prior to their debut articles has increased sharply, they consequently contribute to research at a later age, and they develop various strategies to deal with the increasing quantity of knowledge. These strategies include refraining from changing between fields and distributing work within larger teams of co-authors.

The findings of this study might not necessarily extend to other scientific disciplines. Nevertheless, considering our results for academic publishing in economics and the results by Jones (2009) for patents, one might wonder if there is a more general mechanism that pervades different areas of human progress. It would be interesting to investigate whether similar mechanisms were at work in other fields such as biology, physics, mathematics, engineering, and medicine.

A first prediction for economics based on the trends observed in our study would indeed seem to temper abundant optimism for growth. If we linearly extrapolated the development of the previous 4.5 decades into the future, researchers in economics would arrive at their first publication only in the later parts of their lives or not at all, they would stay in their respective debut fields, and they would work in teams of many co-authors. However, on the long run, such an extrapolation will hardly be accurate and improvements in life expectancy,[13] information and learning technologies, and other future developments could save economics from this bleak prospect. After all, the rewards of developing new strategies to deal with the burden of knowledge will be high.

The perspective of the present paper is that of an aggregated bird's eye view. A more detailed analysis of the dynamics of how knowledge is selected and processed could help to shed light on the inner world of the burden. For example, Furman and Stern (2011) provide evidence of how institutions can facilitate the dissemination of scientific knowledge and play an important role in the practical selection process. Melero and Palomeras (2015) investigate how the composition of inventor teams affects patent output. Analogous studies for teams in scientific research would help to understand, if those findings can be generalised. Eventually, drawing connections between the complex inner workings of knowledge processing and the more abstract general burden of knowledge will contribute to a better understanding of scientific progress and might prove a rewarding subject of future research.

In order to explore the general prevalence of the burden of knowledge, the investigation of additional scientific disciplines seems a promising subject of future research. Further, it might be a rewarding endeavour to investigate how mitigating factors can reduce the effect of the burden of knowledge. For example, increasing life expectancy and improving the maintenance of mental performance at high age could mitigate the increasing need for learning. Also, learning itself has been undergoing transformational changes in recent years. Knowledge is more accessible through digital databases and improvements in search technology. Online courses provide high quality education that can be consumed at low cost and in a highly individualised and selective way. Together, these developments facilitate the absorption of knowledge. Moreover, new technologies provide improved ways of modularising and distributing large tasks to specialised experts in large teams.

Disclosure statement

No potential conflict of interest was reported by the authors.

ORCID

Sascha Schweitzer http://orcid.org/0000-0003-4154-6010

[13]Despite an increase in life expectancy, Hazan (2009) finds that expected hours of lifetime labour supply have decreased. Lee (2001, 648) estimates the length of male retirement in the U.S. to have increased by more than factor six since 1850, representing 'up to 30% of men's length of life after entry into the labor force'.

References

Adams, J. D., G. C. Black, J. Roger Clemmons, and P. E. Stephan. 2005. "Scientific Teams and Institutional Collaborations: Evidence from U.S. Universities, 1981–1999." *Research Policy* 34 (3): 259–285. doi:10.1016/j.respol.2005.01.014.

Angrist, J., P. Azoulay, G. Ellison, R. Hill, and S. F. Lu. 2017. "Economic Research Evolves: Fields and Styles." *American Economic Review* 107: 293–297. doi:10.1257/aer.p20171117.

Aral, S., E. Brynjolfsson, and M. Van Alstyne. 2012. "Information, Technology, and Information Worker Productivity." *Information Systems Research* 23 (3): 849–867. doi:10.1287/isre.1110.0408.

Arbesman, S. 2011. "Quantifying the Ease of Scientific Discovery." *Scientometrics* 86 (2): 245–250. doi:10.1007/s11192-010-0232-6.

Archibald, G., and M. B. Line. 1991. "The Size and Growth of Serial Literature 1950–1987, in Terms of the Number of Articles per Serial." *Scientometrics* 20 (1): 173–196. doi:10.1007/BF02018154.

Azoulay, P., W. Ding, and T. Stuart. 2007. "The Determinants of Faculty Patenting Behavior: Demographics or Opportunities?" *Journal of Economic Behavior and Organization* 63 (4): 599–623. doi:10.1016/j.jebo.2006.05.015.

Barnett, A. H., R. W. Ault, and D. L. Kaserman. 1988. "The Rising Incidence of Co-authorship in Economics: Further Evidence." *The Review of Economics and Statistics* 70 (3): 539–543. doi:10.2307/1926798.

Beaudry, C., and V. Larivière. 2016. "Which Gender Gap? Factors Affecting Researchers' Scientific Impact in Science and Medicine." *Research Policy* 45 (9): 1790–1817. doi:10.1016/j.respol.2016.05.009.

Becker, G. S. 1962. "Investment in Human Capital: A Theoretical Analysis." *Journal of Political Economy* 70 (5): 9–49. doi:10.1086/258724.

Bentley, J. T., and R. Adamson. 2003. *Gender Differences in the Careers of Academic Scientists and Engineers: A Literature Review*. National Science Foundation. http://files.eric.ed.gov/fulltext/ED478916.pdf

Bercovitz, J., and M. Feldman. 2011. "The Mechanisms of Collaboration in Inventive Teams: Composition, Social Networks, and Geography." *Research Policy* 40 (1): 81–93. doi:10.1016/j.respol.2010.09.008.

Bethard, S., and D. Jurafsky. 2010. "Who Should I Cite? Learning Literature Search Models from Citation Behavior." Proceedings of the 19th ACM International Conference on Information and Knowledge Management, 609–617. doi:10.4012/dmj.2009-084.

Bloom, N., C. Jones, J. Van Reenen, and M. Webb. 2017. "Are Ideas Getting Harder to Find?" *NBER Working Paper*. http://www.nber.org/papers/w23782.pdf

Bonaccorsi, A., and G. Thoma. 2007. "Institutional Complementarity and Inventive Performance in Nano Science and Technology." *Research Policy* 36 (6): 813–831. doi:10.1016/j.respol.2007.02.009.

Bornmann, L., and R. Mutz. 2015. "Growth Rates of Modern Science: A Bibliometric Analysis Based on the Number of Publications and Cited References." *Journal of the Association for Information Science and Technology* 66 (11): 2215–2222. doi:10.1002/asi.2015.66.issue-11.

Card, D., and S. DellaVigna. 2013. "Nine Facts about Top Journals in Economics." *Journal of Economic Literature* 51 (1): 144–161. doi:10.1257/jel.51.1.144.

Castelvecchi, D. 2015. "Physics Paper Sets Record with More than 5,000 Authors." *Nature* Accessed 23 May 2018. http://www.nature.com/doifinder/10.1038/nature.2015.17567

Conley, J. P., and A. S. Önder. 2014. "The Research Productivity of New PhDs in Economics: The Surprisingly High Non-Success of the Successful." *Journal of Economic Perspectives* 28 (3): 205–216. doi:10.1257/jep.28.3.205.

Conley, J. P., M. J. Crucini, R. A. Driskill, and A. S. Önder. 2013. "The Effects of Publication Lags on Life-Cycle Research Productivity in Economics." *Economic Inquiry* 51 (2): 1251–1276. doi:10.1111/j.1465-7295.2012.00480.x.

Cordero, R. J. B., C. M. De León-Rodriguez, J. K. Alvarado-Torres, A. R. Rodriguez, and A. Casadevall. 2016. "Life Science's Average Publishable Unit (APU) Has Increased over the past Two Decades." *PloS One* 11 (6): 1–14. doi:10.1371/journal.pone.0156983.

Cronin, B. 2001. "Hyperauthorship: A Postmodern Perversion or Evidence of A Structural Shift in Scholarly Communication Practices?" *Journal of the American Society for Information Science and Technology* 52 (7): 558–569. doi:10.1002/(ISSN)1532-2890.

Croson, R., and U. Gneezy. 2009. "Gender Differences in Preferences." *Journal of Economic Literature* 47 (2): 448–474. doi:10.1257/jel.47.2.448.

Cummings, J. N., and S. Kiesler. 2007. "Coordination Costs and Project Outcomes in Multi-University Collaborations." *Research Policy* 36 (10): 1620–1634. doi:10.1016/j.respol.2007.09.001.

Defazio, D., A. Lockett, and M. Wright. 2009. "Funding Incentives, Collaborative Dynamics and Scientific Productivity: Evidence from the EU Framework Program." *Research Policy* 38 (2): 293–305. doi:10.1016/j.respol.2008.11.008.

Ding, W. W., F. Murray, and T. E. Stuart. 2006. "Gender Differences in Patenting in the Academic Life Sciences." *Science* 313 (5787): 665–667. doi:10.1126/science.1124832.

Egghe, L. 2006. "Theory and Practise of the g-Index." *Scientometrics* 69 (1): 131–152. doi:10.1007/s11192-006-0144-7.

Ellison, G. 2002. "The Slowdown of the Economics Publishing Process." *Journal of Political Economy* 110 (5): 947–993. doi:10.1086/341868.

Ellison, G. 2013. "How Does the Market Use Citation Data? the Hirsch Index in Economics." *American Economic Journal: Applied Economics* 5 (3): 63–90.

Engemann, K. M., and H. J. Wall. 2009. "A Journal Ranking for the Ambitious Economist." *Federal Reserve Bank of St. Louis Review* 91: 127–140.

Esen, S., H. Tunahan, and D. Takil. 2016. "A Comparative Bibliometric Analysis of Finance Papers Published in High Impact Journals and Developing Country-Addressed Journals: The Case of Turkish Journals." *Journal of Economics, Finance and Accounting* 3 (1): 37–49.

Evenson, R. E. 1984. "International Invention: Implications for Technology Market Analysis." In *R&D, Patents, and Productivity*, edited by E. Zvi Griliches, 89–126. Chicago and London: University of Chicago Press.

Evenson, R. E. 1993. "Patents, R&D, and Invention Potential: International Evidence." *The American Economic Review* 83 (2): 463–468.

Fernández-Cano, A., M. Torralbo, and M. Vallejo. 2004. "Reconsidering Price's Model of Scientific Growth: An Overview." *Scientometrics* 61 (3): 301–321. doi:10.1023/B:SCIE.0000045112.11562.11.

Franzoni, C., G. Scellato, and P. Stephan. 2011. "Changing Incentives to Publish." *Science* 333 (6043): 702–703. doi:10.1126/science.1197286.

Furman, J. L., and S. Stern. 2011. "Climbing Atop the Shoulders of Giants: The Impact of Institutions on Cumulative Research." *American Economic Review* 101 (5): 1933–1963. doi:10.1257/aer.101.5.1933.

Garfield, E. 1972. "Citation Analysis as a Tool in Journal Evaluation." *Science* 178 (60): 471–479. doi:10.1126/science.178.4060.471.

Garfield, E. 2006. "The History and Meaning of the Journal Impact Factor." *Journal of the American Medical Association* 295 (1): 90–93. doi:10.1001/jama.295.1.90.

Gingras, Y., V. Larivière, B. Macaluso, and J. P. Robitaille. 2008. "The Effects of Aging on Researchers' Publication and Citation Patterns." *PloS One* 3: 12. doi:10.1371/journal.pone.0004048.

Gonzalez-Brambila, C., and F. M. Veloso. 2007. "The Determinants of Research Output and Impact: A Study of Mexican Researchers." *Research Policy* 36 (7): 1035–1051. doi:10.1016/j.respol.2007.03.005.

Greene, M. 2007. "The Demise of the Lone Author." *Nature* 450 (20): 1165. doi:10.1038/4501165a.

Hamermesh, D. S. 2013. "Six Decades of Top Economics Publishing: Who and How?" *Journal of Economic Literature* 51 (1): 162–172. doi:10.1257/jel.51.1.162.

Hamermesh, D. S. 2015. "Age, Cohort and Co-Authorship." *NBER Working Paper*. http://www.nber.org/papers/w20938

Hamermesh, D. S., and S. M. Oster. 2002. "Tools or Toys? the Impact of High Technology on Scholarly Productivity." *Economic Inquiry* 40 (4): 539–555. doi:10.1093/ei/40.4.539.

Hazan, M. 2009. "Longevity and Lifetime Labor Supply: Evidence and Implications." *Econometrica* 77 (6): 1829–1863.

Henriksen, D. 2016. "The Rise in Co-Authorship in the Social Sciences (1980–2013)." *Scientometrics* 107 (2): 455–476. doi:10.1007/s11192-016-1849-x.

Hirsch, J. E. 2005. "An Index to Quantify an Individual's Scientific Research Output." *Proceedings of the National Academy of Sciences of the United States of America* 102 (46): 16569–16572. doi:10.1073/pnas.0507655102.

Holden, C. 2001. "General Contentment Masks Gender Gap in First AAAS Salary and Job Survey." *Science* 294 (5541): 396–411. doi:10.1126/science.294.5541.396.

Huber, J., W. Kamakura, and C. F. Mela. 2014. "A Topical History of JMR." *Journal of Marketing Research* 51 (1): 84–91. doi:10.1509/jmr.51.1.02.

Hudson, J. 1996. "Trends in Multi-Authored Papers in Economics." *The Journal of Economic Perspectives* 10 (3): 153–158. doi:10.1257/jep.10.3.153.

Jones, B. F. 2009. "The Burden of Knowledge and the 'Death of the Renaissance Man': Is Innovation Getting Harder?" *Review of Economic Studies* 76 (1): 283–317. doi:10.1111/roes.2009.76.issue-1.

Jones, B. F. 2010. "Age and Great Invention." *Review of Economics and Statistics* 92 (1): 1–14. doi:10.1162/rest.2009.11724.

Jones, B. F., and B. A. Weinberg. 2011. "Age Dynamics in Scientific Creativity." *Proceedings of the National Academy of Sciences of the United States of America* 108 (47): 18910–18914. doi:10.1073/pnas.1102895108.

Katz, J. S., and B. R. Martin. 1997. "What Is Research Collaboration?" *Research Policy* 26 (1): 1–18. doi:10.1016/S0048-7333(96)00917-1.

Kim, E. H., A. Morse, and L. Zingales. 2006. "What Has Mattered to Economics since 1970." *The Journal of Economic Perspectives* 20 (4): 189–202. doi:10.1257/jep.20.4.189.

Kodrzycki, Y. K., and P. Yu. 2006. "New Approaches to Ranking Economics Journals." *Contributions in Economic Analysis & Policy* 5: 1–40. doi:10.2202/1538-0645.1520.

Kortum, S. 1993. "Equilibrium R&D and the Patent-R&D Ratio: U.S. Evidence." *The American Economic Review* 83 (2): 450–457.

Kotovsky, K., J. R. Hayes, and H. A. Simon. 1985. "Why are Some Problems Hard? Evidence of Hanoi from Tower." *Cognitive Psychology* 17: 248–294. doi:10.1016/0010-0285(85)90009-X.

Krampen, G. 2010. "Acceleration of Citing Behavior after the Millennium? Exemplary Bibliometric Reference Analyses for Psychology Journals." *Scientometrics* 83 (2): 507–513. doi:10.1007/s11192-009-0093-z.

Laband, D. N., and R. D. Tollison. 2000. "Intellectual Collaboration." *Journal of Political Economy* 108 (3): 632–662. doi:10.1086/262132.

Larivière, V., C. Ni, Y. Gingras, B. Cronin, and C. R. Sugimoto. 2013. "Bibliometrics: Global Gender Disparities in Science." *Nature* 504 (7479): 211–213. doi:10.1038/504211a.

Larsen, P. O., and M. von Ins. 2010. "The Rate of Growth in Scientific Publication and the Decline in Coverage Provided by Science Citation Index." *Scientometrics* 84 (3): 575–603. doi:10.1007/s11192-010-0202-z.

Lawrence, P. A. 2007. "The Mismeasurement of Science." *Current Biology* 17 (15): 583–585. doi:10.1016/j.cub.2007.06.014.

Lee, C. 2001. "The Expected Length of Male Retirement in the United States, 1850–1990." *Journal of Population Economics* 14 (4): 641–650. doi:10.1007/s001480100064.

Lehman, H. C. 1953. *Age and Achievement*. Princeton, NJ: Princeton University Press.

Lehman, H. C. 1962. "More about Age and Achievement." *The Gerontologist* 2 (3): 141–148. doi:10.1093/geront/2.3.141.

Levin, B. S. G., and P. E. Stephan. 1991. "Research Productivity over the Life Cycle: Evidence for Academic Scientists Author." *American Economic Review* 81 (1): 114–132.

Lin, W.-Y. C., and M.-H. Huang. 2012. "The Relationship between Co-Authorship, Currency of References and Author Self-Citations." *Scientometrics* 90 (2): 343–360. doi:10.1007/s11192-011-0523-6.

Lohmann, S. 1992. "Optimal Commitment in Monetary Policy: Credibility versus Flexibility." *The American Economic Review* 82 (1): 273–286.

Lohmann, S. 1994. "Information Aggregation Through Costly Political Action." *The American Economic Review* 84 (3): 518–530.

Mabe, M. 2003. "The Growth and Number of Journals." *Serials* 16 (2): 191–197. doi:10.1629/16191.

Marois, R., and J. Ivanoff. 2005. "Capacity Limits of Information Processing in the Brain." *Trends in Cognitive Sciences* 9 (6): 296–305. doi:10.1016/j.tics.2005.04.010.

Marx, W. 2011. "Literaturflut - Informationslawine - Wissensexplosion Wächst der Wissenschaft das Wissen über den Kopf?." In *Forschung über Forschung*, edited by J. Allmendinger, D. Dzwonnek, B. Ebersold, J. Enders, F. Fabich, R. Hüttl, W. Krull et al, 96–104, Bielefeld: UVW UniversitätsVerlagWebler.

Massaro, M., J. Dumay, and C. Bagnoli. 2019. "Transparency and the Rhetorical Use of Citations to Robert Yin in case Study Research." *Meditari Accountancy Research* 27 (1): 44–71. doi:10.1108/MEDAR-08-2017-0202.

McDowell, J., and L. Singell. 2000. "Productivity of Highly Skilled Immigrants: Economists in the Postwar Period." *Economic Inquiry* 38: 672–684. doi:10.1111/j.1465-7295.2000.tb00045.x.

McDowell, J. M., and M. Melvin. 1983. "The Determinants of Co-Authorship: An Analysis of the Economics Literature." *The Review of Economics and Statistics* 65 (1): 155–160. doi:10.2307/1924423.

Mela, C. F., J. Roos, and Y. Deng. 2013. "A Keyword History of Marketing Science." *Marketing Science* 32: 8–18. doi:10.1287/mksc.1120.0764.

Melero, E., and N. Palomeras. 2015. "The Renaissance Man Is No Dead! the Role of Generalists in Teams of Inventors." *Research Policy* 44: 154–167. doi:10.1016/j.respol.2014.07.005.

Merton, R. K. 1957. "Priorities in Scientific Discovery: A Chapter in the Sociology of Science." *American Sociological Review* 22 (6): 635–659. doi:10.2307/2089193.

Miller, G. 1955. "The Magical Number Seven, Plus or Minus Two: Some Limits on Our Capacity for Processing Information." *Psychological Review* 101 (2): 343–352. doi:10.1037/0033-295X.101.2.343.

Murray, F. 2002. "Innovation as Co-evolution of Scientific and Technological Networks: Exploring Tissue Engineering." *Research Policy* 31 (8–9): 1389–1403. doi:10.1016/S0048-7333(02)00070-7.

Noorden, R. 2013. "The True Cost of Science Publishing." *Nature* 495: 426–429. doi:10.1038/495426a.

Odlyzko, A. 1997 August 4. "The Economics of Electronic Journals." *First Monday* 2 (8). Accessed 23 November 2017. http://firstmonday.org/article/view/542/463

Önder, A. S., and S. Schweitzer. 2017. "Catching up or Falling Behind? Promising Changes and Persistent Patterns across Cohorts of Economics PhDs in German-Speaking Countries from 1991 to 2008." *Scientometrics* 110: 1297–1331. doi:10.1007/s11192-016-2222-9.

Önder, A. S., S. V. Popov, and S. Schweitzer. 2019. "Leadership in Scholarship: Editors' Influence on the Profession's Narrative." *SSRN Working Paper*. doi:10.2139/ssrn.3105539.

Oster, S. M., and D. S. Hamermesh. 1998. "Aging and Productivity among Economists." *The Review of Economics and Statistics* 80 (1): 154–156. doi:10.1162/003465398557258.

Payson, S. 2019. "Cite This Economics Paper! It Is Time for the House of Cards to Fall Down." *Open Economics* 2 (1): 1–18. doi:10.1515/openec-2019-0001.

Phelan, T. J. 1999. "A Compendium of Issues for Citation Analysis." *Scientometrics* 45 (1): 117–136. doi:10.1007/BF02458472.

Price, D. J. 1963. *Little Science, Big Science . . . And Beyond*. New York: Columbia University Press.

Rafols, I., L. Leydesdorff, A. O'Hare, P. Nightingale, and A. Stirling. 2012. "How Journal Rankings Can Suppress Interdisciplinary Research: A Comparison between Innovation Studies and Business & Management." *Research Policy* 41 (7): 1262–1282. doi:10.1016/j.respol.2012.03.015.

Ritzberger, K. 2008. "A Ranking of Journals in Economics and Related Fields." *German Economic Review* 9 (4): 402–430. doi:10.1111/j.1468-0475.2008.00446.x.

Schankerman, M., and A. Pakes. 1986. "Estimates of the Value of Patent Rights in European Countries during Post-1950 Period." *The Economic Journal* 96 (384): 1052–1076. doi:10.2307/2233173.

Schultz, T. W. 1963. *The Economic Value of Education*. New York: Columbia University Press.

Segerstrom, P. S. 1998. "Endogenous Growth Without Scale Effects." *The American Economic Review* 88 (5): 1290–1310.

Singh, J., and L. Fleming. 2010. "Lone Inventors as Sources of Breakthroughs: Myth or Reality?" *Management Science* 56 (1): 41–56. doi:10.1287/mnsc.1090.1072.

Solow, R. 1962. "Technical Progress, Capital Formation, and Economic Growth." *The American Economic Review* 52 (2): 76–86.

Stephan, P. 1996. "The Economics of Science." *Journal of Economic Literature* 34 (3): 1199–1235.

Sweller, J. 1994. "Cognitive Load Theory, Learning Difficulty, and Instructional Design." *Learning and Instruction* 4: 295–312. doi:10.1016/0959-4752(94)90003-5.

Tague, J., J. Beheshti, and L. Rees-Potter. 1981. "The Law of Exponential Growth: Evidence, Implications and Forecasts." *Library Trends* 30 (1): 125–149.

Teodorescu, D., and T. Andrei. 2014. "An Examination of 'Citation Circles' for Social Sciences Journals in Eastern European Countries." *Scientometrics* 99 (2): 209–231. doi:10.1007/s11192-013-1210-6.

Ucar, I., F. Lopez-Fernandino, P. Rodriguez-Ulibarri, L. Sesma-Sanchez, V. Urrea-Mico, and J. Sevilla. 2013. "Growth in the Number of References in Engineering Journal Papers during the 1972–2013 Period." *Scientometrics* 98 (3): 1855–1864.

Xie, Y. 2014. "'undemocracy': Inequalities in Science." *Science* 344 (6186): 809–810. doi:10.1126/science.1252743.

Yitzhaki, M., and D. Ben-Tamar. 1991. "Number of References in Biochemistry and Other Fields; a Case Study of the Journal of Biological Chemistry Throughout 1910–1985." *Scientometrics* 21 (1): 3–22. doi:10.1007/BF02019179.

Zuckerman, H. 1977. *Scientific Elite: Nobel Laureates in the United States*. New York: Free Press.

How the university ecosystem shapes the innovation capacities of undergraduate students – evidence from Germany

Carolin Bock, Daniel Dilmetz, Benjamin S. Selznick, Lini Zhang and Matthew J. Mayhew

ABSTRACT

In society, universities should fulfil their so-called 'third mission' concerning knowledge and technology transfer. However, our knowledge on the impact of the university ecosystem on students' innovative output is still scarce. Our study sheds light on the question whether the university ecosystem stimulates students' innovation capacities or whether innovators are mainly determined by personality traits or family background. The results of our two rounds of surveys, with a total of 345 students of a technical university in Germany, reveal that factors such as functional experiences (e.g. resources and physical spaces within the university) and connecting experiences (e.g. practical application of skills learned during courses) have a significant impact on students' innovation capacities.

1. Introduction

Education for innovation and entrepreneurship has become a world-wide strategic measure to develop scientific and technological progress and economic prosperity (Wang and Tingting 2018).

An important point of investigation in recent years has been the environment of the university ecosystem. Universities are attributed an important role in the development of the regional innovation by educating and preparing students for diverse roles in future academic and professional development and leadership. This results in new needs and concerns related to universities' role in innovation, which can be divided into qualitative and quantitative aims (Reichert 2019). Qualitative aims can be understood as the development of specific skills and competencies, such as the preparation of students for disruptive innovation, the promotion of systemic understanding, competencies and capacities and, especially prevalent in times of the current COVID-19 pandemic, the promotion of digital skills. Processes such as capability building reflect one of the major points for universities' so-called third mission alongside traditional objectives, such as teaching and research (Rampersad 2015; Liefner and Schiller 2008; Mei-Chih and Mathews 2008; Perkmann et al. 2013). Universities respond to these qualitative aims in executing teaching reforms like the extension of interdisciplinary, project-based learning, the support of students' self-organisation and the extension of mentoring. Beside qualitative aims, exemplary quantitative aims of universities comprise the extension of the skill base for the region or country, an increased engagement in the STEM area, especially regarding digital know-how as well as the re-skill and upskill in response to innovation needs (Reichert 2019).

An additional and specific subject to universities' potential promoting regional innovation is its influence on entrepreneurial ecosystems. These ecosystems can be understood as combinations of social, political, economic and cultural elements within a region, supporting the development of innovation and encouragement of nascent entrepreneurial activity and culture (Spigel 2017). As entrepreneurial activity is critical to economic progress (Drucker 1999; Quadrini 2000; Nijkamp 2003; Malecki 1997), the eventual attempt or even success in entrepreneurial activities can serve as a measure of universities' impact on entrepreneurial education and ultimately in economic growth and regional development (Hallam et al. 2014). Models such as the Triple Helix model, developed by Etzkowitz and Leydesdorff (2000) highlight regional economic development, eventually with industry and government as universities third mission (Heaton, Siegel, and Teece 2019). Universities therefore increasingly follow this path of serving as an entrepreneurial university, engaging in technology transfer and commercialisation, providing entrepreneurial skills to students and the wider community (Shapira and Wang 2009).

The question, whether universities can influence the behaviour and development students altered to specific investigations of potential influencing factors provided by the university to increase their innovative behaviour and skillset that are potentially capable to change students (Mayhew et al. 2016). Previous research in higher education mainly focused to investigate occasional factors and their influence to specific abilities or intentions on students. These occasional factors include personal factors of students (Norwani 2009; Zhao, Hills, and Seibert 2005), the influence of students' participation in specific courses (Mentoor and Friedrich 2007; Kourilsky and Esfandiari 1997) or students' participation in extracurricular events (Pascarella et al. 2004). Investigating these potential influencing factors, research in higher education to date has found that occasional factors of higher education institutes can effect students' intention to innovate (e.g. Mayhew et al. 2012), entrepreneurial intentions (e.g. Passaro, Quinto, and Thomas 2018; Zhao, Hills, and Seibert 2005; Volery et al. 2013), or the development of certain cognitive skills of students (Pascarella et al. 2014; Kim et al. 2017). However, these studies have mainly focused on the potential influence of individual factors on specific abilities or intentions of students, leaving open questions, as some studies only offer qualitative approaches to optimising the university environment, while other, quantitative studies only focus on partial aspects of the university environment.

For this reason, this study represents a comprehensive approach to identify influential factors on specific student competencies (i.e. innovation capacities) that takes two aspects into account. First, personal characteristics of students including demographic information such as age, gender and previous family experience with innovation and entrepreneurship and personality traits such as extroversion and openness to new experiences. Second, we investigate universities' educational influence, represented by university courses, and third, the impact of the university environment and its infrastructure itself.

Besides personal characteristics of students, we empirically investigate the potential influence of universities' ecosystem on students' innovation capacities using four kinds of perspectives within this ecosystem: faculty challenges, faculty interaction, functional experiences and connecting experiences. As these factors showed high relevance in past studies in higher education, we use them to generate a comprehensive picture of the university's experiences and services.

We, therefore, contribute to literature in higher education by mapping the university environment as a whole through several factors and examining the influence of all factors on the development of student competencies. Our results show that the innovation capacity of students can be influenced by the university ecosystem and personal experiences on campus, in particular, functional and connecting experiences.

Functional experiences are resources provided directly by university resources, such as space to work with other students on new projects which are not explicitly academic or social. Connecting experiences describe the experiences of students outside the classroom made in university life (Berger and Milem 2000, 319). We thus additionally contribute to the controversially discussed question of whether students' innovation capacity can be influenced by teaching or other factors of higher education institutions. Our results also provide incentives for universities themselves. As our findings indicate the relevance of functional and connecting experiences, universities should focus on developing a climate of innovation taking into account a variety of organisational structures and amenities besides focusing on developing innovation-friendly teaching programmes. By concentrating on the development of skills to enhance innovation, students can use these skills as an instrument for assessing existing and future needs of society and develop viable and innovative solutions to the challenges of the next decades (Bezarra 2017).

The remainder of the paper is structured as follows: Section 2 summarises the existing literature related to educational programmes and the university ecosystem. Section 3 presents the underlying theoretical background of the paper, as well as the development of the investigated hypotheses. Section 4 introduces the dataset and variables. Section 5 deals with empirical analysis and results. In section 6, the results of the empirical analysis will be discussed. Sections 7 and 8 consist of the paper's limitations, conclusion, as well as practical implications, respectively.

2. Literature review

2.1. Educational programmes

The content of education programmes addressing innovation and their impact on students' skillset has been a growing field of interest within higher education research. Notably, prior literature has been investigating several aspects that can be improved by educational activities, e.g. students' entrepreneurial intention, entrepreneurial selfefficacy and innovation capacities (Mayhew et al. 2012). Baumol (2004) points out that universities play a crucial role in teaching innovation and promoting innovation capacities. Implementing innovation-based content in universities' curricula pursues the aim to not replicate existing structures but to think out-of-the-box and thus fulfil Schumpeter's idea of creating new products and services (Block, Fisch, and Mirjam 2017).

Within the past two decades, several studies have investigated the influence of specific innovation-based higher education programmes, which have been implemented within the structures of curricula, on students' innovation skills. In an experimental study, Genco, Seepersad, and Holtta-Otto (2010) compared the innovation level of concept generating exercises between first-year and senior undergraduate engineering students. They found that the results of senior undergraduate students were less innovative than the solutions of the first-year undergraduate students, highlighting the need for increasing the development of innovation-based skills in an engineering curriculum.

With the 'NSF CAREER' project, Purzer, Fila, and Mathis (2014) aimed at characterising how engineering students not only view but also approach innovation. They found that senior engineering students see themselves rather as a technical problem solver, avoiding creative solutions due to the fear of failure and that they tend to outsource creative tasks to others who are not engineers (Purzer, Fila, and Mathis 2014). Another programme designed to address engineering students' innovation capacities was created at the University of Bath in the UK. Students participating in this 'Specialist Design Unit' went through several stages within the programme, targeted at developing different skills such as imagination and creativity, dealing with uncertainty or independence. Results after interviewing the participating students showed an enhancement in their innovation skills (Dekoninck 2012).

Within the Framework for Innovation Competencies Development and Assessment projects (FINCODA), a tool for measuring and validating innovation capacities was developed. Several universities across Europe, as well as partners from industry, worked together to develop an instrument for measuring the innovation competencies of students. The final result of the project was the FINCODA-barometer, assessing innovation capacities through the five core areas initiative, teamwork, networking, critical thinking and creativity (Butter 2017). The FINCODA barometer was then used to evaluate an overarching initiative at the University of Turku, Finland, where innovation pedagogy was implemented as a joint approach in all areas within the university. Describing the initiative, Lappalainen (2018) pointed out that some factors, such as multidisciplinary learning environments and flexible curricula, are essential requirements for the 'innovation pedagogy' to succeed.

Our literature review on entrepreneurial and higher education shows the potential influence of those academic fields on students' innovation capacities as a part of their entrepreneurial skillset. However, previous studies have focused on the identification of individual factors and the development of specific abilities of students. We address this gap in the literature by mapping the university as a coherent structure represented by several factors, and thus to examine the university ecosystem as a whole for the potential development of students. Due to the society-changing mechanism of digitalisation, a plurality of innovations arise in technical environments (Löbbecke 2006). This development leads to interest in how students of a technical university with potential high affinity to technical innovations benefit from the university's ecosystem in developing their innovation capacities.

2.2. Universities ecosystem

Besides the establishment of dedicated programmes to promote students' innovation capacities, several studies focused on the effect of innovative ecosystems within the university (e.g. entrepreneurship and innovation labs or makerspaces) to foster such capacities. Previous studies confirmed that such ecosystems and places have the potential to promote the entrepreneurial skill-set of undergraduate students needed for successful entrepreneurial activities (Chávez-Tellería, Repellin-Moreno, and Mendieta-Jiménez 2017; Hulme, Thomas, and Hal 2014). Fisher and Koch (2008) declared innovation purely as a function of personality, recent studies (see Selznick and Mayhew 2018) demonstrate that capacities can be developed over and above personality traits (e.g. extroversion and openness to new experiences). These findings enhance the understanding of the potential development of students' innovation capacities, representing a crucial part of students' entrepreneurial skillset.

Despite the lack of a common definition for the term ecosystem, it has been associated with the institution of a university in numerous studies in recent years (e.g. Acs et al. 2017; Colombo et al. 2019), discussing its role both as an independent ecosystem, on the one hand, and as an important component of other ecosystems, on the other hand. Hence, universities are embedded as key institutions in knowledge ecosystems, with the primary goal to generate knowledge (Acs et al. 2017; Audretsch et al. 2019; Hayter 2016). Besides the main task of generating knowledge within the framework of such knowledge ecosystems, universities also function as anchor organisations in the knowledge generation process (Agrawal and Cockburn 2002) by producing basic and applied research, transferring this research to the local industry through R&D collaborations and therefore increasing technological innovation (Clarysse et al. 2014). Audretsch et al. (2019) reaffirm the status of universities in entrepreneurial ecosystems as key actors within such ecosystems, not only being able to generate knowledge but also to commercialise it through vehicles such as academic spin-offs, thus being able to contribute to regional and national innovation development (Rampersad 2015). Miller and Acs (2017) provide a different view of universities as independent ecosystems. In their study, they develop a framework based on Frederik Jackson Turner's Frontier Thesis of American democracy (1894) to examine the modern U.S. campus entrepreneurial ecosystem. They analyse themes originally developed in Turner's frontier (available assets, liberty, and diverse populations) and compare these with the modern university college. In summary, they claim that the open innovative American frontier has re-emerged within the campus of modern U.S. universities (Miller and Acs 2017; see also Swayne et al. 2019).

In addition to the view of universities as entrepreneurial ecosystems, universities can also be seen as innovation ecosystems, consisting of a set of actors that engage with regional and national innovation ecosystems through relationships with the industry. These ecosystems can be defined as complex relationships between actors and entities, mainly aspiring to develop innovation (Jackson 2011). Under this aspect, universities foster specific activities. Above all, this is reflected by the promotion of high-tech spinoffs, increased technology commercialisation, but also on the teaching side through the stimulation of the innovative mindset of students (Etzkowitz and Leydesdorff 2000). Although research on the first two points has provided a wide range of results in recent years, further research, interpretation and the critical role of students in the context of innovation education by universities are required (Åstebro, Bazzazian, and Braguinsky 2012).

Whether the university functions as an ecosystem in its own right or as part of an ecosystem (e.g. an entrepreneurial ecosystem), university governance can play an important role in this context. The governance of universities can be described as a bureaucratic-oligarchic model, where mainly professors, functioning as the dominant decision-making party, are responsible for the internal university governance (Braun and Merrien 1999). This internal organisation consisting of mainly professors is usually aggregated in the form of an academic senate, which is responsible for managing areas such as research and teaching. State universities function as autonomous institutions, which are regulated by law but still have a high degree of freedom, which is reflected in a high degree of variance (Meoli, Paleari, and Vismara 2019). Mason and Brown (2014) generally argue that entrepreneurial ecosystems are formed from institutions that already have a strong knowledge base and employ a large number of scientists and engineers. More specifically, with regard to the role of the university as part of a dedicated ecosystem, such as a (regional) entrepreneurial ecosystem, research in recent years has gained increasing knowledge about the influence of governance mechanisms on such an ecosystem. For example, Cunningham, Menter, and Wirsching (2019) developed a principal investigator-centred governance framework with regard to the entrepreneurial ecosystem, in which researchers from a university play a central role. In a university context, scientists take on the role of principal investigators to address the gap between science and business. In order to successfully influence the management of governance within such an entrepreneurial ecosystem, scientists, functioning as the principal investigator, must dispose of several capabilities such as scientific excellence, research leadership and managerial responsiveness. Using these specific skills, acting as a broker between various actors within the entrepreneurial ecosystem (e.g. industry, private and public capital providers) the principal investigators' actions and behaviour influence the governance within the entrepreneurial ecosystem, supporting the creation of new ventures and, respectively, the creation of disruptive knowledge and the provision of resources and capabilities (Cunningham, Menter, and Wirsching 2019; Kidwell 2013). Furthermore, Meoli, Paleari, and Vismara (2019) investigate the impact of governance transformation due to a country-specific law in Italy concerning the composition of the board of directors on the establishment of academic spin-offs. Investigating 1,234 spin-offs from 66 universities, they find empirical evidence that the presence of lay members and entrepreneurs in the university's board of directors can significantly influence the number of technology spin-offs created per year. Although this finding provides evidence of the potentially positive influence of the composition of a university's governing bodies on the creation of academic spin-offs, the results do not prove to be fundamentally generalisable, as no significant effect of the presence of entrepreneurs in the board of directors on the creation of non-technology spin-offs could be detected (Meoli, Paleari, and Vismara 2019).

Within the framework of this study, we want to contribute to the recent call addressing the critical role of students in the context of innovation education by universities (Åstebro, Bazzazian, and Braguinsky 2012) and concentrate on the university ecosystem itself and its potential to develop students' innovation capacities. As universities are increasingly seen as key institutions for technological innovation and transfer to local industry (Clarysse et al. 2014), we see high potential in investigating those factors for a better knowledge of the potential university ecosystems. Since studies have already proven the influence of the environment on competence formation, especially among students (e.g. Norwani 2009), we want to examine the university and its influence as a construct, represented by different facets. To this end, we study various environmental factors of the university ecosystem to investigate the extent of their potential influence on the promotion of specific capabilities, in our case innovation capacities. The selection of these factors of the university ecosystem is primarily based on the observation of past literature, which has already examined these factors in individual cases for their potential influence on the development of student skills as well as on the intention of students in relation to the performance of various activities. A summary of these results can be found in appendix (table 1). The following chapter presents this study's theoretical concepts resulting in the hypotheses developed for these specific environmental factors of the universities' ecosystem.

3. Theoretical framework and hypotheses development

Research in higher education identified three types of constructs that can be associated with the development of students in an educational context: involvement, engagement, and integration. According to Astin (1984), involvement can be defined as the amount of physical and psychological energy that students devote to their academic experience. Engagement, on the one hand, represents the amount of time and effort students invest in activities within the campus context that lead to experiences and outcomes that constitute student success (Wolf-Wendel, Ward, and Kinzie 2009). Also, engagement represents the allocation of resources provided by higher education institutions to encourage students to participate and benefit from, such as human resources and learning opportunities (Kuh 2001). The term integration, in turn, explains the extent to which students share attitudes and beliefs of their faculty and the extent to which students follow the structural rules and requirements of the institution they are part of (Pascarella and Terenzini 1991; Tinto 1993).

In this study, we focus on these concepts, involvement, engagement and integration, and investigate, how these constructs are represented in universities' ecosystem, to potentially foster undergraduate students' innovation capacities.

The theory of student involvement developed by Astin (1984) serves as the centre of this theoretical framework. Within this study, the factors of the university ecosystem are considered as a specific way of student involvement within the university ecosystem. Researchers noted that this theory has a powerful influence on higher education research (Pascarella and Pascarella 2006). The involvement of the student can be applied to a variety of active behaviours of the student, such as the degree of effort the student invests in the performance of his academic achievements, the amount of time he spends on campus or invests participating in student organisations (Wolf-Wendel, Ward, and Kinzie 2009). Astin (1984) also argues that a student's potential to achieve learning outcome is greatest when the learning environment; in our case, the university ecosystem is structured to support the student's active participation (Astin 1984). In his initial work developing the student involvement theory, Astin (1984) identifies five basic postulates within his theory, summarised in Table 1. These propositions can be seen as conceptual

Table 1. Astin's five postulates of the Student involvement theory (Astin 1984, 519).

1. Involvement refers to the investment of physical and psychological energy in various objects. The objects may be highly generalised (the student experience) or highly specific (preparing for a chemistry examination).
2. Regardless of its object, involvement occurs along a continuum; that is, different students manifest different degrees of involvement in a given object, and the same student manifests different degrees of involvement in different objects at different times.
3. Involvement has both quantitative and qualitative features. The extent of a student's involvement in academic work, for instance, can be measured quantitatively (how many hours the student spends studying) and qualitatively (whether the student reviews and comprehends reading assignments or simply stares at the textbook and day-dreams).
4. The amount of student learning and personal development associated with any educational programme is directly proportional to the quality and quantity of student involvement in that programme.
5. The effectiveness of any educational policy or practice is directly related to the capacity of that policy or practice to increase student involvement.

explanations on how factors of the university ecosystem affect students (Berger and Milem 2000).

Berger and Milem (2000) developed a framework for the academic, social, and functional experiences of students.

To further address the term integration, we draw on the early work of Tinto (1993). Investigating the reasons of voluntary departure from colleges and universities, Tinto's (1993) theory was unique to the field of student development as it shifted responsibility for the circumstance of voluntary departure from the individual situation of students to being an issue under the influence of the institution itself (Wolf-Wendel, Ward, and Kinzie 2009). Tinto's (1993) theory of social and academic integration is based on the work of Van Gennep (1960), who described three phases that occur when an individual joins a new group. In the first phase, the individual separates from the past. The second phase consists of a transition, in which the individual begins to interact with new settings and people. In the last phase, the individual incorporates to the new environment, adopting the norms and expectations of the new group (Van Gennep 1960). In his theory, Tinto (1993) defined integration explicitly drawing on both social and academic connection to the campus. Social integration describes students' perceptions of interactions with different agents of the institution, such as peers, faculty and institutional staff. Academic integration reserves to students' perceived experiences in the formal and informal academic setting. These experiences result from interactions with faculty, staff and peers, inside and outside the classroom setting, enhancing students' intellectual development (Tinto 1993; Wolf-Wendel, Ward, and Kinzie 2009). Tinto (1993) also stated that integration in educational context is most important for students in their first year at an institution. Alongside Tinto's (1993) work, the term integration has been used by Chickering (1974) in terms of students' active involvement in academic and social activities, describing integration not only as an influential factor to investigate students' retention from institutions, but also as a critical aspect of student learning (Chickering 1974).

In this study, we address the question to what extent environmental experiences within the university ecosystem can be responsible for improving students' innovation capacities. These environmental experiences, divided into four factors, are intended to illustrate four different aspects of the university ecosystem theorised to be associated with innovation capacity development (Mayhew et al. 2012, 2016) and can be distinguished by covering areas of curricular and co-curricular experiences, as well as the existence of different resources at the university itself.

First, curricular experiences include *faculty challenges*. Faculty challenges can be understood as the type of students' experiences, which are mainly made within the framework of participation in teaching events. Astin (1984) postulates that the amount of physical and psychological energy can be understood as involvement. The energy used by the student may be generalisable, such as the general experiences of students, or highly specific, such as preparing for a specific test. This involvement of the student can be determined quantitatively (e.g. students' hours spend studying) as well as qualitatively (e.g. special tasks or assignments that the student is involved in) (Astin 1984). Astin further claims that the scope of learning and personal development of students in the context of an educational programme is directly proportional to the quality and quantity of students' participation in that programme. Therefore, the question can be asked whether the students' involvement in curricular events and the development of innovation capacities are also proportional to the amount of involvement students experience.

Students' *faculty interaction* has for quite some time been a repeatedly investigated factor related to the development of various characteristics in the educational context (e.g. Mayhew et al. 2016). Based on this construct, researchers have already investigated the question of why students withdraw from college (Finn 1993), as well as if academic performance (Klem and Connell 2004) can be associated with students' interaction to faculty. Since the interaction of students, for example, through the provision of mentor programmes, can be seen as the direct involvement of students in the university ecosystem, Astin's theory also raises the question of the extent to which this factor of involvement in the university ecosystem can contribute to a potential development of innovation capacities. Furthermore, faculty interaction can also be linked as a part of students' academic integration within an institution, drawing on Tinto's (1993) theory of involvement. More precisely, according to Tinto (1993), integration is based on two pillars of connection between an individual and the campus of an institution, depict as social and academic interactions. Social interactions refer to students' perception of interactions with peers, faculty and staff at the institution and the involvement in extra- and co-curricular activities. Academic integration, on the other hand, refers to students' perception of experiences in the academic system itself, resulting from interactions with faculty, staff and peers, both inside and outside the classroom settings. Tinto (1993) stated that these interactions potentially enhance the intellectual development of the student (Tinto 1993; Wolf-Wendel, Ward, and Kinzie 2009).

As a further object of investigation, resources and physical facilities made available by university itself is to be investigated. These so-called *functional experiences* can be understood, for example, by participating and using resources experienced through the use of facilities such as the university library (Berger and Milem 2000). Those facilities potentially contribute to an increase in the participation of students at the university and might also affect students' innovation capacities as well. Students may, for example, organise themselves in more effective ways using those facilities which can also be meeting spots to initiate innovative projects together. Functional experiences, as another of students' involvement into the university ecosystem, have a rather neglected character in research so far (Berger and Milem 2000). Moreover, Berger and Milem (2000) argue that the more students perceive that such experience provides a supportive campus environment, the more such experience can influence the quantity and quality of students' involvement in social and academic aspects of college.

The question whether the students' involvement in curricular events and the development of innovation capacities are also proportional to the amount of involvement students experience is also linked to the fourth factor to be examined in the context of this study, students' *connecting experiences*. Connecting experiences cover students' activities in which the knowledge acquired in curricular events is to be applied practically (e.g. case studies or business challenges presented by companies). Alongside the experiences from teaching events (faculty challenges), we want to investigate to what extent the investment of physical and mental energy (students' involvement) in events, where knowledge from curricular events has to be applied on practical applications can have a positive effect on the application of innovation skills (e.g. Selznick 2019). As Astin (1984) points out in his theory, the involvement of students can be distinguished into qualitative aspects as well as quantitative aspects. This qualitative aspect could be reflected in the consideration of pure knowledge generation through curricular events (faculty challenges) and the application of this learned knowledge to practical application cases, illustrated in our factor connecting experiences.

The second concept we use in this study relates to the argumentation why we want to investigate environmental factors of the university ecosystem as a potential predictor for the development of innovation capacities in this study. The InputEnvironment-Output (IEO) model, again developed by Astin (1993b) represents an appropriate framework within this field of research (Yanto, Mula, and Kavanagh 2011).

The model incorporates three perspectives. First, inputs refer to personal qualities students possess, for example, before the exposure to certain experiences provided by the university ecosystem. Second, environment refers to the actual experience students underly. Third, the outcome represents the talent or skill is to be developed, in our case, students' innovation capacities. In general, two forms of relationships between these factors can be distinguished. General relationships describe the relationships between the environment variables and the potential outcomes, in our case students. Conditional relationships can be understood as the kind of relationships that establish a connection between the individuals' input and their outcome in relation to the influence of an environment to comprehend this relationship (Mayhew et al. 2016). In this study, we focus on general relationships the between environment and the outcome. As the model is based on the context of higher education (Yanto, Mula, and Kavanagh 2011), it has already received numerous applications in previous studies (see Mayhew et al. 2016). Norwani (2009) employed the IEO model to investigate how specific input and environmental variables potentially affect students learning outcomes, divided in students' academic achievement and cognitive development. Environmental factors included academic facilities, course content, interaction with faculty staff and peers, and co-curriculum activities. Interestingly, Norwani (2009) found out that the academic performance of the students was mainly influenced by input factors, such as gender and career aspiration, while the competence building of cognitive skills was influenced by the environmental factors. Tsang (2017) investigated whether a difference can be identified between U.S. humanities and STEM students in terms of the impact of university environmental factors on their propensity towards innovation. The results show that the major of students can have an impact on propensity towards innovation.

Previous studies show that the IEO model according to Astin (1993a) is an appropriate concept to investigate student outcomes under specific environments. Both the theory of student involvement and the IEO model are to serve as the theoretical basis within the framework of this study. In order to investigate the effects of the university ecosystem on the potential development of students' innovation capacities, the four presented factors faculty challenge, connecting experiences, faculty interaction and functional experiences will be investigated. A number of previous studies have already dealt with the effects of these factors on various areas in the student context. An overview of these studies can be found in Appendix (table 1). The hypotheses to be examined in this study in relation to these four factors are presented in the following.

3.1. Faculty challenge

Despite the fact that challenges arising from faculty are not clearly defined, St. Clair (2014) sees the mission of such challenges in promoting excellent teaching for enhanced student learning. Various characteristics of faculty challenges can be found in dedicated literature, such as demanding high achievement (Braxton 1993), challenging students to strive for excellence (Unks 1979), and engaging students in active learning (Hackett and St.Clair 2014). The education of skills and knowledge of students through teaching events is a central element of universities. In society, universities are sometimes portrayed as innovative threats (Wieder 2011) rather than being seen as a dedicated facility to foster the skills of students to develop new products and services that can potentially lead to global change (Mayhew et al. 2012; Mars, Slaughter, and Rhoades 2008). A number of previous studies have already dealt with the potential impact of participation in teaching events on various areas in the educational context. Warren, Kisenwether, and Hanke (2006) successfully demonstrated that participation in teaching events has a positive effect on the development of creativity aspects and entrepreneurial self-efficacy. Mentoor and Friedrich (2007) provide another example. In a study with 463 undergraduate students of a university in South Africa, the participation of an entrepreneurship course found to be a significant impact to increase students' opportunity recognition-skills. Pascarella et al. (2014) performed a study with a total of 949 students, attending liberal arts colleges and research universities. In their study, it could be proven that academic challenges lead to an improvement in students' cognitive skills. Passaro, Quinto, and Thomas (2018) investigated the influence of special courses and their influence on student skills. They found that participating in special entrepreneurship courses can have a significant impact on the entrepreneurial intention of students.

However, not all studies come to the conclusion that participation in general or specific courses must necessarily lead to the development of innovation skills. Within their study including almost 500 students at 27 Swiss institutions (Volery et al. 2013) show that no significant influences of such participation on opportunity recognition and exploitation skills, entrepreneurial intentions or perceived innovation propensity can be identified.

Within the framework of our study, faculty challenges are seen as challenges that students have to face in the context of curricular events. It will be investigated whether faculty encourage their students to come up with new ideas and solutions and whether they apply a particular course concept to actual problems. As most studies found a positive impact of those challenges by faculty on students' innovation capacities, we propose the following hypothesis:

Hypothesis 1: *'Challenges provided by faculty have a positive impact on students' innovation capacities.'*

3.2. Faculty interaction

We refer to faculty interactions as interactions between students and their faculty outside of teaching events. These interactions can take various forms, such as digital or personal communication of students with teachers, serving as an advisor in student clubs or voluntary institutions and organisations (Pingree and Zakrajsek 2019; Davis 2009). As previous research indicates, interactions between students and faculty serve as one of the most important factors to improve students' learning, development, engagement, satisfaction and success on college (Astin 1993a; Kuh et al. 2010; Joosten 2012; Tinto 1993). Studies within higher education research also found that this dimension of students' involvement (e.g. meeting/working with faculty members to discuss ideas in workshops or conferences) is positively related with the development of interpersonal skills of college students (Astin 1993b; Strayhorn 2018; Sax 2008; Tinto 1993). The increased relevance of this factor is reflected in a large number of studies that have adequately investigated the influence of faculty interaction. In a study involving over 700 students from four universities in Taiwan, Hu, Hung, and Ching (2014) find that strong interaction with faculty has a significant effect on three dimensions of students' educational outcomes. Along with these findings, Kim et al. (2017) recently found that faculty interaction can positively influence the development of cognitive and interpersonal skills, as well as civic attitudes under international students in the United States.

However, even when looking at previous studies with regard to the potential influence of faculty interactions, it becomes clear that there does not always have to be a positive connection. Pascarella et al. (2014) find, that high-quality interactions with faculty are no significant predictor for the development of certain skills in students' cognitive development. Whether a close relationship between students and the university has an influence on students' innovative abilities will be tested within the framework of the second hypothesis.

Hypothesis 2: *'Students' non-classroom faculty interaction has a positive impact on students' innovation capacities.'*

3.3. Functional experiences

In this study, functional experiences are understood as the provision of resources by the university, such as workspaces where students can work together on projects and also resources provided by institutions such as university libraries. Studies have already demonstrated the impact of different designs and characteristics of workspace on the effectiveness of students' working practices. Leicht, Messner, and Anumba (2009) developed a framework for effective planning and use of interactive workspaces in order to enhance student collaboration. To do so, they evaluated 24 undergraduate teams of an architectural engineering programme at Penn State University using four different configurations of an interactive workspace. They found that different configurations resulted in different levels of effectiveness of collaboration due to the improving ability to participate and communicate in the tasks students were given. Björklund et al. (2011) also found that co-working spaces dedicated to students positively influence the activities, interactions, experiments and work of students. Functional experiences enable students to organise themselves in small interdisciplinary groups and to work on creative solutions. Addressing the potential effects of providing resources by the university library, Walter and David Lankes (2015) report that innovation 'may involve collaboration with student affairs professionals to consider the impact of co-curricular spaces on student learning' (Walter and David Lankes 2015, 855). A current topic of discussion on students' functional experiences is the expansion of the university library's resources by opening or expanding makerspaces in order to allow students to work independently on innovative projects. Hynes and Hynes (2018) investigated this current trend, examining different settings of makerspaces and their potential and their evaluation by students concerning their use of those facilities. Due to the fact that this kind of factor of the university ecosystem has not received enough attention in previous research (Berger and Milem 2000), we want to address this gap in knowledge within the framework of this study and investigate, whether functional experiences serve as a significant predictor for the improvement of innovation capacities.

Hypothesis 3: *'Students' functional experiences through the provision of resources, premises, and contact points within the university have a positive impact on students' innovation capacities.'*

3.4. Connecting experiences

The last factor of the university ecosystem to be investigated in this study is described as connecting experiences. By connecting experiences, the knowledge and skills of the students provided in courses shall be applied to practical out-of-class situations. In the university context, experimental studies, field trials, design projects or internships that arise from cooperation between universities and companies can be considered as connecting experiences. Educational research has identified the existence of a transfer problem, where the knowledge acquired at university cannot be applied to the challenges in practical working life (Illeris 2009). In an extensive study, Mayhew et al. (2012) investigated the effect of such experiences on students' potential intention to innovate. Volery et al. (2013) also report a significant correlation to practical-orientated activities of students on entrepreneurial knowledge and business-opportunity exploitation skills. Passaro, Quinto, and Thomas (2018) also come to similar results. In their study, they examine the influence of the participation in business-plan competitions, both by students and by academic staff (e.g. doctoral candidates and technical staff). They also come to the conclusion that attending courses of this kind can positively influence the development of entrepreneurial intentions, as well as entrepreneurial human capital skills.

Connecting experiences can also play a decisive role with regard to the degree of internationalisation of the university. In addition to a growing focus and interest in factors that influence the internationalisation of companies shortly after the start-up phase (Knight and Liesch 2016), the term internationalisation has become increasingly important in relation to basic disciplines of entrepreneurship, such as the recognition of opportunities (Rebecca et al. 2018).

Internationalisation can also play an important role in the university context. Minola, Donina, and Meoli (2016) show that the degree of internationalisation of the university in teaching, research and the so-called 'third mission' can have a demonstrable influence on the willingness of students to consider whether and how seriously they have thought about starting their own business. Connecting experiences can support this degree of internationalisation in many ways, for example, by setting business challenges through internationally represented companies. On the one hand, this can promote the degree of internationalisation in teaching, on the other hand, it can have a positive influence on the number of international students. In the study by Minola, Donina, and Meoli (2016), both factors proved to be significant factors influencing the future entrepreneurial orientation of students.

As students' innovation capacities are supposed to enable the students to participate in innovation processes in companies and organisations (Penttila and Lyytinen 2015), it is also important in the context of this study whether connecting experiences made at university can positively influence students' innovation capacities, leading to the following hypothesis:

Hypothesis 4: *'Students' out-of-class connecting experiences have a positive impact on students' innovation capacities.'*

4. Data and sample

To test our hypotheses, we refer to a longitudinal survey-sampled dataset of students of a major technical university in Germany. The university at which the study was conducted has more than 25,000 students and offers a wide range of programmes, with the exception of medicine and law. The students were survey-sampled twice during their first academic year at university. The first survey was conducted right at the beginning of their first academic year. The second round was carried out towards the end of the first academic year. The two survey rounds took place between fall 2016 and 2017. The questionnaire in round one consisted of various questions that covered the personality and behaviour of the students surveyed. For example, questions were asked as to how far students see themselves as extroverted or open to new experiences. In addition, questions were asked about the behaviour of students in specific situations. Additionally, a total of nine superordinate constructs of questions were asked. These nine sub-scales such as motivation, proactivity, and willingness to take risks are required to determine the overall score of students' innovation capacities.

In addition to the questions of round one, the survey in round two contained several questions about the university's ecosystem and environment. The questionnaire in round one was sent to 3,761 students. Of these, 1,303 respondents could be evaluated. In round two, the questionnaire was sent again to 3,530 students. From this group, 528 questionnaires could be used for evaluation, 345 of which took part in both question rounds. Accordingly, 345 respondents were available for evaluation in this study. Table 2 shows descriptive statistics of our dataset.

Sixty per cent of the 345 surveyed students are male. The majority of students age between 18 and 20 (57.97%) followed by a group of 21- to 23-year-old (28.12%). About 80% of the respondents pursue a Bachelor of Science degree which is common at a technical university. Nearly 30% of the respondents can relate to a family member that founded a profit or non-profit organisation and close to 12% report that a family member has invented a new product, service or process.

4.1. Measurement of innovation capacities (dependent variable)

The focus of this study is to gain information about the potential factors of the university ecosystem that influence students' innovation capacities. To gain insights on this aspect, we refer to a reliable and valid instrument to measure students' innovation capacities

Table 2. Descriptive Statistics of the Sample.

	Sample (N = 345)	
	n	%
Gender		
Male	209	60.58
Female	132	38.27
No Information	4	1.25
Age		
18–20	200	57.97
21–23	97	28.12
24–26	15	4.35
27–29	2	0.58
30+	6	1.74
No Information	25	7.8
Degree Type		
Bachelor of Arts	24	6.96
Bachelor of Science	274	79.42
Joint Bachelor	21	6.09
Bachelor of Education	14	4.06
Master of Science	10	2.90
Extraversion		
Strongly Disagree	22	6.38
Disagree	100	28.99
Neutral	121	35.07
Agree	76	22.03
Strongly Agree	26	7.54
Openness to Experiences		
Strongly Disagree	0	0
Disagree	15	4.35
Neutral	67	19.42
Agree	172	49.86
Strongly Agree	91	26.38
Family Innovation History		
Yes	41	11.88
Family Founding History		
Yes	102	29.57

conducted by Selznick and Mayhew (2018). Based on a theoretical model conducted by Kegan (1994), students' innovation capacities were generated using nine constructs representing three lines of personal development. Intrapersonal items as the first dimension of personal development include motivation, proactivity and self-concept. The social dimension of personal development contains networking, teamwork, and persuasive communication. Lastly, the cognitive dimension contains risk-taking/tolerance, creative cognition and the intention to innovate. To generate total innovation capacity scores, second-order confirmatory factor analysis is conducted to incorporate all nine conditioned first-order constructs (i.e. motivation, proactivity, self-concept, networking, teamwork, persuasive communication, risk talking/tolerance, creative cognition and intention to innovate) into a single factor.

4.2. Independent variables

The main focus of this study lies in the potential influence of the university ecosystem on students' innovative behaviour. For this purpose, four multi-item variables are developed to reflect the experiences within the university ecosystem using confirmatory factor analysis (CFA). The first variable *faculty challenges* relates to the challenges that students have to face in teaching events and projects within their everyday university life. The second variable *faculty interaction* covers the interaction of students with institutions and persons of the university outside of teaching events. The variable *functional experiences* refers to the existence of resources made available by the university, for example, sufficient space to work with other students on new ideas and projects. The last variable *connecting experiences* for measuring the university ecosystem refers to the experiences made by students outside of teaching events in the context of everyday university life, in order to apply, for example, experiences and knowledge gained in everyday or working life. Connecting experiences can, for example, be experimental research work, practical project work with a technical background, or the execution of design and creativity projects. All four variables were developed using confirmatory factor analysis from individual items, which were directly taken from the questionnaire. The individual items in the questionnaire were asked in the same manner as the personality traits, i.e. extroversion and openness to new experiences, on a five-point Likert scale. The reliability of the four multi-item factors (i.e. faculty challenge, faculty interaction, functional experiences and connecting experiences) shown was tested by calculating Cronbach's alpha of the Likert-type scales. As Leong et al. (2013) suggest, Cronbach's alpha values can be interpreted as follows: 0.90 or higher = excellent, 0.89 to 0.80 = good, 0.79 to 0.70 = adequate, and 0.69 and below = may have limited applicability. The values for Cronbach's alpha as well as the underlying standardised factor loadings of the items in the questionnaire on the respective multilevel constructs can be found in Table 3 Referring to Leong et al. (2013), all multi-level factors show good to excellent results in terms of the internal consistency of the multilevel constructs.

4.3. Control variables

Previous literature has identified several factors that are relevant to innovative behaviour. Those factors are included in our regressions as control variables. In order to learn more

Table 3. Properties of Measurement Items.

Measurement items	Standardised factor loadings
Faculty challenge (Cronbach's α = 0.82)	
1. Faculty ask me to show how a particular course concept could be applied to an actual problem.	0.61
2. Faculty ask me to point out any fallacies in basic ideas, principles, or point of view represented in the course.	0.70
3. Faculty challenge my ideas in class.	0.64
4. Faculty encourage me to explore my own original ideas.	0.75
5. Faculty challenge me to think in new ways in order to create solutions to problems presented in class.	0.75
Faculty interaction (Cronbach's = 0.77)	
1. My non-classroom interactions with faculty have had a positive influence on my personal growth, attitudes, and values.	0.85
2. My non-classroom interactions with faculty have had a positive influence on my career goals and aspirations.	0.84
3. Since coming to this institution, I have developed a close personal relationship with at least one faculty member.	0.50
Functional experiences (Cronbach's α = 0.77)	
1. My campus provides enough physical spaces for individuals to work collaboratively on a new project.	0.53
2. The library resources at this school encourage me to explore connections across academic disciplines.	0.68
3. The library resources at this school help me come up with ideas for academic projects, papers, and/or other course assignments.	0.73
4. My campus provides offices/resources that help me think about new ways to fund my education.	0.50
5. My campus provides enough physical spaces – including outdoor spaces – for individuals to discuss new ideas.	0.58
Connecting experiences (Cronbach's = 0.80)	
1. My out-of-class experiences have helped me connect what I learned in the classroom with life events.	0.70
2. My out-of-class experiences have had a positive influence on my personal growth, attitudes, and values.	0.65
3. My out-of-class experiences have had a positive influence on my intellectual growth and ideas.	0.76
4. My out-of-class experiences have provided me with opportunities to translate knowledge and understanding acquired in the classroom into action.	0.72

about the potential predictors which may be responsible for training students' innovation capacities, control variables as *age*, *gender*, personality traits (i.e. *extroversion* and *openness to new experiences*) and *family background* have been identified. It is reasonable to assume that with increasing age, the development of innovation capacities increases due to the increase in experience inside and outside the university. Numerous studies have already investigated the impact of gender on entrepreneurial and innovative activities and found that the typical entrepreneur is male (Wilson, Kickul, and Marlino 2007; Baron, Markman, and Hirsa 2001). In addition, several studies have demonstrated lower self-efficacy expectations of women in nontraditional career opportunities (Eccles 1994; Zeldin and Pajares 2007). These non-traditional career opportunities also include entrepreneurial careers (Wilson, Kickul, and Marlino 2007). Zhao, Hills, and Seibert (2005) proved that the female gender can have a negative impact on innovation behaviour.

The effects of personality traits such as extroversion and openness to new experiences on students' innovation capacities have also been investigated in prior studies and therefore, we control for those factors in our study (see Selznick 2017; Zhao and Seibert 2006). Further, the participants of the study were asked about their entrepreneurial family background and whether new products or services have been developed by family members. The influence of family background has already been investigated in studies. For example, Bowen and Hisrich (2011) found out that new entrepreneurs often already have independent entrepreneurs in the family environment. In this case, too, it can be assumed that students with such a background have a higher capacity for innovation than students who do not have such a family background. In order to examine the influence of students' existing innovation capacities before the first year of their studies, the results of the innovation capacities determined in round one are included in the models as the last control variable.

5. Empirical analysis and results

5.1. Empirical analysis

In order to investigate the potential effect of universities' ecosystem on students' innovation capacities, a total of six OLS regressions are performed. Model 1 consists exclusively of the control variables *age, gender*, personal factors *extroversion* and *openness to new experiences* as well as the variables used to query the *family founding* and *innovation* background. Models 2 to 5 contain the respective independent variables for mapping the university ecosystem separately (i.e. *faculty interaction, faculty challenge, functional experiences* and *connecting experiences*) in addition to the control variables. Model 6 of Table 5 displays the full model which contains the control variables and all independent variables of the university ecosystem.

Correlations between the control variables and the variables used to measure the university ecosystem (i.e. faculty challenge, faculty interaction, functional experiences and connecting experiences) do not reveal any uncommon high correlations.

All correlations can be taken from Table 4. The Breusch–Pagan test was performed to check for potential heteroskedasticity within the sample. According to this test, the sample is not subject to heteroskedasticity below the underlying significance level of 5% ($p = 0.1897$). To address multi-collinearity, variance inflation factors (VIF) were calculated for all predictor variables. As several authors confirm (e.g. Jou, Huang, and Cho 2014; O'brien 2007) values around 1 indicate that the sample is not subject to issues of multi-collinearity. The explicit VIF values of all variables used in model 6 are shown in Table 5.

5.2. Results

Table 5 shows the results of all regressions carried out. The evaluation of the factors of the university ecosystem on students' innovation capacities after the first academic year leads to the following results. Two of the four factors of the university ecosystem investigated (i.e. *functional experiences* and *connecting experiences*) prove to be statistically significant predictors of students' innovation capacities after the first academic year ($p < 0.01$ for connecting experiences and $p < 0.1$ for functional experiences), both in their dedicated single regression (models 4 and 5) and in the full model 6. However, we do not detect significant influences

Table 4. Correlation Matrix of Model Constructs.

		1	2	3	4	5	6	7	8	9	10	11	12
1.	Post-test innovation score	**1**											
2.	Pre-test innovation score	0.68***	**1**										
3.	Age	0.07	0.09	**1**									
4.	Gender	−0.24***	−0.22***	0.09	**1**								
5.	Family founding background	0.14***	0.09	−0.01	−0.02	**1**							
6.	Family innovation background	0.20***	0.14***	0.04	−0.01	0.31	**1**						
7.	Extroversion	0.30***	0.24***	0.20***	0.09	0.08	0.11**	**1**					
8.	Openness to new experiences	0.37***	0.24***	0.06	−0.06	0.04	0.01	0.29***	**1**				
9.	Faculty Challenge	0.06	0.08	0.05	0.04	−0.05	−0.01	0.07	0.01	**1**			
10.	Faculty Interaction	0.26***	0.29***	0.01	0.02	0.07	0.07	0.19***	0.12**	0.31	**1**		
11.	Functional Experiences	0.13***	0.07	0.19***	0.07	0.05	−0.01	0.09	0.09	0.25***	0.19***	**1**	
12.	Connecting Experiences	0.39***	0.27***	0.07	−0.09	0.02	0.07	0.14***	0.16***	0.24***	0.21***	0.08	**1**

*** and ** indicate significance at the 1 ($p < 0.01$) and 5 ($p < 0.05$) % levels.

Table 5. OLS analysis results.

Variables	VIF	Model 1	Model 2	Model 3	Model 4	Model 5	Model 6
Constant (CV)	-	−0.404***	−0.403***	−0.402***	−0.350**	−0.345**	−0.294*
		(0.140)	(0.140)	(0.148)	(0.137)	(0.144)	(0.128)
Age (CV)	1.09	−0.0019	−0.001	−0.001	−0.003	−0.003	−0.004
		(0.005)	(0.005)	(0.006)	(0.005)	(0.006)	(0.004)
Gender (CV)	1.10	0.0811***	−0.081***	−0.084***	−0.085***	−0.074***	−0.078***
		(0.027)	(0.027)	(0.031)	(0.028)	(0.028)	(0.026)
Family Background: Entrepreneurship (CV)	1.13	0.0316	0.321	0.030	0.028	0.033	0.269
		(0.313)	(0.313)	(0.031)	(0.031)	(0.030)	(0.303)
Family Background: Innovation (CV)	1.14	0.0981**	0.098**	0.097**	0.102**	0.091**	0.095**
		(0.0457)	(0.045)	(0.043)	(0.045)	(0.042)	(0.044)
Extroversion (CV)	1.22	0.040**	0.039***	0.037**	0.039***	0.036**	0.035**
		(0.0143)	(0.014)	(0.014)	(0.014)	(0.014)	(0.013)
Openness to New Experiences (CV)	1.15	0.085***	0.085***	0.084**	0.083***	0.078***	0.075***
		(0.020)	(0.020)	(0.018)	(0.020)	(0.018)	(0.019)
Pre-test Innovation Capacity Score (CV)	1.31	0.546***	0.544***	0.532***	0.543***	0.506***	0.498***
		(0.045)	(0.045)	(0.042)	(0.444)	(0.043)	(0.043)
Faculty Challenge	1.22		0.006				−0.039
			(0.028)				(0.028)
Faculty Interaction	1.26			0.019			0.011
				(0.014)			(0.128)
Functional Experiences	1.14				0.079*		0.079*
					(0.045)		(0.042)
Connecting Experiences	1.17					0.085***	0.087***
						(0.018)	(0.018)
Number of Observations (n)		316	316	316	316	316	316
R-squared		0.5367	0.5368	0.0539	0.5418	0.5677	0.5748
F-Test (p-value)		0.000	0.000	0.000	0.000	0.000	0.000

This table reports the results of our ordinary least squares regression on students' innovation capacities. Model 1 represents our baseline model, which is composed exclusively of our control variables. Models 2–5 add our investigated variables regarding the universities' ecosystem. Each model includes one variable of the universities' ecosystem respectively. Model 6 includes all control variables and universities' ecosystem variables. The robust standard errors are shown in brackets. ***, **, and * indicate significance at the 1 ($p < 0.01$), 5 ($p < 0.05$), and 10 ($p < 0.1$) % levels, respectively.

concerning *faculty challenge* and *faculty interaction* in our regressions – neither in the single regressions (models 2 and 3) nor in the full model 6.

Concerning students' *age*, no significant influence on post-test innovation capacity of students is found. However, the variable *gender* shows a highly significant ($p < 0.01$) influence on post-test students' innovation capacities in all regression models. In line with prior literature, the personality factors (i.e. *extroversion* and *openness to new experiences*) are found to have a significantly positive impact on students' post-test innovation capacities. The personality factor *extroversion* proved to be statistically significant ($p < 0.05$). The personality factor *openness to new experience* even proved to be a statistically highly significant predictor of students' innovation capacities in five of six models.

The results of the impact of *families' background* in terms of *entrepreneurship* and *developing a new product or service* shows conflicting results. While the variable related to *entrepreneurship within family* is not statistically significant in any of the six models, the variable related to the *development of new products or services by family members* has a significant positive effect on students' post-test innovation capacities in all regressions. In addition, students' *pre-test innovation capacities* show a highly significant positive effect on students' post-test innovation capacities which is a plausible effect as students' innovation capacity at the beginning of their study programme should be related to their innovation capacity one year later.

6. Discussion

The influencing factors of the universities' ecosystem on students' innovation capacities investigated in this study lead to a broad spectrum of findings. For faculty challenges, no significant influence on students' innovation capacities can be detected. Faculty challenges reflect students' perception of the extent to which the university encourages students to develop new ideas and solutions to the problems discussed in lectures, and how these outcome learnings in lectures can potentially be applied to problems occurring in reality. The results for this part of experiences within the framework of the university ecosystem allow for several explanations. First, within the first academic year, students mainly acquire basic knowledge of topics such as mathematics and economics. This gives rise to the assumption that these courses, which mainly impart basic knowledge, are not suitable for training special skills such as innovation skills. Studies have already shown that the determined participation in courses can be quite capable of certain abilities of students. Within the framework of an extensive problem-based learning course, Warren, Kisenwether, and Hanke (2006) proved that such courses can positively improve the perception of students with regard to skills such as creativity and entrepreneurial self-efficacy. Similar results are reported by Mentoor and Friedrich (2007), demonstrating an increase in innovation recognition after attending a dedicated entrepreneurship course at a university in South Africa. Interestingly, the study was also conducted with students in their first academic year. This leads to the assumption that above all the nature of the course is decisive, how and in which amount-specific abilities such as innovation capacities can be developed. This basic knowledge is usually only applied in the further course of studies, e.g. in specialisation courses, group work, or project work. Furthermore, courses within the first academic year build on many subject areas and knowledge that students already got to know during their pre-university academic education. As previous studies have already dealt intensively with the investigation of student intentions in relation to entrepreneurship the influences on the development of specific capacities, such as students' innovation capacities which emerge from university challenges within the framework of teaching events should be investigated as a next step to improve insight on higher education, its environment and affectable student outcomes. These further studies could, for example, investigate the effect of the university ecosystem on the undergraduate students in higher semesters or even with students pursuing master-level degrees.

The second factor that could not be shown to have any significant influence on the development of students' innovation capacities by the university ecosystem is faculty interactions. Faculty interactions occur through people or institutions of the university, with whom, for example, career goals and ideas can be discussed outside of the curriculum events. Other forms of interaction between teachers, tutors or mentors and students may arise through personal or digital exchanges, club consultations, and volunteer programmes (Davis 2009). Previous research has already indicated students' faculty interaction as a valid predictor of students' drop-out rates (Finn 1993) and academic achievement (Klem and Connell 2004). This type of interaction has been therefore pointed out to be one of the most important factors for the development, engagement, satisfaction, and success of students (Joosten 2012; Alexander W. Astin 1993a; Kuh et al. 2010). Studies have already demonstrated a significant effect of faculty interaction on students' engagement factors and students' educational outcome gains. Hu, Hung, and Ching (2014) found that students' faculty interaction had a direct effect on students' educational outcomes, measured in three dimensions: general educational gains, practical competency gains and personal social gains. Among the 724 undergraduate students surveyed, more than 30% were in their first or second year of study, the remaining students surveyed were already in higher semesters. Pascarella et al. (2014) come to similar conclusions as in our study. Their study examined, among other factors, the influence of co-curricular involvement and interactions with faculty on the development of students' cognitive skills. Investigating a sample of 949 students after four years of college attention, they found no significant influence of students' faculty interaction on students' cognitive skills. A study by Pascarella et al. (2004) came to different results, related to the potential effect of faculty interaction. In their study, they examined the difference between first-generation students and students whose parents had higher educational experiences. While some factors related to first-generation students, such as the internal locus of attribution for academic success or preferences for higher-order cognitive tasks in curricular events and cognitive skills, could be positively influenced significantly by interaction with the faculty, some of these factors were not statistically significant for students with parental higher educational background.

The results of our study in comparison to earlier studies give rise to various conclusions. On the one hand, it can be seen that increased interaction with the faculty does not necessarily lead to the development of specific skills. On the other hand, especially with regard to the work of Hu, Hung, and Ching (2014) and Kim et al. (2017), it can also be assumed that, depending on the background of the students, the influence of their interactions with the faculty can have positive effects on the development of new skills. It can also be concluded that students in their first academic year do not necessarily have an intention to engage in extracurricular activities. It can be assumed that this form of interaction only develops in the further course of studies and not necessarily already after the first academic year. Perhaps, students follow such tracks in their academic life only after they have embarked on special courses or directions in their studies. Similar to the results obtained for the factor faculty challenges, further studies would be interesting to investigate the potential faculty interactions' influence of students who are already advanced in their studies or even pursuing master-level degrees and to find out whether faculty interactions can be shown to have a significant influence on students' innovation capacities then.

Within the framework of the empirical investigation in this study, functional experiences could be shown to have a significant influence – albeit only with weak significance – on students' innovation capacities. In the context of the university ecosystem, functional experiences are the provision of resources by the university, such as workspaces where students can work together on projects and resources provided by institutions such as university libraries. The investigation of such functional experiences and their potential impact on the outcome of students has received little attention in literature so far (Berger and Milem 2000). Research related to this factor is still at a conceptual level, but it has already been demonstrated that functional experiences have the potential to support students in the development of their innovation capacities (Selznick 2017). Walter and David Lankes (2015) have already addressed the potential impact of resources provided by the university libraries. With special regard to how such resources can foster students' innovation outcomes, Walter and David Lankes (2015) quote: 'Innovation may involve collaboration with student affairs professionals to consider the impact of co-curricular spaces on student learning' (Walter and David Lankes 2015, 855). Other studies have also demonstrated the impact of different designs and characteristics of workspace on the effectiveness of students' working practices (Leicht, Messner, and Anumba 2009). Furthermore, studies indicate that the provision of makerspaces can be an influencing measure to promote student creativity and innovation. With a sample of 276 students from art and design, engineering, and liberal arts majors, Hynes and Hynes (2018) investigated the preference of students for potential concepts on such makerspaces. They conclude that such makerspaces should be located when possible in or near the university libraries in order to not only reach students of certain courses (e.g. engineering students) or only male students, but to attract the full diversity of university students through such a strategic placement. In our case, regarding a university with over 25,000 students, individual supervision and support of students are hard to provide. Tutorials within courses hosted for several hundreds of students are held in smaller groups, but still hold too many students to provide individual attention. Due to this circumstance, students might organise themselves in smaller groups to work on tasks and projects that have to be fulfilled in the context of university education. As has been proven in literature, workspaces can support the activities, interaction and the overall outcome of students (Kyrö and Artto 2015). Therefore, the significant influence of functional experiences on students' innovation capacities shows that resources and workspaces at large universities must be attributed to increasing importance.

Connecting experiences, as the fourth factor investigated also proved to be a significant predictor of students' innovation capacities. In this study, we understand connecting experiences as the kind of experience in which students have to apply the knowledge they have learned in courses to practical applications. Educational research discusses a transfer problem, where knowledge learned in courses often cannot be transferred to reality or real working life (Illeris 2009). Early studies dealing with the effects of entrepreneurship education have already come to the conclusion that the promotion of venture development through entrepreneurship education should above all cover practical contents. These practical features include exposure to technological innovation and new product development (Mcmullan and Long 1987), skill-building courses in addition to knowledge-based courses (Ronstadt, Vesper, and McMullan 1988), multi-disciplinary and process-oriented approaches, and theory-based practical applications (Plaschka and Welsch 1990). Previous studies demonstrate a significant influence on various factors in the student context. In an empirical study including 3700 senior students (Mayhew et al. 2012) found that connecting experiences have a significant influence on the intention to innovate. Furthermore, in a comprehensive study with a total of 494 Swiss students, Volery et al. (2013) demonstrated in various (mostly practical-oriented) entrepreneurship courses that such courses are able to positively affect several outcomes of students, such as entrepreneurial knowledge and business-opportunity exploitation skills. Another recent study by Passaro, Quinto, and Thomas (2018) deals with the design of entrepreneurship courses and their potential impact on the development of entrepreneurial intention, as well as on human capital skills for successfully fostering entrepreneurship activities of students and academics. Hence, in line with prior literature, our results reveal that connecting experiences can have a far-reaching effect on the personal development of students. Although several universities already try to address this circumstance by providing practical projects (e.g. product design projects) to be worked on by students which are based on the knowledge acquired in curricular events and outcomes of previous specific courses, universities should focus their curriculum even stronger on expanding practical projects and tasks for students to reduce the aforementioned transfer problem between learned theoretical knowledge and skills and the transfer of these skills to real-world problems.

Our study addresses the influence of the university ecosystem on the development of specific abilities of students, more precisely their innovation capacities. By presenting the university ecosystem as a unit consisting of four different factors and examining their respective influence on the development of innovation capacities, we make various contributions to the literature on innovation and higher education. First, we make an empirical contribution to the successful empirical testing of a highly relevant theory in higher education, the student involvement theory according to Astin (1984). The involvement of students in university activities inside and outside the classroom has in recent years created a chain of previous research in this field. With our study, we test Astin's theory regarding the potential success of factors in the university ecosystem and their effect on students' innovation capacities. We can show that the circumstances at universities besides teaching events have indeed an influence on students' innovativeness. Mainly, the functional and connecting experiences are of high relevance in this context. Second, we contribute to the question of the extent to which the university as an institution is responsible for shaping the innovation capabilities of the next generation. As policy states that higher education does not contribute to the promotion of innovation as it should (Hero, Lindfors, and Taatila 2017), we provide empirical evidence that elements in the everyday university life of students have a significant influence on the development of skills that can foster innovation. The promotion and development of human capital in relation to innovation are in line with current expectations of universities and higher education in general, to spread a heightened entrepreneurial culture and thus fulfil universities' third mission, besides education and research (Fini et al. 2011; Franzoni and Lissoni 2006; Laredo 2007). Promoting and developing human capital with specific regard to innovation and entrepreneurship can not only help to address entrepreneurial and managerial challenges and barriers to growth and nascent business survival (Passaro, Quinto, and Thomas 2018) but also fulfiling universities overriding goal in third mission activities: to serve the public (Backs, Günther, and Stummer 2019). Third, we contribute to the validation of a complex and up-to-date measurement tool for students' innovation capacities. Previous studies have mainly dealt with the collection of individual aspects related to innovation capacity. In comparison, the study developed by Selznick and Mayhew (2018) is a much more in-depth way of measuring innovation capacity by capturing nine constructs from three dimensions (intrapersonal, social, and cognitive). The results of this study and the related validation of this measuring instrument of student innovation capacities can be used by future studies as well to identify further factors that can positively influence such capacities of students.

7. Limitations and future research

As any empirical study, our study is subject to some limitations. The results of the empirical analysis detect that factors of the university ecosystem can be responsible for improving students' innovation capacities. However, the factors of the university ecosystem can only be analysed on an aggregated level. The existing structure of the dataset does not allow any analysis regarding the origin of these factors, for example, which courses, projects, or institutions of the university are in particular responsible for the evaluation of these factors of the university ecosystem. Future studies should address this issue by evaluating how dedicated participation in courses, seminars and other extracurricular programmes such as mentoring programmes can influence students' specific capacities, as in our case, the innovation capacities of students.

Students surveyed in this study were asked to assess the influence of the university ecosystem on their knowledge and experience after their first academic year. Since the evaluation was only carried out at one specific point in time, the study leaves the question open to what extent the evaluation of the factors, that could be responsible for the improvement of students' innovation capacities, may change over time when students continue with their respective programmes. Therefore, our study delivers only a limited picture of the influencing factors of the German university system. In public German universities, it is common that students have to follow some obligatory basic courses which often have a rather high number of participants. The influence of those events on students' innovative skillset may, therefore, be limited. Courses in later academic years may be more individualised and aimed at developing different skills and may have a higher impact on students' innovation capacities. It is reasonable to assume that when students continue with their study programmes, the connection with the university will also increase due to the expanded interest in specific fields of study and thus the contact with the university and its institutions. Further studies should, therefore, investigate the influence of the university ecosystem on the development of innovation capacities in the further academic course of the students. Students often have a wide range of options to choose from, which they can pursue and select according to their own interests. For example, it is still possible to investigate the extent to which the spread of courses in specific subject areas can influence the development of innovative skills. It could be investigated whether innovative capabilities are more likely to be developed through specialisation in specific subject areas or through a broader distribution of the courses attended.

The results might also look different in other countries with different systems of higher education in which students start with less obligatory courses or have courses with fewer participants. It hence makes sense the influence of environmental factors under different contextual factors. According to this, the influence of the university ecosystem on innovation capacities in other countries should also be investigated and examined for possible differences compared to our study. It would be interesting to see whether the results of the influence of individual constructions, for example, in the area of faculty challenges, differ in other countries due to a different teaching system in the first year compared to German universities.

Another point of interest would have been the impact of special teaching events, such as the participation in courses with entrepreneurial and innovation-based content.

Previous studies have already investigated the potential effects due to the participation in specific courses on various outcomes concerning an entrepreneurial context. Webb, Quince, and Watkins (1984) demonstrate, for example, an increased entrepreneurial intention after attending an entrepreneurship course. However, Müller (2008) warned that the participation of a single entrepreneurship course cannot fundamentally change the basic attitude towards founding one's own company. Nevertheless, further evidence of a positive correlation between participation in an innovative or creative course context and entrepreneurial intention (Chia and Liang 2016; Chye Koh 1996) as well as entrepreneurial self-efficacy (Lengelle et al. 2016; Borchers and Park 2010) can be found in the literature. Duval-Couetil (2013) offers a comprehensive summary of research in entrepreneurship education outcomes. Due to the high variation in fields of study and the resulting variation in courses and projects that students can choose in their studies, a precise evaluation of which specific course and projects can be responsible for the delivery of innovation capacity seems challenging however.

Furthermore, a point of limitation in this study is the sample of students from the natural sciences. As Audretsch and Keilbach (2004) note regarding the impact of technology transfer from universities on the regional development of entrepreneurship and innovation, academic spillovers are heterogeneous and their impact on regional development potentially depends on the discipline (e.g. social science vs. natural science). This heterogeneous effect could also be present in the case of the impact of the university ecosystem on the development of innovation capacities. Mentoor and Friedrich (2007) provide a further indication for the question of the generalisability of our results in their analysis of the factors influencing the innovation recognition of students. In their results, only one of the three investigated degree programmes considered showed a significant increase in such skills. The study by Tsang (2017) also indicates that the main subject of students can influence the influence of the university environment on the development of propensity to innovation to varying degrees. We do not claim to be able to generalise our results. Nevertheless, we assume that the effects of the university ecosystem could also have an effect on students with other specialisations. Future studies should investigate this aspect to enhance the understanding of innovation capacity-building measures and the impact of the university ecosystem.

8. Conclusion and practical implications

With the increasing social and environmental challenges that our society is currently facing, the development of innovations to remain competitive is crucial. Although the ever-accelerating pace of technological and scientific progress over the last decades has produced a multitude of solutions for negative circumstances, it simultaneously resulted in a completely new and more complex paradigm of problems, which can only be tackled by fostering new innovations (Waychal 2016). Policy-building measures point to the fact that not only the existence of innovative measures as such is necessary to solve current societal and technological challenges, but that innovative thinking and action must be promoted by institutions responsible for the education of the next generation. In the context of this educational responsibility, universities are increasingly seen as key institutions to ensure the development and improvement of the national innovation system (Audretsch, Keilbach, and Lehmann 2006). Despite this central role of universities in the development of skills and excellence, the role of innovation in education systems still receives subordinate attention (Genco, Seepersad, and Holtta-Otto 2010).

This study stresses the importance and potential of the development of students' innovation capacities at universities. As the findings of this survey show, university structures may well be responsible for shaping and promoting students' innovation capacities in addition to factors already identified in literature, such as personality traits or demographic characteristics of individuals. These findings lead to several practical implications.

First, it can be shown that functional experiences of students can have a positive influence on the application of innovation skills. Decision-makers in universities should use these findings as an opportunity to evaluate the potential of their current circumstances and the resources they make available to students. Based on our findings, these resources can lead to the development of specific skills for the employees and perhaps entrepreneurs of tomorrow who, according to literature and politics, are the foundation for keeping up with innovative competitiveness.

Second, it can be demonstrated that the experiences of students in which the knowledge acquired in courses is applied to practical challenges can have a significant influence on the development of innovation capacities. Lecturers should use this knowledge and include it in their teaching. Even though the teaching of basic knowledge is essential in the first semesters of students' academic life, students should be confronted with challenges early on that reflect the problems of the real world. This could not only bring the traditional approach of university teaching into a more modern light but could also create an enhanced culture of innovation among students. The findings regarding the connecting experiences of students should be taken into account as a predictor for students' innovation capacities.

Third, universities and responsible persons should consider the results of our study with regard to the faculty challenges as the potential for improvement in the design of study programme as well as the actual courses themselves. In the first year of study, students are taught basic knowledge, for example, in mathematics or economics. University programme managers should consider using the potential of such events to develop innovative capacities, but also evaluate them. For example, special assessments and tasks could be carried out at the beginning and end of a course, which are then examined by experts in the field of innovation management and evaluated for possible differences in the innovative character of the solution to the problem. Furthermore, an early integration and cooperation with actually existing problems from the economy, e.g. from companies, could be aimed at. Here, the basic knowledge to be learned by the students could be imparted directly by working on dedicated tasks and at the same time be evaluated by the teaching staff as well as experts from companies.

Fourth, the university should invest an increased capacity in the evaluation of the design of courses, but also of study processes within the framework of a degree programme itself. Since no significant influence on the development of innovative capacities could be proven for two of four aspects of the university environment, the question arises whether this could potentially change in the further course of the study. It may also be of great interest which specific programmes in the context of students' everyday university life have an influence on the development of innovative capacities and which do not. These findings can be used by university decision-makers to maintain or even strengthen the potential of already influential factors of the university environment, and to change and improve less or not influential aspects of the university environment.

The last point, which should also be regarded as a recommendation for decision-makers in universities, concerns the results of faculty interaction. This type of student involvement has already been identified as an important factor for the development, engagement, satisfaction, and success of students (Joosten 2012; Astin 1993a; Kuh et al. 2010). Universities should, therefore, provide an increased degree of readiness to allow students already in earlier semesters to participate in extracurricular activities. This could not only lead to a development of relevant skills, but also to an improved identification of students with their academic institution.

Disclosure statement

No potential conflict of interest was reported by the authors.

ORCID

Lini Zhang http://orcid.org/0000-0003-4805-0069
Matthew J. Mayhew http://orcid.org/0000-0002-1720-1162

References

Acs, Z., D. Erik Stam, D. B. Audretsch, and A. O'Connor. 2017. "The Lineages of the Entrepreneurial Ecosystem Approach." *Small Business Economics* 49 (1): 1. doi:10.1007/s11187-017-9864-8.

Agrawal, A., and I. Cockburn. 2002. "University Research, Industrial R&D, and the Anchor Tenant Hypothesis." *National Bureau of Economic Research*. w9212. Cambridge, MA. doi:10.3386/w9212.

Åstebro, T., N. Bazzazian, and S. Braguinsky. 2012. "Startups by Recent University Graduates and Their Faculty: Implications for University Entrepreneurship Policy." *Research Policy* 41 (4): 663–677. doi:10.1016/j.respol.2012.01.004.

Astin, A. 1984. "Student Involvement: A Developmental Theory for Higher Education." *Journal of College Student Personnel* 25 (4): 297–308.

Astin, A. W. 1993a. *What Matters in College?: Four Critical Years Revisited*. San Francisco: Jossey-Bass. https://eric.ed.gov/?id=ED351927

Astin, A. W. 1993b. *Assessment for Excellence: The Philosophy and Practice of Assessment and Evaluation in Higher Education*. New York: ORIX PRESS.

Audretsch, D. B., J. A. Cunningham, D. F. Kuratko, E. E. Lehmann, and M. Menter. 2019. "Entrepreneurial Ecosystems: Economic, Technological, and Societal Impacts." *Journal of Technology Transfer* 44 (2): 313–325. doi:10.1007/s10961-018-9690-4.

Audretsch, D. B., and M. Keilbach. 2004. "Does Entrepreneurship Capital Matter?" *Entrepreneurship Theory and Practice* 28 (5): 419–429. doi:10.1111/j.1540-6520.2004.00055.x.

Audretsch, D. B., M. C. Keilbach, and E. E. Lehmann. 2006. *Entrepreneurship and Economic Growth*. Oxford, England: Oxford University Press. doi:10.1093/acprof:oso/9780195183511.001.0001.

Backs, S., M. Günther, and C. Stummer. 2019. "Stimulating Academic Patenting in a University Ecosystem: An Agent-Based Simulation Approach." *Journal of Technology Transfer* 44 (2): 434–461. doi:10.1007/s10961018-9697-x.

Baron, R. A., G. D. Markman, and A. Hirsa. 2001. "Perceptions of Women and Men as Entrepreneurs: Evidence for Differential Effects of Attributional Augmenting." *Journal of Applied Psychology* 86 (5): 923–929. doi:10.1037/0021-9010.86.5.923.

Baumol, W. J. 2004. "Education for Innovation." *IEEE Spectrum* 5 (1): 83–89. doi:10.1109/MSPEC.1968.5215638.

Berger, J. B., and Milem, J. F. (2000). "Organizational Behavior in Higher Education and Student Outcomes." In *Higher Education: Handbook of Theory and Research*, 268–338. Vol. XV. New York: Agathon.

Bezarra, C. 2017. "Building Innovation Competencies." *Proceedings of the Canadian Engineering Education Association, Kananaskis, Alberta.* doi:10.24908/pceea.v0i0.3898.

Björklund, T., M. Clavert, S. Kirjavainen, M. Laakso, and S. Luukkonen. 2011. "Aalto University Design Factory in the Eyes of Its Community." https://aaltodoc.aalto.fi/handle/123456789/12171

Block, J. H., C. O. Fisch, and V. P. Mirjam. 2017. "The Schumpeterian Entrepreneur: A Review of the Empirical Evidence on the Antecedents, Behaviour and Consequences of Innovative Entrepreneurship." *Industry and Innovation* 24 (1): 61–95. doi:10.1080/13662716.2016.1216397.

Borchers, A., and S. A. Park. 2010. "Understanding Entrepreneurial Mindset: A Study of Entrepreneurial Self Efficacy, Locus of Control and Intent to Start A Business." *Journal of Engineering Entrepreneurship* 1 (January): 51–62.

Bowen, D. D., and R. D. Hisrich. 2011. "The Female Entrepreneur: A Career Development Perspective." *Academy of Management Review* 11 (2): 393–407. doi:10.5465/amr.1986.4283366.

Braun, D., and F. X. Merrien. 1999. *Towards A New Model of Governance for Universities? A Comparative View.* London: Jessica Kingsley.

Braxton, J. M. 1993. "Selectivity and Rigor in Research Universities." *The Journal of Higher Education* 64 (6): 657. doi:10.2307/2960017.

Butter, R. 2017. "Psychometric Validation of a Tool for Innovation Competencies Development and Assessment Using a Mixed-Method Design." https://static1.squarespace.com/static/583dddb7cd0f686c5defc5bb/t/58da1ce5e3df 28fabb796bff/1490689255628/EURAM_Validation_WP7_Rev1.pdf

Chávez-Tellería, R., A. A. Repellin-Moreno, and B. A. Mendieta-Jiménez. 2017. "Entrepreneurship and Innovation Lab: A Proposal for the Enhancement of an Entrepreneurial Profile in Undergraduate Students." In, 7484–7489. doi:10.21125/iceri.2017.2002.

Chia, C.-C., and C. Liang. 2016. "Influence of Creativity and Social Capital on the Entrepreneurial Intention of Tourism Students." *Journal of Entrepreneurship, Management and Innovation* 12 (2): 151–167. doi:10.7341/20161227.

Chickering, A. W. 1974. *Commuting versus Resident Students: Overcoming the Educational Inequities of Living off Campus.* San Francisco: Jossey-Bass Publishers.

Chye Koh, H. 1996. "Testing Hypotheses of Entrepreneurial Characteristics." *Journal of Managerial Psychology* 11 (3): 12–25. doi:10.1108/02683949610113566.

Clarysse, B., M. Wright, J. Bruneel, and A. Mahajan. 2014. "Creating Value in Ecosystems: Crossing the Chasm between Knowledge and Business Ecosystems." *Research Policy* 43 (7): 1164–1176. doi:10.1016/j.respol.2014.04.014.

Colombo, M. G., G. B. Dagnino, E. E. Lehmann, and M. P. Salmador. 2019. "The Governance of Entrepreneurial Ecosystems." *Small Business Economics* 52 (2): 419–428. doi:10.1007/s11187-017-9952-9.

Cunningham, J. A., M. Menter, and K. Wirsching. 2019. "Entrepreneurial Ecosystem Governance: A Principal Investigator-Centered Governance Framework." *Small Business Economics* 52 (2): 545–562. doi:10.1007/s11187-017-9959-2.

Davis, B. G. 2009. "Tools for Teaching." San Francisco: Jossey-Bass. https://www.indiana.edu/~istr695/readingsfall2013/Tools For Teaching.pdf

Dekoninck, E. 2012. "Enhancing the Innovation Skills in Engineering Students." *Proceedings of the 14th International Conference on Engineering and Product Design Education: Design Education for Future Wellbeing, EPDE 2012*, Antwerp, no. September, 1–6.

Drucker, P. F. 1999. "Knowledge-Worker Productivity: The Biggest Challenge." *California Management Review* 41 (2): 79–94. doi:10.2307/41165987.

Duval-Couetil, N. 2013. "Assessing the Impact of Entrepreneurship Education Programs: Challenges and Approaches." *Journal of Small Business Management* 51 (3): 394–409. doi:10.1111/jsbm.12024.

Eccles, J. S. 1994. "Understanding Women's Educational and Occupational Choices: Applying the Eccles Et Al. Model of Achievement-Related Choices." *Psychology of Women Quarterly* 18 (4): 585–609. doi:10.1111/j.14716402.1994.tb01049.x.

Ed, M. W., and W. A. Long. 1987. "Entrepreneurship Education in the Nineties." *Journal of Business Venturing* 2 (3): 261–275. doi:10.1016/0883-9026(87)90013-9.

Etzkowitz, H., and L. Leydesdorff. 2000. "The Dynamics of Innovation: From National Systems and 'Mode 2' to a Triple Helix of University–Industry–Government Relations." *Research Policy* 29 (2): 109–123. doi:10.1016/S0048-7333(99)00055-4.

Fini, R., R. Grimaldi, S. Santoni, and M. Sobrero. 2011. "Complements or Substitutes? The Role of Universities and Local Context in Supporting the Creation of Academic Spin-Offs." *Research Policy* 40 (8): 1113–1127. doi:10.1016/j.respol.2011.05.013.

Finn, J. D. (1993). School Engagement & Students at Risk. Washington DC: National Center for Education Statistics

Fisher, J. L., and J. V. Koch. 2008. "Born, Not Made: The Entrepreneurial Personality." *Praeger*. https://cmc.marmot.org/Record/.b31213194?mylang=es

Franzoni, C., and F. Lissoni. 2006. "Academic Entrepreneurship, Patents, and Spin-Offs: Critical Issues and Lessons for Europe," October.

Galloway, L., Anderson, M., Brown, W., & Wilson, L. 2005. Enterprise skills for the economy. Education + Training, 47(1),7–17. doi: 10.1108/00400910510580593

Genco, N., C. C. Seepersad, and K. Holtta-Otto. 2010. "An Experimental Investigation of the Innovation Capabilities of Engineering Students." *American Society for Engineering Education Annual Conference and Exposition 2010*, 1–19, Louisville.

Gennep, A. V. 1960. *The Rites of Passage*. London: Routledge and Kegan Paul.

Hackett, P. M. W., and S. C. Karen. 2014. "Academic Challenge: Its Meaning for College Students and Faculty," no. January.

Hallam, C., L. de la Vina, A. Leffel, and M. Agrawal. 2014. "Accelerating Collegiate Entrepreneurship (ACE): The Architecture of a University Entrepreneurial Ecosystem Encompassing an Intercollegiate Venture Experience." *Journal of Business and Entrepreneurship* 26 (2): 95.

Hayter, C. S. 2016. "A Trajectory of Early-Stage Spinoff Success: The Role of Knowledge Intermediaries within an Entrepreneurial University Ecosystem." *Small Business Economics* 47 (3): 633–656. doi:10.1007/s11187-016-9756-3.

Heaton, S., D. S. Siegel, and D. J. Teece. 2019. "Universities and Innovation Ecosystems: A Dynamic Capabilities Perspective." *Industrial and Corporate Change* 28 (4): 921–939. doi:10.1093/icc/dtz038.

Hero, L.-M., E. Lindfors, and V. Taatila. 2017. "Individual Innovation Competence: A Systematic Review and Future Research Agenda." *International Journal of Higher Education* 6 (5): 103. doi:10.5430/ijhe.v6n5p103.

Hu, Y.-L., C.-H. Hung, and G. S. Ching. 2014. "Student-Faculty Interaction: Mediating between Student Engagement Factors and Educational Outcome Gains." *International Journal of Research Studies in Education* 4: 1. doi:10.5861/ijrse.2014.800.

Hulme, E., B. Thomas, and D. Hal. 2014. "Developing Creativity Ecosystems: Preparing College Students for Tomorrow's Innovation Challenge." *About Campus* 19 (1): 14–23. doi:10.1002/abc.21146.

Hynes, M. M., and W. J. Hynes. 2018. "If You Build It, Will They Come? Student Preferences for Makerspace Environments in Higher Education." *International Journal of Technology and Design Education* 28 (3): 867–883. doi:10.1007/s10798-017-9412-5.

Illeris, K. 2009. "Transfer of Learning in the Learning Society: How Can the Barriers between Different Learning Spaces Be Surmounted, and How Can the Gap between Learning inside and outside Schools Be Bridged?" *International Journal of Lifelong Education* 28 (2): 137–148. doi:10.1080/02601370902756986.

Jackson, D. J. 2011. "What Is an Innovation Ecosystem?" http://ercassoc.org/sites/default/files/topics/policy_studies/DJackso- n_Innovation Ecosystem_03-15-11.pdf

Joosten, T. 2012. *Social Media for Educators: Strategies and Best Practices.* San Francisco: Jossey-Bass.

Jou, Y. J., C. C. L. Huang, and H. J. Cho. 2014. "A VIF-Based Optimization Model to Alleviate Collinearity Problems in Multiple Linear Regression." *Computational Statistics* 29 (6): 1515–1541. doi:10.1007/s00180-014-0504-3.

Kegan, R. 1994. "In over Our Heads: The Mental Demands of Modern Life." *Harvard University Press.* http://www.hup.harvard.edu/catalog.php?isbn=9780674445888

Kidwell, D. K. 2013. "Principal Investigators as Knowledge Brokers: A Multiple Case Study of the Creative Actions of PIs in Entrepreneurial Science." *Technological Forecasting and Social Change* 80 (2): 212–220. doi:10.1016/j.techfore.2012.05.004.

Kim, Y. K., C. S. Collins, L. A. Rennick, and D. Edens. 2017. "College Experiences and Outcomes among International Undergraduate Students at Research Universities in the United States: A Comparison to Their Domestic Peers." *Journal of International Students* 7 (2): 395–420.

Klem, A. M., and J. P. Connell. 2004. "Relationships Matter: Linking Teacher Support to Student Engagement and Achievement." *Journal of School Health* 74 (7): 262–273. doi:10.1111/j.1746-1561.2004.tb08283.x.

Knight, G. A., and P. W. Liesch. 2016. "Internationalization: From Incremental to Born Global." *Journal of World Business* 51 (1): 93–102. doi:10.1016/j.jwb.2015.08.011.

Kourilsky, M. L., and M. Esfandiari. 1997. "Entrepreneurship Education and Lower Socioeconomic Black Youth: An Empirical Investigation." *Urban Review* 29 (3): 205–215. doi:10.1023/A:1024629027806.

Kuh, G. D. 2001. "Assessing What Really Matters to Student Learning inside the National Survey of Student Engagement." *Change: The Magazine of Higher Learning* 33 (3): 10–17. doi:10.1080/00091380109601795.

Kuh, G. D., J. (Jillian L.) Kinzie, J. H. Schuh, and E. J. Whitt. 2010. *Student Success in College: Creating Conditions That Matter.* https://www.wiley.com/enus/Student+Success+in+College%3A+Creating+Conditions+That+Matter%2C+% 28Includes+New+Preface+and+Epilogue%29-p-9780470599099

Kyrö, R., and K. Artto. 2015. "The Development Path of an Academic CoWorking Space on Campus – Case Energy Garage." *Procedia Economics and Finance* 21: 431–438. doi:10.1016/S2212-5671(15)00196-3.

Lappalainen, H. 2018. "Towards Innovation Competences: A Finnish Perspective." In *Proceedings of the 1st International Conference on Early Childhood and Primary Education (ECPE 2018).* Paris, France: Atlantis Press. doi:10.2991/ecpe-18.2018.14.

Laredo, P. 2007. "Revisiting the Third Mission of Universities: Toward a Renewed Categorization of University Activities?" *Higher Education Policy* 20 (December): 441–456. doi:10.1057/palgrave.hep.8300169.

Leicht, R. M., J. I. Messner, and C. J. Anumba. 2009. "A Framework For Using Interactive Workspaces For Effective Collaboration." *Journal of Information Technology in Construction* 14: 180–203. http://www.itcon.org/2009/15

Lengelle, R., F. Meijers, R. Poell, F. Geijsel, and M. Post. 2016. "Career Writing as a Dialogue about Work Experience: A Recipe for Luck Readiness?" *International Journal for Educational and Vocational Guidance* 16 (1): 29–43. doi:10.1007/s10775-014-9283-1.

Leong, L.-Y., T.-S. Hew, G. W.-H. Tan, and K.-B. Ooi. 2013. "Predicting the Determinants of the NFC-Enabled Mobile Credit Card Acceptance: A Neural Networks Approach." *Expert Systems with Applications* 40 (14): 5604–5620. doi:10.1016/J.ESWA.2013.04.018.

Liefner, I., and D. Schiller. 2008. "Academic Capabilities in Developing Countries—A Conceptual Framework with Empirical Illustrations from Thailand." *Research Policy* 37 (2): 276–293. doi:10.1016/j.respol.2007.08.007.

Loebbecke C. (2006) Digitalisierung — Technologien und Unternehmensstrategien. In: Scholz C. (eds) Handbuch Medienmanagement. Springer, Berlin, Heidelberg.

Malecki, E. J. 1997. "Technology and Economic Development: The Dynamics of Local, Regional, and National Change."

Mars, M. M., S. Slaughter, and G. Rhoades. 2008. "The State-Sponsored Student Entrepreneur." *The Journal of Higher Education* 79 (6): 638–670. doi:10.1080/00221546.2008.11772122.

Marvel, M. R., & Lumpkin, G. T. 2007. Technology Entrepreneurs' Human Capital and Its Effects on Innovation Radicalness. *Entrepreneurship Theory and Practice*, 31 (6): 807–828. https://doi.org/10.1111/j.1540-6520.2007.00209.x

Mason, C., and R. Brown. 2014. "Entrepreneurial Ecosystems and Growth Oriented Entrepreneurship. Final Report to OECD, Paris." http://lib.davender.com/wp-content/uploads/2015/03/Entrepreneurial-ecosystemsOECD.pdf

Martin, B. C., McNally, J. J., & Kay, M. J. 2013. Examining the formation of human capital in entrepreneurship: A meta-analysis of entrepreneurship education outcomes. *Journal of Business Venturing*, 28 (2): 211–224. https://doi.org/10.1016/j.jbusvent.2012.03.002

Mayhew, M. J., A. N. Rockenbach, N. A. Bowman, T. A. Seifert, and G. C. Wolniak. 2016. *How College Affects Students: 21st Century Evidence that Higher Education Works (3rd Ed.).* San Francisco: Jossey-Bass.

Mayhew, M. J., J. S. Simonoff, W. J. Baumol, B. M. Wiesenfeld, and M. W. Klein. 2012. "Exploring Innovative Entrepreneurship and Its Ties to Higher Educational Experiences." *Research in Higher Education* 53 (8): 831–859. doi:10.1007/s11162-012-9258-3.

Mei-Chih, H., and J. A. Mathews. 2008. "China's National Innovative Capacity." *Research Policy* 37 (9): 1465–1479. doi:10.1016/j.respol.2008.07.003.

Mentoor, E. R., and C. Friedrich. 2007. "Is Entrepreneurial Education at South African Universities Successful?: An Empirical Example." *Industry and Higher Education* 21 (3): 221–232. doi:10.5367/000000007781236862.

Meoli, M., S. Paleari, and S. Vismara. 2019. "The Governance of Universities and the Establishment of Academic Spin-Offs." *Small Business Economics* 52 (2): 485–504. doi:10.1007/s11187-017-9956-5.

Miller, D. J., and Z. J. Acs. 2017. "The Campus as Entrepreneurial Ecosystem: The University of Chicago." *Small Business Economics* 49 (1): 75–95. doi:10.1007/s11187-017-9868-4.

Minola, T., D. Donina, and M. Meoli. 2016. "Students Climbing the Entrepreneurial Ladder: Does University Internationalization Pay Off?" *Small Business Economics* 47 (3): 565–587. doi:10.1007/s11187-016-9758-1.

Moberg, K. 2014. Two approaches to entrepreneurship education: The different effects of education for and through entrepreneurship at the lower secondary level. The International Journal of Management Education, 12(3),512–528. doi:10.1016/j.ijme.2014.05.002.

Moriano, J. A., Gorgievski, M., Laguna, M., Stephan, U., & Zarafshani, K. 2012. A Cross-Cultural Approach to Understanding Entrepreneurial Intention. Journal of Career Development, 39(2), 162–185. doi:10.1177/0894845310384481

Mueller, S. 2008. "Encouraging Future Entrepreneurs: The Effect of Entrepreneurship Course Characteristics on Entrepreneurial Intention," January.

Nijkamp, P. 2003. "Entrepreneurship in a Modern Network Economy." *Regional Studies* 37 (4): 395–405. doi:10.1080/0034340032000074424.

Norwani, N. M. 2009. "Learning Outcomes at Higher Education Institutions: To What Extent Do Institutional Environments Contribute?" *Journal of Human Resource and Adult Learning* 5 (June): 84–94.

O'brien, R. M. 2007. "A Caution regarding Rules of Thumb for Variance Inflation Factors." *Quality & Quantity* 41 (5): 673–690. doi:10.1007/s11135-006-9018-6.

Pascarella, E. T., C. T. Pierson, G. C. Wolniak, and P. T. Terenzini. 2004. "First-Generation College Students: Additional Evidence on College Experiences and Outcomes." *The Journal of Higher Education* 75 (3): 249–284. doi:10.1353/jhe.2004.0016.

Pascarella, E.T. 2006. How College Affects Students: Ten Directions for Future Research. Journal of College Student Development 47(5), 508-520. doi:10.1353/csd.2006.0060.

Pascarella, E. T., G. L. Martin, J. M. Hanson, T. L. Trolian, B. Gillig, and C. Blaich. 2014. "Effects of Diversity Experiences on Critical Thinking Skills over 4 Years of College." *Journal of College Student Development* 55 (1): 86–92. doi:10.1353/csd.2014.0009.

Pascarella, E. T., and P. T. Terenzini. 1991. *How College Affects Students: Findings and Insights from Twenty Years of Research.* San Francisco: Jossey-Bass.

Passaro, R., I. Quinto, and A. Thomas. 2018. "The Impact of Higher Education on Entrepreneurial Intention and Human Capital." *Journal of Intellectual Capital* 19 (1): 135–156. doi:10.1108/JIC-04-2017-0056.

Penttila, T., and S. Lyytinen. 2015. "How to Educate Somebody to Be Innovative? Developing and Measuring Innovation Competences in UniversityCompany Co-Operation." *Edulearn15: 7Th* International Conference on Education and New Learning Technologies, Barcelona, 163–69.

Perkmann, M., V. Tartari, M. McKelvey, E. Autio, A. Broström, P. D'Este, R. Fini, et al. 2013. "Academic Engagement and Commercialisation: A Review of the Literature on University–Industry Relations." *Research Policy* 42 (2): 423–442. doi:10.1016/j.respol.2012.09.007.

Pingree, A., and T. Zakrajsek. 2019. "Encouraged Student-Faculty Interaction outside of Class." https://www.ideaedu.org/Resources-Events/TeachingLearning-Resources/Encouraged-student-faculty-interaction-outside-ofclass#133357-why-this-matters

Plaschka, G. R., and H. P. Welsch. 1990. "Emerging Structures in Entrepreneurship Education: Curricular Designs and Strategies." *Entrepreneurship Theory and Practice* 14 (3): 55–71. doi:10.1177/104225879001400308.

Purzer, S., N. D. Fila, and P. D. Mathis. 2014. "CAREER: A Study of How Engineering Students Approach Innovation."

Quadrini, V. 2000. "Entrepreneurship, Saving, and Social Mobility." *Review of Economic Dynamics* 3 (1): 1–40. doi:10.1006/redy.1999.0077.

Rampersad, G. 2015. Building University Innovation Ecosystems: The Role of Work Integrated Learning as a Core Element in the University-Industry Nexus. Journal of Research in Business, Economics and Management. 4. 231-240.

Rebecca, R. A., G. A. Knight, P. W. Liesch, and L. Zhou. 2018. "International Entrepreneurship: The Pursuit of Entrepreneurial Opportunities across National Borders." *Journal of International Business Studies* 49 (4): 395–406. doi:10.1057/s41267-018-0149-5.

Reichert, S. 2019. "The Role of Universities in Regional Innovation Ecosystems." *European University Association 2019*, no. March: 102.

Ronstadt, R., K. H. Vesper, and W. Ed McMullan. 1988. "Entrepreneurship: Today Courses, Tomorrow Degrees?" *Entrepreneurship Theory and Practice* 13 (1): 7–13. doi:10.1177/104225878801300102.

Sax, L. J. 2008. *The Gender Gap in College: Maximizing the Development Potential of Women and Men.* San Francisco: Jossey-Bass.

Selznick, B. 2017. "Higher Education for Undergraduate Innovation." *School of Strategic Leadership Studies – Faculty Scholarship*, April. https://commons.lib.jmu.edu/sls/1

Selznick, B. S. 2019. Developing innovators: Preparing 21st century graduates for the ideaeconomy. In. T. Trolian & E. Jach (Eds.), New Directions for Higher Education, 181, (pp. 81-90). Wiley.

Selznick, B. S., and M. J. Mayhew. 2018. "Measuring Undergraduates' Innovation Capacities." *Research in Higher Education* 59 (6): 744–764. doi:10.1007/s11162-017-9486-7.

Swayne, N., Selznick, B. S., McCarthy S., & Fisher, K. A. 2019. Uncoupling innovation andentrepreneurship to improve undergraduate learning. Journal of Small Business and Enterprise Development, 26 (6/7): 786–796.

Shapira, P., and J. Wang. 2009. "From Lab to Market? Strategies and Issues in the Commercialization of Nanotechnology in China." *Asian Business & Management* 8 (4): 461–489. doi:10.1057/abm.2009.15.

Spigel, B. 2017. "The Relational Organization of Entrepreneurial Ecosystems." *Entrepreneurship: Theory and Practice* 41 (1): 49–72. doi:10.1111/etap.12167.

Strayhorn, T. L. 2018. "College Students' Sense of Belonging. College Students' Sense of Belonging." New York: Routledge. doi:10.4324/9781315297293.

Tinto, V. 1993. *Leaving College: Rethinking the Causes and Cures of Student Attrition*. Chicago: University of Chicago Press.

Tsang, T. L. 2017. "A Quantitative Analysis Examining Differences between US Humanities and STEM Students' Propensity toward Innovation." *Journal of Further and Higher Education* 43 (2): 149–165. doi:10.1080/0309877X.2017.1357069.

Turner, F. 1894. *The Significance of the Frontier in American History*. Madison: State of Historical Society of Wisconsin.

Unks, G. 1979. "The Scholastic Horror Show." *High School Journal* 62 (4): 157–158. https://eric.ed.gov/?id=EJ205820

Volery, T., S. Müller, F. Oser, C. Naepflin, and N. Del Rey. 2013. "The Impact of Entrepreneurship Education on Human Capital at Upper-Secondary Level." *Journal of Small Business Management* 51 (3): 429–446. doi:10.1111/jsbm.12020.

Walter, S., and R. David Lankes. 2015. "The Innovation Agenda." *College and Research Libraries* 76 (7): 854–858. doi:10.5860/crl.76.7.854.

Wang, X., and L. Tingting 2018. "Problems and Ways of Promoting Innovation and Entrepreneurship Education against the Background of QNew Normalityq." In *Proceedings of the 2018 International Conference on Sports, Arts, Education and Management Engineering (SAEME 2018)*. Paris, France: Atlantis Press. doi:10.2991/saeme-18.2018.104.

Warren, A., E. Kisenwether, and R. Hanke. 2006. "A Scalable Problem-Based Learning System for Entrepreneurship Education." *ASEE Annual Conference and Exposition, Conference Proceedings*. Chicago.

Waychal, P. K. 2016. A Framework for Developing Innovation Competencies Paper presented at 2016 ASEE Annual Conference & Exposition, New Orleans, Louisiana. doi:10.18260/p.26321

Webb, T., T. Quince, and D. Watkins. 1984. *Small Business Research. The Development of Entrepreneurs*. Aldershot:Gower.

Wieder, B. 2011. "Thiel Fellowship Pays 24 Talented Students $100,000 Not to Attend College." https://www.chronicle.com/article/Thiel-Fellowship-Pays-24/127622/

Wilson, F., J. Kickul, and D. Marlino. 2007. "Gender, Entrepreneurial SelfEfficacy, and Entrepreneurial Career Intentions: Implications for Entrepreneurship Education." *Entrepreneurship Theory and Practice* 31 (3): 387–406. doi:10.1111/j.1540-6520.2007.00179.x.

Wolf-Wendel, L., K. Ward, and J. Kinzie. 2009. "A Tangled Web of Terms: The Overlap and Unique Contribution of Involvement, Engagement, and Integration to Understanding College Student Success." *Journal of College Student Development* 50 (4): 407–428.

Yanto, H., J. M. Mula, and M. H. Kavanagh. 2011. "Developing Student's Accounting Competencies Using Astin's I-E-O Model: An Identification of Key Educational Inputs Based on Indonesian Student Perspectives." *RMIT Accounting Educators' Conference* 2009, Melbourne, Australia, (March 2017): 1–24.

Zeldin, A. L., and F. Pajares. 2007. "Against the Odds: Self-Efficacy Beliefs of Women in Mathematical, Scientific, and Technological Careers." *American Educational Research Journal* 37 (1): 215–246. doi:10.3102/00028312037001215.

Zhao, H., G. E. Hills, and S. E. Seibert. 2005. "The Mediating Role of SelfEfficacy in the Development of Entrepreneurial Intentions." *Journal of Applied Psychology* 90 (6): 1265–1272. doi:10.1037/0021-9010.90.6.1265.

Zhao, H., and S. E. Seibert. 2006. "The Big Five Personality Dimensions and Entrepreneurial Status: A Meta-Analytical Review." *Journal of Applied Psychology* 91 (2): 259–271. doi:10.1037/0021-9010.91.2.259.

Table 1. Literature overview on educational research.

Study (year)	Sample	Theoretical background	Country	Empirical (E) Theoretical (T) Descriptive (D)	Student outcomes (O)/ Intentions (I)	Faculty challenges	Faculty interaction	Functional experiences	Connecting experiences
Kourilsky and Esfandiari (1997)	95 school sophomores from lower socio-economic neighbourhood (51 treatment; 44 control)	Generative learning theory Theory of cognitive developmental stages Taxonomy of learning	USA	E	O	X			
Franklin (1995)	2,165 four-year full-time students	General Model for Assessing the effects of differential college environments on student learing (developed by Pascarella 1985)	USA	T	O	X	X	X	
Pascarella et al. (2004)	1,041 students	Student Involvement Theory (among others)	USA	E	O	X	X		
Galloway, Anderson, Brown, and Wilson (2005)	519 students (from 4 universities)	Theory of planed behaviour	Scotland	D	O	X			
Zhao, Hills, and Seibert (2005)	265 students	Self-efficacy Theory Social-cognitive Theory	USA	E	O/I	X			
Warren, Kisenwether, and Hanke (2006)	135 students	-	USA	D	O	X		X	X
Mentoor and Friedrich (2007)	463 students	-	South-Africa	D	O	X			
Marvel and Lumpkin (2007)	145 students	Human Capital Theory	USA	E	O	X			
Norwani (2009)	528 students	Input-Environment-Output-Model	Malaysia	E	O	X	X		
Yanto and Mula (2011)	411 students	Input-Environment-Output-Model	Indonesia	E	O	X			
Genco, Genco, Seepersad, and Holtta-Otto (2010)	94 students	-	USA	E	O	X			
Moriano et al. (2012)	1,074 students	Theory of planed behaviour	Germany, India, Iran, Poland, Spain & Netherlands	E	O/I				

(*Continued*)

Table 1. (Continued).

Study (year)	Sample	Theoretical background	Country	Empirical (E) Theoretical (T) Descriptive (D)	Student outcomes (O)/ Intentions (I)	Faculty challenges	Faculty interaction	Functional experiences	Connecting experiences
Mayhew, Simonoff, Baumol, and Wiesenfeld (2012)	3,700 students	Theory of planed behaviour Input-Environment-Output-Model	USA	E	I	X	X		X
Martin, McNally, and Kay (2013)	-	Human Capital Theory	-	D	O	X			
Volery et al. (2013)	494 students	Theory of planed behaviour Human Capital Theory	Switzerland	E	O/I	X			
Pascarella et al. (2014)	949 students	Student Involvement Theory	USA	E	O	X	X		
Hu, Hung, and Ching (2014)	724 students	-	Taiwan	E	O		X		
Moberg et al. (2014)	557 students	-	13 countries in Europe	E	O	X			
Kim et al. (2017)	790 students	Input-Environment-Output-Model Transition theory	USA	E	O		X		
Passaro, Quinto, and Thomas (2018)	128 students & 100 academics (e.g PHD candidates)	Theory of planed behaviour Human Capital Theory	Italy	E	O/I	X			
Hynes and Hynes (2018)	276 students	Environmental preference model	USA	D	O			X	

X = examined in study

Transformative change in higher education: entrepreneurial universities and high-technology entrepreneurship

James A. Cunningham and Matthias Menter

ABSTRACT

Public policies focusing on the higher education landscape often pursue a paradigm shift among universities that may ultimately lead to the transformation towards entrepreneurial universities. The purpose of this paper is to examine whether a higher education policy-induced transformation significantly influenced regional high-technology entrepreneurship. We thereby focus on the German Excellence Initiative, a higher education policy intervention designed to foster and support the transformative change of German universities towards an entrepreneurial paradigm. Our results reveal that the German Excellence Initiative had a positive and significant impact on regional high-technology entrepreneurship. Our results further show that the higher the interaction with industry, the more conducive universities become for regional high-technology entrepreneurship. In addition, universities' overarching scientific focus decisively affects regional high-technology entrepreneurship. Based on our results, we conclude our paper by outlining implications for policy makers, high-technology entrepreneurs and university managers as well as present future avenues for research.

1. Introduction

For regional economies, high-technology entrepreneurship provides considerable benefits and spillover effects that have economic and social impacts, such a bringing highly innovative ideas to the market (see Oakey 2012; Van Praag and Versloot 2007), thus contributes to faster economic growth (see Matejun 2016). An important environmental factor to encourage and support high-technology entrepreneurship within a region are investments in research and development (Xue and Klein 2010). Contemporary perspectives of universities view them as institutions that can support, pioneer and enhance entrepreneurship and innovation within and outside their institutional boundaries (Kirby, Guerrero, and Urbano 2011). Within regions, universities have been accorded a central role in supporting innovation and entrepreneurship (Siegel and Wright 2015). Collaborations with universities can confer benefits to industrial partners and simultaneously substantiate the new (entrepreneurial) role of the university within the society (see Audretsch 2014; Cunningham and Link 2015; Paleari, Donina, and Meoli 2015). Universities are therefore mandated to integrate entrepreneurial elements within their overall architecture to embrace third mission activities focused on commercialisation and technology transfer (see Cunningham and Harney 2006) that are supported or enabled through public sector entrepreneurship initiatives (see Leyden and Link 2015). Other universities, so-called entrepreneurial universities, are going even further and fully embrace the entrepreneurial paradigm that shapes institutional and cultural aspects, processes and architecture that support the entire university community in pursuing third mission activities (Nelles and Vorley 2011). Such transformative change can bring direct benefits to universities by increasing the levels of academic entrepreneurship within their institution and can also have regional spillover effects on the economic, technological and societal exploitation of knowledge (Urbano and Guerrero 2013; Braunerhjelm 2008).

Regions with high-technology entrepreneurship prosper, such as the Silicon Valley, and respective entrepreneurs focus on innovation through their entrepreneurial endeavours that are highly disruptive (Bahrami and Evans 1995). The impact of high-technology entrepreneurship on Silicon Valley is described by Bahrami and Evans (1995: 62) as follows: 'The entrepreneurial spirit and commitment to innovation have so far proven effective in producing pioneering products and high value added jobs'. Access to knowledge, human capital and networks are thereby critical ingredients for regional development, competitiveness and prosperity. To support the development of such high-technology entrepreneurship regions, policy makers are constantly trying to develop and augment regional capabilities and competencies that support regional innovation and entrepreneurship (see Keeble and Wilkinson 1999; Longhi 1999). Within regions, universities are increasingly important supporting institutions for high-technology entrepreneurship through proprietary scientific research and development and human capital to support the exploitation of novel innovations and entrepreneurial opportunities. Studies have shown that there are local geographic spillovers between university research and high-technology entrepreneurship and innovation (see Anselin, Varga, and Acs 1997; Audretsch et al. 2016b; Brown 2016; Cowan and Zinovyeva 2013; Liu 2015).

Within the growing literature on entrepreneurial universities, while there has been a focus on examining their economic impact on research, teaching and third mission activities (see Guerrero, Cunningham, and Urbano 2015a; Urbano and Guerrero 2013). There has been no empirical attention to date that examines whether higher education policy initiatives inducing transformative change among universities, i.e. creating entrepreneurial universities, are effective, hence influence regional high-technology entrepreneurship. Set in the German context, our study finds that the German Excellence Initiative – a higher education policy – had a positive and significant impact on regional high-technology entrepreneurship. We can further show that the higher the interaction with industry, i.e. the intensity of knowledge flowing and being transferred between the public and the private sector, the more conducive universities become for regional high-technology entrepreneurship. However, also universities' overarching scientific focus decisively affects regional high-technology entrepreneurship. Our findings emphasise that universities need guidance and support in their transformation towards an entrepreneurial paradigm to fully exploit and leverage their potential for regional development. Not only well-established entrepreneurial universities but also universities undergoing transformative change bear potential to create positive impact within and beyond the academic spheres. Our study thus adds to the literature by highlighting that the concept of entrepreneurial universities should be much broader than just focusing on already transformed universities, embracing also universities that currently deal with transformative change towards an entrepreneurial paradigm.

The remainder of our paper is structured as follows. We begin with a review of high-technology entrepreneurship, entrepreneurial universities and their transformative change as well as higher education policy interventions. We then present our methodology and findings. We conclude the paper with a discussion of our findings and outline recommendations for policy makers, high-technology entrepreneurs and university managers as well as discuss some future avenues of research.

2. Literature review

2.1. High-technology entrepreneurship

The rationale for supporting and encouraging high-technology entrepreneurship centres on economic growth, job creation, new innovations and growth in new venture creation (see Audretsch and Keilbach 2004; Audretsch, Keilbach, and Lehmann 2005a; Mason and Brown 2013; Van Stel, Carree, and Thurik 2005). There are several factors that support the growth of high-technology regions such as research and educational infrastructure, government policies, location of major inventions, availability of (financial, human and social) capital, amenities, entrepreneurial spirit and technology-based spin-offs (see Audretsch, Lehmann, and Seitz 2019a; Sternberg 1996). To effectively support high-technology entrepreneurship in a region, Friar and Meyer (2003) argue that it requires both exogenous and endogenous approaches. In reflecting on a case study of the Aragon region in Spain, Sanchez and Perez (1998) argue that it is more challenging for peripheral regions to create high-technology entrepreneurship. Policy interventions to support high-technology firms in a European context should centre on reducing the regulatory burden, marketing regions to attract capital – financial and human – and to direct public supports through government agencies and bodies (see Cunningham et al. 2019; Grilli 2014).

High-technology entrepreneurship is typically associated with geographical agglomerations such as the Silicon Valley in California and Route 128 in Boston in the US, Cambridge and Oxford in the UK, Tel Aviv in Israel, Bangalore in India, or Lund in Sweden (see Bieri 2010; Cooper and Folta 2017). Typically, policy interventions aimed at fostering the share of high-technology start-ups, so-called high-growth entrepreneurship policies, are thereby focused on the private sector (Autio and Rannikko 2016; Audretsch, Lehmann, and Menter 2016a). Kuratko and Menter (2017: 31) argue that 'despite the strong rationale of implementing comprehensive public policy approaches that create conducive conditions for the different types of ventures, policymakers tend to favour the high-technology sector, especially since knowledge and technology-based industries tend to exhibit high rates of growth'. Dahlstrand (2007) shows that such technology-based firms are a highly regional phenomenon, constituting an effective means 'when it comes to industrial invention and innovation' (see Oakey 2012: 3).

For high-technology entrepreneurship firms to be successful, research and development, the management team and customer relationships are critical along with the capabilities of the founding team (Chorev and Anderson 2006). Access to new knowledge to support high-technology entrepreneurship is essential (see Dai and Liu 2009; Garnsey 1998; Hart and Acs 2011). Furthermore, access to venture capital can support the creation and expansion of high-technology entrepreneurship in a location (Lehmann, Seitz, and Wirsching 2017). Where there is a high concentration of high-technology entrepreneurship and firms in a location, venture capital firms tend to fund locally, rather than these firms relying on venture capital funding from other locations (Florida and Kenney 1988). According to Hayton (2005), studying high-technology new ventures in the US that issued an initial public offering, organisational reputation and human capital diversity of high-technology entrepreneurship firms are the most significant factors for their entrepreneurial performance. Gimmon and Levie (2010) in their study of Israeli technology incubation programmes find that academic status was a factor in attracting capital investment but did not positively affect firm survival. High-technology entrepreneurship firms require innovation and entrepreneurship efficiency based on a mix of strong and weak network ties (Elfring and Hulsink 2003), whereby the creation of high-technology new ventures can suffer in situations where there are tight labour markets (Fairlie and Chatterji 2013).

Universities have a role to play in supporting high-technology entrepreneurship within regional entrepreneurship and innovation ecosystems (see Lehmann et al. 2020; Brown 2016). Hülsbeck and Pickavé (2014: 121) highlight its context-dependency as they state that high-technology entrepreneurship 'is highly dependent on regional knowledge production by industry *and* university, while technology entrepreneurship does largely not dependent on these factors'. Thus, besides industry, universities as sources of new knowledge also play a crucial role in the process of high-technology firm birth. Founders of high-technology entrepreneurship firms are more likely to have a university background and the origins of these firms can be through spin-offs from universities or exiting firms (see Oakey 2003). Based on their study of the Silicon Valley and the Berkeley Campus of the University of California, Huffman and Quigley (2002: 403) conclude: 'The results also reinforce the self-interested reasons for government investment in high-quality educational institutions, as measured by the return on the augmented human capital stock in the region'. Moreover, their study highlights how the state benefited from graduates staying in the locality through taxation and that the local economy benefited from graduates remaining on living in the region post university.

2.2. Entrepreneurial universities and transformative change

Policy makers now view universities as actors, creating new knowledge to support innovation and entrepreneurship and exploiting this knowledge through technology and knowledge transfer (Cunningham and Link 2015). There has been an increasing research focus on how universities become entrepreneurial universities, and especially how universities are adapting to an entrepreneurial paradigm (see Guerrero et al. 2016a; Ranga, Debackere, and Tunzelmann 2003; Van Looy et al. 2011). Cunningham, Guerrero, and Urbano (2017a) define the role of an entrepreneurial university as follows: 'An entrepreneurial university simultaneously fulfils three different activities – teaching, research, and entrepreneurship – while providing an adequate atmosphere in which the university community can explore and exploit ideas and contribute to the creation of a sustained competitive advantage that could be transformed into social and economic impacts'. The changing nature of academic work (Cannizzo and Osbaldiston 2016), entrepreneurship and innovation public policies (Siegfried, Sanderson, and McHenry 2007), competition (Maringe 2006) funding (Geuna 2001), and managerialism (Lawrence and Sharma 2002) are some of the factors that are driving universities to adapt an entrepreneurial paradigm. Moreover, universities are becoming even more influential by shaping actors within regions in supporting regional innovation and entrepreneurship (see Benneworth and Hospers 2007) and bridging social and entrepreneurial capital (Nahapiet and Ghoshal 1998). However, in some regions, as Brown (2016) notes, there is a lack of connectivity between local innovation and entrepreneurship ecosystems and universities. Nevertheless, studies to date have shown that universities and especially entrepreneurial universities do have an economic impact (Bramwell and Wolfe 2008; Lehmann and Menter 2016; Guerrero, Urbano, and Fayolle 2016b).

Various interpretations and definitions of entrepreneurial universities have acknowledged that these institutions are a source of funding (Etzkowitz 1983), new venture creation (Dill 1995), foster networking (Formica 2002) and are involved in commercialisation and technology transfer activities (Jacob, Lundqvist, and Hellsmark 2003). Etzkowitz (2003: 112) argues that the entrepreneurial university functions as 'a natural incubator, providing support structures for teachers and students to initiate new ventures: intellectual, commercial and conjoint'. However, Röpke (1998: 2) goes further and suggests that 'the university itself, as an organization, becomes entrepreneurial'. Schulte (2004: 187) adds that respective universities 'operate in an entrepreneurial manner'. In essence, universities transforming to become an entrepreneurial university means, not alone structural and organisational changes, but also changes to organisational culture and decision-making that is entrepreneurial in nature.

Entrepreneurial universities have responded and transformed in different ways to this entrepreneurial paradigm shift, such as through the creation of technology transfer offices (Siegel, Waldman, and Link 2003; Berbegal-Mirabent, Sabaté, and Cañabate 2012), supporting graduate entrepreneurship (Guerrero et al. 2018; Hayter, Lubynsky, and Maroulis 2017), student business plan competitions (Watson, McGowan, and Cunningham 2018), or the creation of university based accelerators, incubators and science parks (Hobbs, Link, and Scott 2017; McAdam et al. 2006; Phan, Siegel, and Wright 2005). Such transformative change responses of universities to become entrepreneurial universities have seen some growth of academic entrepreneurship (Grimaldi et al. 2011; Miller, McAdam, and McAdam 2018; Shane 2004) among faculty and a growth in scientists becoming publicly funded principal investigators to secure the necessary resources to purse knowledge creation and commercialisation (see Cunningham et al. 2016; Menter 2016).

Studies have highlighted that entrepreneurial universities adopt different approaches that reflect local, regional and national environmental factors. In a cross-country case study comparison between Irish and Spanish universities, Guerrero et al. (2014) find significant institutional differences in how they were making transformative changes in becoming an entrepreneurial university. There are differences concerning local, regional and environmental factors with respect to attitudes towards entrepreneurship, reward systems, structures and incentives. Such differences in approaches are also reflected in the case studies undertaken by Clark (1998, 2004), as he suggests that what really matters is the manner in which universities have adopted to meeting external challenges and forces. In a study of Iranian entrepreneurial universities, Guerrero, Urbano, and Salamzadeh (2015b) find that respective universities are highly dependent on state funding with the entrepreneurial transformation process being directly influenced by the internal entrepreneurial architecture of these institutions. According to Cunningham, Guerrero, and Urbano (2017a), institutional context, resources and the characteristics of university communities are critical determinant factors for entrepreneurial universities. The institutional context influences the transformation of universities to become an entrepreneurial university – both through formal (economic, political, regulatory) and informal factors (culture, values, attitudes) (see North 1990).

The resources and capabilities that are available within the university will determine the scope and scale of their transformation to becoming an entrepreneurial university (O'Reilly, Robbins, and Scanlan 2019). Governance, finances, people, physical assets, engagement in networks are just some of the factors that influence the extent of such a transformative change. In particular, financial resources will determine the pace of the transformative change and potential spillover benefits within and beyond the university, highlighting the important role of the government to direct and guide universities in their transformative processes particularly within regions (Budyldina 2018). In summary, entrepreneurial universities have become an important actor within regional entrepreneurial and innovation ecosystems by creating and building local knowledge and intellectual capital that is necessary to ultimately support regional high-technology entrepreneurship.

2.3. Higher education policy interventions

The rationale of higher education policy interventions is to increase the overall quality of funded institutions, mainly with regard to teaching and research but increasingly also to transferring knowledge. Hence, building close relationships with industry seems to be a crucial element of such programmes. According to Kitagawa (2004: 846), 'those relationships growing between universities and their regions are an important strategic and policy issue for universities, industry, communities and for governments alike in order to construct "advantage" within the multi-level governance structure of knowledge economies'. Studies have found that universities' activities do have an impact on regions (see Batterbury and Hill 2005; Drucker and Goldstein 2007; Huggins, Johnston, and Steffenson 2008). Based on public sector entrepreneurship initiatives, policy makers try to drive and shape transformative processes through the provision of financial resources. Studies of higher education policy interventions at a national and regional level have focused mainly on different aspects such as entrepreneurial education and training (see Galvão, Ferreira, and Marques 2018), entrepreneurial intention (Passaro, Quinto, and Thomas 2018), business formation (Fotopoulos and Storey 2019), or technology business incubators (Lamine et al. 2018). Specifically, there has been a concentration of studies examining higher education policy interventions from an entrepreneurial education perspective across different countries (see Ahmad 2013; İlhan Ertuna and Gurel 2011; Solomon and Matlay 2008). However, especially the impact of higher education policies on entrepreneurial activities beyond academic boundaries has not received much scholarly attention.

The most recent higher education policy intervention in Germany, the Excellence Initiative, was meant to foster the transformation of German universities towards an entrepreneurial paradigm and create outstanding conditions for cutting-edge research across all disciplines. Not by chance, the slogan of the Technical University of Munich (TUM) in their first funding application was 'TUM: The Entrepreneurial University'. Based on overall three different funding lines that supported the creation of *Graduate Schools, Clusters of Excellence*, and *Institutional Strategies*, with a total funding exceeding € 4.6 billion, the Excellence Initiative was implemented in order to increase the competitiveness of the higher education sector and augment positive externalities of universities through the promotion of top-level research and the improvement of the quality of universities and research institutions in general (DFG 2013). The initiative itself took place in two phases (first phase from 2005–2012 and second phase from 2012–2017) and funded the creation of in total 51 Graduate Schools, 49 Clusters of Excellence and 14 Institutional Strategies. Whereas Graduate Schools aimed at improving the promotion of young scientists and researchers, Clusters of Excellence were meant to bundle universities' research potential and expand universities' networks beyond academic spheres, thus encouraged collaborations with non-university research institutions and industrial partners. Institutional strategies promoted universities as a whole and aimed at enabling funded universities to compete globally by enhancing top-level research and promoting young scientists and researchers. Thus, only those universities were eligible for the nomination as an elite university, i.e. receiving financial support through the third funding line, which had been awarded at least one Graduate School and one Cluster of Excellence. It is important to note that the focus of the German Excellence Initiative was not directly related to high-technology entrepreneurship, but rather aimed at creating conducive environments within and beyond academic spheres that facilitate knowledge spillovers, which might ultimately serve as the breeding ground for regional entrepreneurial activities.

Studies examining the effects of the Excellence Initiative are limited and have found rather mixed results with regard to its effectiveness. Whereas the report of the International Expert Commission on the Excellence Initiative (IEKE), evaluating the first phase of the Excellence Initiative, indicates that this policy initiative was a great success, making the entire German university system more competitive and dynamic (IEKE 2016), Gawellek and Sunder (2016) find a drop in efficiency among applying universities, whereby positive effects did not extend beyond the actual funding. Lehmann and Stockinger (2018: 70) focus on the impact the Excellence Initiative had on university outcomes (e.g. patents or industry engagement) and conclude that this policy intervention 'created an advantage for the whole of Germany while being an Excellence University does not have an impact on academic entrepreneurship with regards to patenting activity'. Menter, Lehmann, and Klarl (2018) find that the Excellence Initiative positively contributed to augmented research performance among promoted universities, yet argue that not the political initiative itself but rather the announcement of funding fostered the performance of the German higher education system.

3. Dataset and methodology

This paper studies the policy-induced impact of universities' transition towards an entrepreneurial paradigm on regional high-technology entrepreneurship. As high-technology start-ups push technological boundaries and as universities are perceived as engines of innovation (Thorp and Goldstein 2013), the transition towards an entrepreneurial university might stimulate and encourage entrepreneurial activities within a region.

We consider regions in terms of spatial planning regions (*Raumordnungsregionen, RORs*) as utilised by the German Statistics Office.[1] Taking a view on Germany reveals large differences across both regions and universities (see Table 1). Whereas some regions are highly innovative (see *regional innovativeness*), others lack sufficient resources as indicated by a rather low GDP per capita ratio (see *regional prosperity*). Likewise, some universities in those regions have strong linkages with industry whereas other higher education institutions are rather stuck in their traditional (ivory tower) paradigm as reflected by the low share of industry funds compared to all third-party funds (see *industry focus*). Overall, our dataset captures 102 German universities nested within 63 RORs within a timeframe from 2001 to 2014.

Analysing the bivariate correlations of our utilised variables reveals further insights into the context dependency of high-technology entrepreneurship (see Table 2). As confirmed by previous studies (Adler et al. 2019; Carlino, Chatterjee, and Hunt 2007; Acs and Varga 2005), regional density is rather highly correlated with high-technology entrepreneurship ($r = 0.598$). Further, university size, as reflected by the number of graduates, is rather highly correlated with entrepreneurial activities ($r = 0.491$) as well as with innovative activities ($r = 0.640$). Despite the partially high correlations (all correlation coefficients are yet below 0.70), the calculation of the variance inflation factors reveals the non-presence of multicollinearity (see Hair et al. 1998). The mean variance inflation factors for all model specifications is around 2.

In order to analyse our dataset, we rely on difference-in-differences estimations, enabling the differentiation between funded regions (*treatment group*) and non-funded regions (*control group*). Out of the investigated 63 RORs, 32 RORs received at least funding from one funding line of the Excellence Initiative. An adoption of a difference-in-differences approach requires testing a similar development of the treatment and control group prior to the actual treatment, i.e. getting funded through the German Excellence Initiative, the so-called common trends assumption. Appendix 1 to 4 confirm this common trends assumption graphically. We control for both regional specifics (regional density, regional prosperity and regional innovativeness) and university specifics (industry focus, graduates, research output and scientific orientation) as suggested by multiple studies.

Due to our dataset time structure (2001 to 2014), we specifically focus on the first phase of the Excellence Initiative, as it allows us to consider sufficient time periods before and after the treatment (in 2007), i.e. the implementation of the first phase of the Excellence Initiative. We utilise four model specifications in order to investigate the overall impact of the Excellence Initiative (Model I/V) as well as the isolated effects of

[1]Germany consists of in total 96 RORs. However, for our empirical analysis, we only consider RORs that also inhere at least one university (in sum 63 RORs). Hence, we compare university regions that have received funding from the Excellence Initiative (in sum 32 RORs) with university regions that have not received any funding from the Excellence Initiative (in sum 31 RORs).

Table 1. Descriptive statistics.

Variable	Obs	Mean	SD	Min	Max	Description/Source
High-tech. entrepreneurship (abs.)	896	3.123	4.732	0	57	Number of high-technology start-ups; Source: German Institute for Employment Research
High-tech. entrepreneurship ratio	895	0.056	0.046	0	0.420	Number of high-technology start-ups in relation to the regional workforce (in 10,000); Source: German Institute for Employment Research, German Statistics Office
Scientific orientation	896	0.250	0.433	0	1	Indication of technical university (dummy variable); Source: German Statistics Office
Industry focus	880	0.215	0.141	0	1	Ratio of university third-party funding by industry in relation to total university third-party funding; Source: German Statistics Office
Research output	896	0.319	0.157	0	0.976	Publications per research fellow; Source: Scopus, German Statistics Office
Graduates	896	3,045	2,665	0	20,242	Number of university graduates: Source: German Statistics Office
Regional density	896	405.92	563.33	58.71	3,867	Citizens per square kilometre; Source: German Statistics Office
Regional prosperity	896	29,531	8,160	14,459	59,787	Gross domestic product per capita; Source: German Statistics Office
Regional innovativeness	896	38.81	50.95	0.868	291.67	Patents per workforce (in 10,000); Source: OECD REGPAT Database, German Statistics Office

Note: This table shows descriptive data on 63 German planning regions (RORs) observed from 2001 to 2014.

Table 2. Correlation matrix.

		1	2	3	4	5	6	7	8	9
1	High-tech. entrepreneurship (log.)	1								
2	High-tech. entrepreneurship ratio	0.677	1							
3	Scientific orientation	0.378	0.163	1						
4	Industry focus	0.178	0.067	0.136	1					
5	Research output	0.118	−0.038	0.175	−0.012	1				
6	Graduates	0.491	0.063	0.274	−0.027	0.439	1			
7	Regional density	0.598	0.292	0.293	−0.027	0.164	0.579	1		
8	Regional prosperity	0.184	−0.288	0.129	0.088	0.158	0.514	0.392	1	
9	Regional innovativeness	0.630	0.193	0.343	0.104	0.158	0.640	0.563	0.541	1

Note: This table reports the correlation coefficients among the dependent and independent variables employed in our regressions.

each funding line (Model II–IV(VI–VIII) on regional high-technology entrepreneurship. We operationalise high-technology entrepreneurship by the logarithmized number of regional high-technology start-ups as classified by the Institute for Employment Research (see Schmucker et al. 2018). In order to test the robustness of our results, we employ the same estimation approach, yet exchange our dependent variable by taking the share of regional high-technology start-ups in relation to the workforce (in 10,000). As effects on regional high-technology entrepreneurship may be not immediate, we include time lags in our empirical approach to take account of this fact.

4. Findings and discussion

The findings of our empirical analysis are shown in Table 3. A higher education policy-induced transformative change of universities towards an entrepreneurial paradigm significantly affects regional high-technology entrepreneurship – across all three funding lines of the Excellence Initiative (as indicated by the positive and significant variable *treatment effect*). Our results thus illustrate that irrespective of the type of funding (Graduate Schools, Clusters of Excellence, or Institutional Strategies) supporting universities to become entrepreneurial universities, higher education policy interventions seem to have a wider impact beyond the university sphere. These results extend existing studies by highlighting the importance of universities within a regional context with respect to high-technology entrepreneurship (Calcagnini et al. 2016; Lehmann and Menter 2016; Shane 2004). Our study further affirms the important function that entrepreneurial universities play in a regional context particularly in enhancing and fostering high-technology entrepreneurship. One explanation for these beneficial effects may be the fact that additional funding may overcome the disconnection between universities and local innovation and entrepreneurship ecosystems (see Brown 2016).

Our control variables show the expected results and thereby confirm previous studies. Collaborations with industry and the associated orientation towards applied research (as represented by the variable *industry focus*) have a positive and significant effect on high-technology business creation. The overarching scientific focus of a university further positively affects the creation of highly innovative start-ups, indicating the existence of positive spillover effects of universities (Anselin, Varga, and Acs 1997; Audretsch, Lehmann, and Warning 2005b). The variable graduates, our control for size effects of universities, shows a negative and significant effect on high-technology entrepreneurship

Table 3. Estimation results.

	Model I (Excellence Initiative)	Model II (Graduate Schools)	Model III (Clusters of Excellence)	Model IV (Institutional Strategies)
PUBLIC POLICY				
Treatment group	**0.339*****	0.117	**0.397*****	0.196
	(0.098)	(0.094)	**(0.103)**	(0.143)
Treatment period	**−0.204*****	**−0.205*****	**−0.195*****	**−0.196*****
	(0.029)	**(0.028)**	**(0.027)**	**(0.025)**
Treatment effect	**0.074****	**0.057***	**0.079****	**0.108****
	(0.032)	**(0.032)**	**(0.033)**	**(0.048)**
UNIVERSITY				
L.Scientific orientation	**0.299*****	**0.265****	**0.228****	**0.244****
	(0.104)	**(0.105)**	**(0.104)**	**(0.105)**
L.Industry focus	**0.249*****	**0.251*****	**0.248*****	**0.252*****
	(0.079)	**(0.080)**	**(0.079)**	**(0.080)**
L.Research output	−0.084	−0.032	−0.054	−0.013
	(0.129)	(0.131)	(0.127)	(0.128)
L.Graduates	**−0.000*****	**−0.000*****	**−0.000*****	**−0.000*****
	(0.000)	**(0.000)**	**(0.000)**	**(0.000)**
REGION				
L.Reg. density	**0.001*****	**0.001*****	**0.001*****	**0.001*****
	(0.000)	**(0.000)**	**(0.000)**	**(0.000)**
L.Reg. prosperity	**−0.000*****	**−0.000*****	**−0.000*****	**−0.000*****
	(0.000)	**(0.000)**	**(0.000)**	**(0.000)**
L.Reg. innovativeness	**0.003*****	**0.004*****	**0.003*****	**0.004*****
	(0.001)	**(0.001)**	**(0.001)**	**(0.001)**
R^2	0.48	0.45	0.49	0.45
N	878	878	878	878
n	63	63	63	63

Note: This table reports the results of our difference-in-differences estimation approach. We rely on a sample of 63 German planning regions (RORs) ranging from 2001 to 2014. The dependent variable is regional high-technology entrepreneurship measured by the logarithmized number of high-technology start-ups. Standard errors are reported in parentheses.
*p <.10; ** p <.05; ***p <.01.

(see Guerrero et al. 2018). From a regional perspective, especially the density of regions might positively affect high-technology entrepreneurship (Glaeser, Rosenthal, and Strange 2010), whereas regional prosperity seems to negatively influence innovative new business formation. Finally, regional innovativeness shows a positive and significant impact on regional high-technology entrepreneurship.

These results indicate that a higher education policy-induced institutional re-orientation of universities may not only impact the scientific, but also the regional spheres with regard to high-technology entrepreneurship (see Eesley, Li, and Yang 2016). Changing the entrepreneurial paradigm of a university along with the provision of additional financial resources to enhance the research infrastructure and entrepreneurial architecture has thus stimulated an entrepreneurial spark within and beyond an academic setting. Hence, the German Excellence Initiative has succeeded in creating stimuli for the institutional change towards entrepreneurial universities. Our results thereby suggest that all different higher education policy instruments, either focusing on fostering human capital (via Graduate Schools), promoting advanced research (via Clusters of Excellence) or the combination thereof (via Institutional Strategies) seem to be effective policy instruments in the context of stimulating regional high-technology entrepreneurship. These results are rather robust as confirmed by our alternative regression approach (see Table 4): funding through the Excellence Initiative results in augmented levels of regional high-technology entrepreneurship.

Table 4. Robustness tests.

	Model V	Model VI	Model VII	Model VIII
	(Excellence Initiative)	(Graduate Schools)	(Clusters of Excellence)	(Institutional Strategies)
PUBLIC POLICY				
Treatment group	**0.015****	**0.011***	**0.011***	**0.027*****
	(0.006)	**(0.006)**	**(0.007)**	**(0.009)**
Treatment period	**−0.021*****	**−0.020*****	**−0.021*****	**−0.019*****
	(0.003)	**(0.003)**	**(0.003)**	**(0.002)**
Treatment effect	**0.006***	0.002	**0.008****	−0.004
	(0.003)	(0.003)	**(0.003)**	(0.005)
UNIVERSITY				
L.Scientific orientation	**0.012***	0.010	0.008	0.008
	(0.006)	(0.006)	(0.006)	(0.006)
L.Industry focus	**0.014***	**0.014***	**0.014***	**0.015***
	(0.008)	**(0.008)**	**(0.008)**	**(0.008)**
L.Research output	−0.019	−0.016	−0.014	−0.010
	(0.012)	(0.012)	(0.012)	(0.011)
L.Graduates	**−0.000*****	**−0.000*****	**−0.000*****	**−0.000*****
	(0.000)	**(0.000)**	**(0.000)**	**(0.000)**
REGION				
L.Reg. density	**0.000*****	**0.000*****	**0.000*****	**0.000*****
	(0.000)	**(0.000)**	**(0.000)**	**(0.000)**
L.Reg. prosperity	**−0.000*****	**−0.000*****	**−0.000*****	**−0.000*****
	(0.000)	**(0.000)**	**(0.000)**	**(0.000)**
L.Reg. innovativeness	**0.000****	**0.000*****	**0.000****	**0.000****
	(0.000)	**(0.000)**	**(0.000)**	**(0.000)**
R^2	0.42	0.42	0.42	0.44
N	878	878	878	878
n	63	63	63	63

Note: This table reports the results of our difference-in-differences estimation approach. We rely on a sample of 63 German planning regions (RORs) ranging from 2001 to 2014. The dependent variable is the regional high-technology entrepreneurship ratio measured by the amount of high-technology start-ups in relation to the regional workforce (in 10,000). Standard errors are reported in parentheses.

*p < .10; ** p < .05; ***p < .01.

5. Conclusions and future research avenues

In conclusion, our study demonstrates that a policy-induced transformative change of universities towards an entrepreneurial paradigm significantly affects regional high-technology entrepreneurship: the more universities transform towards an entrepreneurial university, the more high-technology start-ups arise within the respective region. Hence, universities that have adopted an entrepreneurial paradigm serve as a positive and significant element impacting regional high-technology entrepreneurship. Our results also suggest that the overarching scientific focus of a university has a significant impact on regional high-technology entrepreneurship. Further, collaborations with industry and the associated orientation towards applied research seem to stimulate entrepreneurial endeavours and enhance regional high-technology entrepreneurship.

Our paper is not without limitations. Due to the design of our study, we have a single-country focus limiting the generalisability of our results. Cross-country comparisons might be one way to tackle this issue, yet provoke potential conflicts with regard to the comparability, e.g. of university focused policy initiatives. In addition, our empirical setting does not capture non-university research institutes (e.g. Fraunhofer institutes or the institutes comprising the Max Planck Society and the Leibnitz Society) that also constitute important institutions with regard to knowledge dissemination and diffusion. We also do not test for the potential cross-fertilisation of basic and applied research (see

Leyden and Menter 2018). Moreover, we do not consider the simultaneous impact of further policy instruments that try to stimulate regional high-technology entrepreneurship, i.e. the policy mix. Finally, the observed time period might be too short to capture long-term effects of the Excellence Initiative.

Our paper reveals several implications for policy makers. Higher education policy instruments aimed at building capacity to support the transformation of universities to adopt an entrepreneurial university paradigm have a positive impact on the institution and the region that they inhabit. Therefore, policy makers need to give careful consideration to the design of the policy tools as well as the intended and unintended consequences. Policy makers need to ensure that such policy instruments provide sufficient institutional autonomy to enable universities to adapt to regional contextual dynamics, while simultaneously moving in a sustainable manner to realise an entrepreneurial university paradigm. This allows universities to experiment and to take risks irrespective of the current performance and standing. However, a university targeting innovation and technology transfer is not a means in itself as universities should be designed to contribute to what Kitagawa (2004: 847) describes as economic and social cohesion.

Consideration also needs to be given in relation to how higher education policies such as the German Excellence Initiative complement other innovation and entrepreneurship policy interventions. Hence, the policy mix needs to be taken into account in order not to displace resources and actor efforts in achieving desired policy outcomes (see Munari et al. 2016). What is worth reflecting on the German Excellence Initiative is that it was broad enough in scope, in terms of specific programme initiatives and funding lines, but also flexible enough to ensure that universities where able to make further institutional progress to adopt the entrepreneurial university paradigm, based on individual strengths and resources. The elements of the higher education policy allowed for institutional autonomy that is necessary to create positive externalities through knowledge spillovers alongside the necessary institutional building activities. Nevertheless, policy makers need to be more aware of the circular effect such public investments may have in supporting regions in a more sustainable manner in terms of issues such as increased taxation revenue, retention of high skilled labour that Huffman and Quigley (2002) outline with respect to Silicon Valley. Moreover, our study again illustrates that public investments in entrepreneurial universities do pay off and further enhance the university at the centre of the 'local entrepreneurial fulcrum' as Budyldina (2018) posits.

For high-technology entrepreneurship and entrepreneurs, our study again reaffirms the importance of location in order to set up a new venture. High-technology entrepreneurs need to locate in a region and an environment where there is a concentration of such firms, so-called entrepreneurial ecosystems (see Audretsch et al. 2019b; Cantner et al. 2020;). Therefore, the determinant factors of the local environment that Sternberg (1996) outlines should factor into the decision-making of high-technology entrepreneurs in terms of where they are going to locate their venture. Moreover, our study highlights that high-technology entrepreneurs should develop close collaborative relationships with universities and academic entrepreneurs that can contribute to the development of novelty and originality with regard to product and/or service design. Such collaborations can also contribute to enhancing the invention, innovation and entrepreneurship efficiency that are necessary to purse high-technology entrepreneurship.

For university managers, our study highlights the positive effects of adopting the entrepreneurial university paradigm through proactively responding to a higher education policy initiative. Our study highlights that all dimensions of the university – teaching, research and technology transfer – have an impact on regional high-technology entrepreneurship. We suggest that universities experiment with different interventions and approaches that are aligned with local needs of high-technology entrepreneurs while also furthering the entrepreneurial university transformation agenda. Not all activities will work and some will fail or not achieve the desired impacts and outcomes, yet potential benefits might be ultimately overcompensated. This should be factored in and recognised as part of the transformational agenda.

University managers also need to consider which practical supports they can provide at an institutional level to support high-technology entrepreneurship for the members of the university community. For faculty, it is important to consider how universities' institutional architecture actually supports the enhancing of individual career status irrespective of gender, diversity and stage of career considerations to purse high-technology entrepreneurial opportunities. In addition, the overarching scientific focus of a university might have decisive impacts on regional high-technology entrepreneurship.

Our study finally provides the basis to build some fruitful research avenues that further our understanding of the relationship between entrepreneurial universities' transformation and high-technology entrepreneurship. There is a need to extend and initiate cross-country studies and comparisons to better understand if similar results, as presented in our study, are prevalent. At a more micro level, using mixed methodological approaches (see Cunningham, Menter, and Young 2017b), more research should be devoted to the classification, measurement and evaluation concerning the different approaches and strategies used by entrepreneurial universities to pursue the entrepreneurial paradigm. A final avenue of research should focus on graduate education and how it should support high-technology entrepreneurship (Guerrero et al. 2018). What are the optimal pedagogical approaches, curricula and extra-curricular support programmes that are required to truly support high-technology entrepreneurship and nascent high-technology entrepreneurs? In this context, the role of supporting institutions like technology transfer offices but also specific centres (see Dolan et al. 2019), e.g. entrepreneurship centres or cooperative research centres, needs to be better understood to enhance the efficiency and effectiveness of prevalent mechanisms.

Disclosure statement

No potential conflict of interest was reported by the authors.

References

Acs, Z. J., and A. Varga. 2005. "Entrepreneurship, Agglomeration and Technological Change." *Small Business Economics* 24 (3): 323–334. doi:10.1007/s11187-005-1998-4.

Adler, P., R. Florida, K. King, and C. Mellander. 2019. "The City and High-tech Startups: The Spatial Organization of Schumpeterian Entrepreneurship." *Cities* 87: 121–130. doi:10.1016/j.cities.2018.12.013.

Ahmad, S. Z. 2013. "The Need for Inclusion of Entrepreneurship Education in Malaysia Lower and Higher Learning Institutions." *Education + Training* 55 (2): 191–203. doi:10.1108/00400911311304823.

Anselin, L., A. Varga, and Z. Acs. 1997. "Local Geographic Spillovers between University Research and High Technology Innovations." *Journal of Urban Economics* 42 (3): 422–448. doi:10.1006/juec.1997.2032.

Audretsch, D., E. Lehmann, M. Meoli, and S. Vismara. 2016b. *University Evolution, Entrepreneurial Activity and Regional Competitiveness*. Basel: Springer International Publishing.

Audretsch, D. B., M. Keilbach, and E. Lehmann. 2005a. "The Knowledge Spillover Theory of Entrepreneurship and Technological Diffusion." In *University Entrepreneurship and Technology Transfer*, edited by G. D. Libecap, 69–91. Bingley: Emerald Group Publishing Limited.

Audretsch, D. B. 2014. "From the Entrepreneurial University to the University for the Entrepreneurial Society." *The Journal of Technology Transfer* 39 (3): 313–321. doi:10.1007/s10961-012-9288-1.

Audretsch, D. B., E. E. Lehmann, and M. Menter. 2016a. "Public Cluster Policy and New Venture Creation." *Economia e Politica Industriale* 43 (4): 357–381. doi:10.1007/s40812-016-0050-9.

Audretsch, D. B., E. E. Lehmann, and N. Seitz. 2019a. "Amenities, Subcultures, and Entrepreneurship." *Small Business Economics*. (forthcoming). doi:10.1007/s11187-019-00190-5.

Audretsch, D. B., E. E. Lehmann, and S. Warning. 2005b. "University Spillovers and New Firm Location." *Research Policy* 34 (7): 1113–1122. doi:10.1016/j.respol.2005.05.009.

Audretsch, D. B., J. A. Cunningham, D. F. Kuratko, E. E. Lehmann, and M. Menter. 2019b. "Entrepreneurial Ecosystems: Economic, Technological, and Societal Impacts." *The Journal of Technology Transfer* 44 (2): 313–325. doi:10.1007/s10961-018-9690-4.

Audretsch, D. B., and M. Keilbach. 2004. "Entrepreneurship and Regional Growth: An Evolutionary Interpretation." *Journal of Evolutionary Economics* 14 (5): 605–616. doi:10.1007/s00191-004-0228-6.

Autio, E., and H. Rannikko. 2016. "Retaining Winners: Can Policy Boost High-growth Entrepreneurship?" *Research Policy* 45 (1): 42–55. doi:10.1016/j.respol.2015.06.002.

Bahrami, H., and S. Evans. 1995. "Flexible Re-cycling and High-technology Entrepreneurship." *California Management Review* 37 (3): 62–89. doi:10.2307/41165799.

Batterbury, S., and S. Hill. 2005. "Assessing the Impact of Higher Education on Regional Development." *Higher Education Management and Policy* 16 (3): 35–52. doi:10.1787/hemp-v16-art22-en.

Benneworth, P., and G. J. Hospers. 2007. "The New Economic Geography of Old Industrial Regions: Universities as global—Local Pipelines." *Environment and Planning C: Government and Policy* 25 (6): 779–802. doi:10.1068/c0620.

Berbegal-Mirabent, J., F. Sabaté, and A. Cañabate. 2012. "Brokering Knowledge from Universities to the Marketplace: The Role of Knowledge Transfer Offices." *Management Decision* 50 (7): 1285–1307. doi:10.1108/00251741211247012.

Bieri, D. S. 2010. "Booming Bohemia? Evidence from the US High-technology Industry." *Industry and Innovation* 17 (1): 23–48. doi:10.1080/13662710903573828.

Bramwell, A., and D. A. Wolfe. 2008. "Universities and Regional Economic Development: The Entrepreneurial University of Waterloo." *Research Policy* 37 (8): 1175–1187. doi:10.1016/j.respol.2008.04.016.

Braunerhjelm, P. 2008. "Specialization of Regions and Universities: The New versus the Old." *Industry and Innovation* 15 (3): 253–275. doi:10.1080/13662710802040853.

Brown, R. 2016. "Mission Impossible? Entrepreneurial Universities and Peripheral Regional Innovation Systems." *Industry and Innovation* 23 (2): 189–205. doi:10.1080/13662716.2016.1145575.

Budyldina, N. 2018. "Entrepreneurial Universities and Regional Contribution." *International Entrepreneurship and Management Journal* 14 (2): 265–277. doi:10.1007/s11365-018-0500-0.

Calcagnini, G., I. Favaretto, G. Giombini, F. Perugini, and R. Rombaldoni. 2016. "The Role of Universities in the Location of Innovative Start-ups." *The Journal of Technology Transfer* 41 (4): 670–693. doi:10.1007/s10961-015-9396-9.

Cannizzo, F., and N. Osbaldiston. 2016. "Academic Work/life Balance: A Brief Quantitative Analysis of the Australian Experience." *Journal of Sociology* 52 (4): 890–906. doi:10.1177/1440783315600803.

Cantner, U., J. A. Cunningham, E. E. Lehmann, and M. Menter. 2020. "Entrepreneurial Ecosystems: A Dynamic Lifecycle Model." *Small Business Economics* 1–17. doi:10.1007/s11187-020-00316-0.

Carlino, G. A., S. Chatterjee, and R. M. Hunt. 2007. "Urban Density and the Rate of Invention." *Journal of Urban Economics* 61 (3): 389–419. doi:10.1016/j.jue.2006.08.003.

Chorev, S., and A. R. Anderson. 2006. "Success in Israeli High-tech Start-ups; Critical Factors and Process." *Technovation* 26 (2): 162–174. doi:10.1016/j.technovation.2005.06.014.

Clark, B. R. 1998. *Creating Entrepreneurial Universities: Organizational Pathways of Transformation. Issues in Higher Education.* New York: Emerald Publishing.

Clark, B. R. 2004. "Delineating the Character of the Entrepreneurial University." *Higher Education Policy* 17 (4): 355–370. doi:10.1057/palgrave.hep.8300062.

Cooper, A., and T. Folta. 2017. "Entrepreneurship and High-technology Clusters." In *The Blackwell Handbook of Entrepreneurship*, edited by D. L. Sexton and H. Landström, 348–367. Oxford: Wiley.

Cowan, R., and N. Zinovyeva. 2013. "University Effects on Regional Innovation." *Research Policy* 42 (3): 788–800. doi:10.1016/j.respol.2012.10.001.

Cunningham, J. A., M. Guerrero, and D. Urbano. 2017a. "Entrepreneurial Universities—Overview, Reflections, and Future Research Agendas." In *The World Scientific Reference on Entrepreneurship: Entrepreneurial Universities*, edited by D. Siegel, 3–19. Singapore: Technology and Knowledge Transfer.

Cunningham, J. A., and A. N. Link. 2015. "Fostering University-industry R&D Collaborations in European Union Countries." *International Entrepreneurship and Management Journal* 11 (4): 849–860. doi:10.1007/s11365-014-0317-4.

Cunningham, J. A., and B. Harney. 2006. *Strategic Management of Technology Transfer: The New Challenge on Campus.* Cork, Ireland: Oak Tree Press, Oxfordshire.

Cunningham, J. A., E. E. Lehmann, M. Menter, and N. Seitz. 2019. "The Impact of University Focused Technology Transfer Policies on Regional Innovation and Entrepreneurship." *The Journal of Technology Transfer* 44 (5): 1451–1475. doi:10.1007/s10961-019-09733-0.

Cunningham, J. A., M. Menter, and C. Young. 2017b. "A Review of Qualitative Case Methods Trends and Themes Used in Technology Transfer Research." *The Journal of Technology Transfer* 42 (4): 923–956. doi:10.1007/s10961-016-9491-6.

Cunningham, J. A., V. Mangematin, C. O'Kane, and P. O'Reilly. 2016. "At the Frontiers of Scientific Advancement: The Factors that Influence Scientists to Become or Choose to Become Publicly Funded Principal Investigators." *The Journal of Technology Transfer* 41 (4): 778–797. doi:10.1007/s10961-015-9400-4.

Dahlstrand, Å. L. 2007. "Technology-based Entrepreneurship and Regional Development: The Case of Sweden." *European Business Review* 19 (5): 373–386. doi:10.1108/09555340710818969.

Dai, O., and X. Liu. 2009. "Returnee Entrepreneurs and Firm Performance in Chinese High-technology Industries." *International Business Review* 18 (4): 373–386. doi:10.1016/j.ibusrev.2009.03.004.

DFG. 2013. Excellence Initiative at a Glance: German Research Foundation. Bonn. Available at https://www.dfg.de/download/pdf/dfg_im_profil/geschaeftsstelle/publikationen/exin_broschuere_en.pdf

Dill, D. D. 1995. "University-industry Entrepreneurship: The Organization and Management of American University Technology Transfer Units." *Higher Education* 29 (4): 369–384. doi:10.1007/BF01383958.

Dolan, B., J. A. Cunningham, M. Menter, and C. McGregor. 2019. "The Role and Function of Cooperative Research Centers in Entrepreneurial Universities: A Micro Level Perspective." *Management Decision* 57 (12): 3406–3425. doi:10.1108/MD-10-2018-1172.

Drucker, J., and H. Goldstein. 2007. "Assessing the Regional Economic Development Impacts of Universities: A Review of Current Approaches." *International Regional Science Review* 30 (1): 20–46. doi:10.1177/0160017606296731.

Eesley, C., J. B. Li, and D. Yang. 2016. "Does Institutional Change in Universities Influence High-tech Entrepreneurship? Evidence from China's Project 985." *Organization Science* 27 (2): 446–461. doi:10.1287/orsc.2015.1038.

Elfring, T., and W. Hulsink. 2003. "Networks in Entrepreneurship: The Case of High-technology Firms." *Small Business Economics* 21 (4): 409–422. doi:10.1023/A:1026180418357.

Etzkowitz, H. 1983. "Entrepreneurial Scientists and Entrepreneurial Universities in American Academic Science." *Minerva* 21 (2): 198–233. doi:10.1007/BF01097964.

Etzkowitz, H. 2003. "Research Groups as 'Quasi-firms': The Invention of the Entrepreneurial University." *Research Policy* 32 (1): 109–121. doi:10.1016/S0048-7333(02)00009-4.

Fairlie, R. W., and A. K. Chatterji. 2013. "High-technology Entrepreneurship in Silicon Valley." *Journal of Economics & Management Strategy* 22 (2): 365–389. doi:10.1111/jems.12015.

Florida, R., and M. Kenney. 1988. "Venture Capital and High Technology Entrepreneurship." *Journal of Business Venturing* 3 (4): 301–319. doi:10.1016/0883-9026(88)90011-0.

Formica, P. 2002. "Entrepreneurial Universities: The Value of Education in Encouraging Entrepreneurship." *Industry and Higher Education* 16 (3): 167–175. doi:10.5367/000000002101296261.

Fotopoulos, G., and D. J. Storey. 2019. "Public Policies to Enhance Regional Entrepreneurship: Another Programme Failing to Deliver?" *Small Business Economics* 53 (1): 189–209. doi:10.1007/s11187-018-0021-9.

Friar, J. H., and M. H. Meyer. 2003. "Entrepreneurship and Start-ups in the Boston Region: Factors Differentiating High-growth Ventures from Micro-ventures." *Small Business Economics* 21 (2): 145–152. doi:10.1023/A:1025045828202.

Galvão, A., J. J. Ferreira, and C. Marques. 2018. "Entrepreneurship Education and Training as Facilitators of Regional Development: A Systematic Literature Review." *Journal of Small Business and Enterprise Development* 25 (1): 17–40. doi:10.1108/JSBED-05-2017-0178.

Garnsey, E. 1998. "The Genesis of the High Technology Milieu: A Study in Complexity." *International Journal of Urban and Regional Research* 22 (3): 361–377. doi:10.1111/1468-2427.00146.

Gawellek, B., and M. Sunder. 2016. "The German Excellence Initiative and Efficiency Change among Universities, 2001–2011." *Working Paper, No. 142, Universität Leipzig*, Faculty of Economics and Management Science.

Geuna, A. 2001. "The Changing Rationale for European University Research Funding: Are There Negative Unintended Consequences?" *Journal of Economic Issues* 35 (3): 607–632. doi:10.1080/00213624.2001.11506393.

Gimmon, E., and J. Levie. 2010. "Founder's Human Capital, External Investment, and the Survival of New High-technology Ventures." *Research Policy* 39 (9): 1214–1226. doi:10.1016/j.respol.2010.05.017.

Glaeser, E. L., S. S. Rosenthal, and W. C. Strange. 2010. "Urban Economics and Entrepreneurship." *Journal of Urban Economics* 67 (1): 1–14. doi:10.1016/j.jue.2009.10.005.

Grilli, L. 2014. "High-tech Entrepreneurship in Europe: A Heuristic Firm Growth Model and Three "(un-) Easy Pieces" for Policy-making." *Industry and Innovation* 21 (4): 267–284. doi:10.1080/13662716.2014.939850.

Grimaldi, R., M. Kenney, D. S. Siegel, and M. Wright. 2011. "30 Years after Bayh–Dole: Reassessing Academic Entrepreneurship." *Research Policy* 40 (8): 1045–1057. doi:10.1016/j.respol.2011.04.005.

Guerrero, M., D. Urbano, and A. Fayolle. 2016b. "Entrepreneurial Activity and Regional Competitiveness: Evidence from European Entrepreneurial Universities." *The Journal of Technology Transfer* 41 (1): 105–131. doi:10.1007/s10961-014-9377-4.

Guerrero, M., D. Urbano, A. Fayolle, M. Klofsten, and S. Mian. 2016a. "Entrepreneurial Universities: Emerging Models in the New Social and Economic Landscape." *Small Business Economics* 47 (3): 551–563. doi:10.1007/s11187-016-9755-4.

Guerrero, M., D. Urbano, and A. Salamzadeh. 2015b. "Entrepreneurial Transformation in the Middle East: Experiences from Tehran Universities." *Technics Technologies Education Management* 10 (4): 533–537.

Guerrero, M., D. Urbano, J. Cunningham, and D. Organ. 2014. "Entrepreneurial Universities in Two European Regions: A Case Study Comparison." *The Journal of Technology Transfer* 39 (3): 415–434. doi:10.1007/s10961-012-9287-2.

Guerrero, M., D. Urbano, J. A. Cunningham, and E. Gajon. 2018. "Determinants of Graduates' Start-Ups Creation across a Multi-Campus Entrepreneurial University: The Case of Monterrey Institute of Technology and Higher Education." *Journal of Small Business Management* 56 (1): 150–178. doi:10.1111/jsbm.12366.

Guerrero, M., J. A. Cunningham, and D. Urbano. 2015a. "Economic Impact of Entrepreneurial Universities' Activities: An Exploratory Study of the United Kingdom." *Research Policy* 44 (3): 748–764. doi:10.1016/j.respol.2014.10.008.

Hair, J. F., R. E. Anderson, R. L. Tatham, and W. C. Black. 1998. *Multivariate Data Analysis*. New York: Macmillan.

Hart, D. M., and Z. J. Acs. 2011. "High-tech Immigrant Entrepreneurship in the United States." *Economic Development Quarterly* 25 (2): 116–129. doi:10.1177/0891242410394336.

Hayter, C. S., R. Lubynsky, and S. Maroulis. 2017. "Who Is the Academic Entrepreneur? The Role of Graduate Students in the Development of University Spinoffs." *The Journal of Technology Transfer* 42 (6): 1237–1254. doi:10.1007/s10961-016-9470-y.

Hayton, J. C. 2005. "Competing in the New Economy: The Effect of Intellectual Capital on Corporate Entrepreneurship in High-technology New Ventures." *R&D Management* 35 (2): 137–155. doi:10.1111/j.1467-9310.2005.00379.x.

Hobbs, K. G., A. N. Link, and J. T. Scott. 2017. "The Growth of US Science and Technology Parks: Does Proximity to a University Matter?" *The Annals of Regional Science* 59 (2): 495–511. doi:10.1007/s00168-017-0842-5.

Huffman, D., and J. M. Quigley. 2002. "The Role of the University in Attracting High Tech Entrepreneurship: A Silicon Valley Tale." *The Annals of Regional Science* 36 (3): 403–419. doi:10.1007/s001680200104.

Huggins, R., A. Johnston, and R. Steffenson. 2008. "Universities, Knowledge Networks and Regional Policy." *Cambridge Journal of Regions, Economy and Society* 1 (2): 321–340. doi:10.1093/cjres/rsn013.

Hülsbeck, M., and E. N. Pickavé. 2014. "Regional Knowledge Production as Determinant of High-technology Entrepreneurship: Empirical Evidence for Germany." *International Entrepreneurship and Management Journal* 10 (1): 121–138. doi:10.1007/s11365-011-0217-9.

İlhan Ertuna, Z., and E. Gurel. 2011. "The Moderating Role of Higher Education on Entrepreneurship." *Education+ Training* 53 (5): 387–402. doi:10.1108/00400911111147703.

IEKE. 2016. *Endbericht der Internationalen Expertenkommission zur Evaluation der Exzellenzinitiative*: International Expert Commission to Evaluate the Excellence Initiative.

Jacob, M., M. Lundqvist, and H. Hellsmark. 2003. "Entrepreneurial Transformations in the Swedish University System: The Case of Chalmers University of Technology." *Research Policy* 32 (9): 1555–1568. doi:10.1016/S0048-7333(03)00024-6.

Keeble, D., and F. Wilkinson. 1999. "Collective Learning and Knowledge Development in the Evolution of Regional Clusters of High Technology SMEs in Europe." *Regional Studies* 33 (4): 295–303. doi:10.1080/00343409950081167.

Kirby, D. A., M. Guerrero, and D. Urbano. 2011. "Making Universities More Entrepreneurial: Development of a Model." *Canadian Journal of Administrative Sciences* 28 (3): 302–316. doi:10.1002/cjas.220.

Kitagawa, F. 2004. "Universities and Regional Advantage: Higher Education and Innovation Policies in English Regions." *European Planning Studies* 12 (6): 835–852. doi:10.1080/0965431042000251882.

Kuratko, D. F., and M. Menter. 2017. "The Role of Public Policy in Fostering Technology-based Nascent Entrepreneurship." In *Technology-based Nascent Entrepreneurship*, edited by J. A. Cunningham and C. O'Kane, 19–52. New York: Palgrave Macmillan.

Lamine, W., S. Mian, A. Fayolle, M. Wright, M. Klofsten, and H. Etzkowitz. 2018. "Technology Business Incubation Mechanisms and Sustainable Regional Development." *The Journal of Technology Transfer* 43 (5): 1121–1141. doi:10.1007/s10961-016-9537-9.

Lawrence, S., and U. Sharma. 2002. "Commodification of Education and Academic Labour—using the Balanced Scorecard in a University Setting." *Critical Perspectives on Accounting* 13 (5–6): 661–677. doi:10.1006/cpac.2002.0562.

Lehmann, E. E., and M. Menter. 2016. "University–industry Collaboration and Regional Wealth." *The Journal of Technology Transfer* 41 (6): 1284–1307. doi:10.1007/s10961-015-9445-4.

Lehmann, E. E., M. Meoli, S. Paleari, and S. A. E. Stockinger. 2020. "The Role of Higher Education for the Development of Entrepreneurial Ecosystems." *European Journal of Higher Education* 10 (1): 1–9. doi:10.1080/21568235.2020.1718924.

Lehmann, E. E., N. Seitz, and K. Wirsching. 2017. "Smart Finance for Smart Places to Foster New Venture Creation." *Economia e Politica Industriale* 44 (1): 51–75. doi:10.1007/s40812-016-0052-7.

Lehmann, E. E., and S. A. Stockinger. 2018. "Entrepreneurship in Higher Education: The Impact of Competition-based Policy Programmes Exemplified by the German Excellence Initiative." *Higher Education Quarterly* 73 (1): 70–84. doi:10.1111/hequ.12188.

Leyden, D. P., and A. N. Link. 2015. *Public Sector Entrepreneurship: US Technology and Innovation Policy*. USA: Oxford University Press.

Leyden, D. P., and M. Menter. 2018. "The Legacy and Promise of Vannevar Bush: Rethinking the Model of Innovation and the Role of Public Policy." *Economics of Innovation and New Technology* 27 (3): 225–242. doi:10.1080/10438599.2017.1329189.

Liu, S. 2015. "Spillovers from Universities: Evidence from the Land-grant Program." *Journal of Urban Economics* 87: 25–41. doi:10.1016/j.jue.2015.03.001.

Longhi, C. 1999. "Networks, Collective Learning and Technology Development in Innovative High Technology Regions: The Case of Sophia-Antipolis." *Regional Studies* 33 (4): 333–342. doi:10.1080/713693559.

Maringe, F. 2006. "University and Course Choice: Implications for Positioning, Recruitment and Marketing." *International Journal of Educational Management* 20 (6): 466–479.

Mason, C., and R. Brown. 2013. "Creating Good Public Policy to Support High-growth Firms." *Small Business Economics* 40 (2): 211–225. doi:10.1007/s11187-011-9369-9.

Matejun, M. 2016. "Role of Technology Entrepreneurship in the Development of Innovativeness of Small and Medium-sized Enterprises." *Management* 20 (1): 167–183. doi:10.1515/manment-2015-0032.

McAdam, M., B. Galbraith, R. McAdam, and P. Humphreys. 2006. "Business Processes and Networks in University Incubators: A Review and Research Agendas." *Technology Analysis & Strategic Management* 18 (5): 451–472. doi:10.1080/09537320601019578.

Menter, M. 2016. "Principal Investigators and the Commercialization of Knowledge." In *University Evolution Entrepreneurial Activity and Regional Competitiveness*, edited by D. B. Audretsch, E. E. Lehmann, S. Vismara, and M. Meoli, 193–203. Heidelberg: Springer.

Menter, M., E. E. Lehmann, and T. Klarl. 2018. "In Search of Excellence: A Case Study of the First Excellence Initiative of Germany." *Journal of Business Economics* 88 (9): 1105–1132. doi:10.1007/s11573-018-0909-5.

Miller, K., R. McAdam, and M. McAdam. 2018. "A Systematic Literature Review of University Technology Transfer from A Quadruple Helix Perspective: Toward A Research Agenda." *R&D Management* 48 (1): 7–24. doi:10.1111/radm.12228.

Munari, F., E. Rasmussen, L. Toschi, and E. Villani. 2016. "Determinants of the University Technology Transfer Policy-mix: A Cross-national Analysis of Gap-funding Instruments." *The Journal of Technology Transfer* 41 (6): 1377–1405. doi:10.1007/s10961-015-9448-1.

Nahapiet, J., and S. Ghoshal. 1998. "Social Capital, Intellectual Capital, and the Organizational Advantage." *Academy of Management Review* 23 (2): 242–266. doi:10.5465/amr.1998.533225.

Nelles, J., and T. Vorley. 2011. "Entrepreneurial Architecture: A Blueprint for Entrepreneurial Universities." *Canadian Journal of Administrative Sciences/Revue Canadienne des Sciences de l'administration* 28 (3): 341–353. doi:10.1002/cjas.186.

North, D. C. 1990. *Institutions, Institutional Change and Economic Performance*. Cambridge: Cambridge University Press.

O'Reilly, N. M., P. Robbins, and J. Scanlan. 2019. "Dynamic Capabilities and the Entrepreneurial University: A Perspective on the Knowledge Transfer Capabilities of Universities." *Journal of Small Business & Entrepreneurship* 31 (3): 243–263. doi:10.1080/08276331.2018.1490510.

Oakey, R. P. 2003. "Technical Entreprenenurship in High Technology Small Firms: Some Observations on the Implications for Management." *Technovation* 23 (8): 679–688. doi:10.1016/S0166-4972(03)00045-2.

Oakey, R. P. 2012. *High-technology Entrepreneurship*. New York: Routledge.

Paleari, S., D. Donina, and M. Meoli. 2015. "The Role of the University in Twenty-first Century European Society." *The Journal of Technology Transfer* 40 (3): 369–379. doi:10.1007/s10961-014-9348-9.

Passaro, R., I. Quinto, and A. Thomas. 2018. "The Impact of Higher Education on Entrepreneurial Intention and Human Capital." *Journal of Intellectual Capital* 19 (1): 135–156. doi:10.1108/JIC-04-2017-0056.

Phan, P., D. S. Siegel, and M. Wright. 2005. "Science Parks and Incubators: Observations, Synthesis and Future Research." *Journal of Business Venturing* 20 (2): 165–182. doi:10.1016/j.jbusvent.2003.12.001.

Ranga, L., K. Debackere, and N. Tunzelmann. 2003. "Entrepreneurial Universities and the Dynamics of Academic Knowledge Production: A Case Study of Basic Vs. Applied Research in Belgium." *Scientometrics* 58 (2): 301–320. doi:10.1023/A:1026288611013.

Röpke, J. 1998. "The Entrepreneurial University, Innovation, Academic Knowledge Creation and Regional Development in a Globalized Economy." *Working Paper No. 3*, Department of Economics, Philipps-Universität Marburg, Germany.

Sanchez, A. M., and O. U. Perez. 1998. "Entrepreneurship Networks and High Technology Firms: The Case of Aragon." *Technovation* 18 (5): 335–345. doi:10.1016/S0166-4972(98)00007-8.

Schmucker, A., J. Eberle, A. Ganzer, J. Stegmaier, and M. Umkehrer. 2018. "Establishment History Panel 1975-2016." *FDZ-Datenreport, 01-2018*: 1–120. Available at http://doku.iab.de/fdz/reporte/2018/DR_01-18_EN.pdf

Schulte, P. 2004. "The Entrepreneurial University: A Strategy for Institutional Development." *Higher Education in Europe* 29 (2): 187–191. doi:10.1080/0379772042000234811.

Shane, S. A. 2004. *Academic Entrepreneurship: University Spinoffs and Wealth Creation*. New York: Edward Elgar Publishing.

Siegel, D. S., D. Waldman, and A. Link. 2003. "Assessing the Impact of Organizational Practices on the Relative Productivity of University Technology Transfer Offices: An Exploratory Study." *Research Policy* 32 (1): 27–48. doi:10.1016/S0048-7333(01)00196-2.

Siegel, D. S., and M. Wright. 2015. "Academic Entrepreneurship: Time for a Rethink?" *British Journal of Management* 26 (4): 582–595. doi:10.1111/1467-8551.12116.

Siegfried, J. J., A. R. Sanderson, and P. McHenry. 2007. "The Economic Impact of Colleges and Universities." *Economics of Education Review* 26 (5): 546–558. doi:10.1016/j.econedurev.2006.07.010.

Solomon, G., and H. Matlay. 2008. "The Impact of Entrepreneurship Education on Entrepreneurial Outcomes." *Journal of Small Business and Enterprise Development* 15 (2): 382–396. doi:10.1108/14626000810871745.

Sternberg, R. 1996. "Technology Policies and the Growth of Regions: Evidence from Four Countries." *Small Business Economics* 8 (2): 75–86. doi:10.1007/BF00394419.

Thorp, H., and B. Goldstein. 2013. *Engines of Innovation: The Entrepreneurial University in the Twenty-first Century*. Chapel Hill: University of North Carolina Press.

Urbano, D., and M. Guerrero. 2013. "Entrepreneurial Universities: Socioeconomic Impacts of Academic Entrepreneurship in a European Region." *Economic Development Quarterly* 27 (1): 40–55. doi:10.1177/0891242412471973.

Van Looy, B., P. Landoni, J. Callaert, B. Van Pottelsberghe, E. Sapsalis, and K. Debackere. 2011. "Entrepreneurial Effectiveness of European Universities: An Empirical Assessment of Antecedents and Trade-offs." *Research Policy* 40 (4): 553–564. doi:10.1016/j.respol.2011.02.001.

Van Praag, C. M., and P. H. Versloot. 2007. "The Economic Benefits and Costs of Entrepreneurship: A Review of the Research." *Foundations and Trends in Entrepreneurship* 4 (2): 65–154. doi:10.1561/0300000012.

Van Stel, A., M. Carree, and R. Thurik. 2005. "The Effect of Entrepreneurial Activity on National Economic Growth." *Small Business Economics* 24 (3): 311–321. doi:10.1007/s11187-005-1996-6.

Watson, K., P. McGowan, and J. A. Cunningham. 2018. "An Exploration of the Business Plan Competition as a Methodology for Effective Nascent Entrepreneurial Learning." *International Journal of Entrepreneurial Behavior & Research* 24 (1): 121–146. doi:10.1108/IJEBR-05-2017-0158.

Xue, J., and P. G. Klein. 2010. "Regional Determinants of Technology Entrepreneurship." *International Journal of Entrepreneurial Venturing* 1 (3): 291–308. doi:10.1504/IJEV.2010.030978.

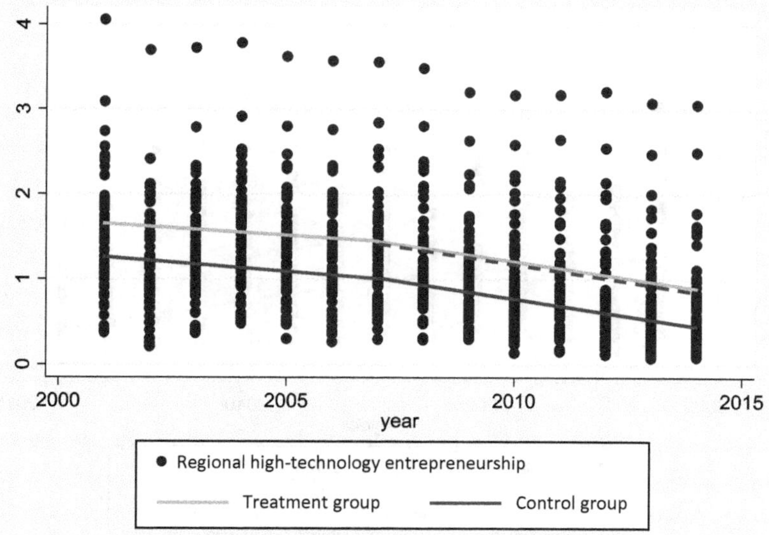

Appendix 1. Common trends assumption | excellence initiative.

Note: This figure visualises the development of our dependent variable regional high-technology entrepreneurship measured by the logarithmized number of high-technology start-ups over time. The treatment group classifies all regions that have been funded by the Excellence Initiative (either in the first funding line (Graduate Schools), and/or the second funding line (Clusters of Excellence), and/or the third funding line (Institutional Strategies)).

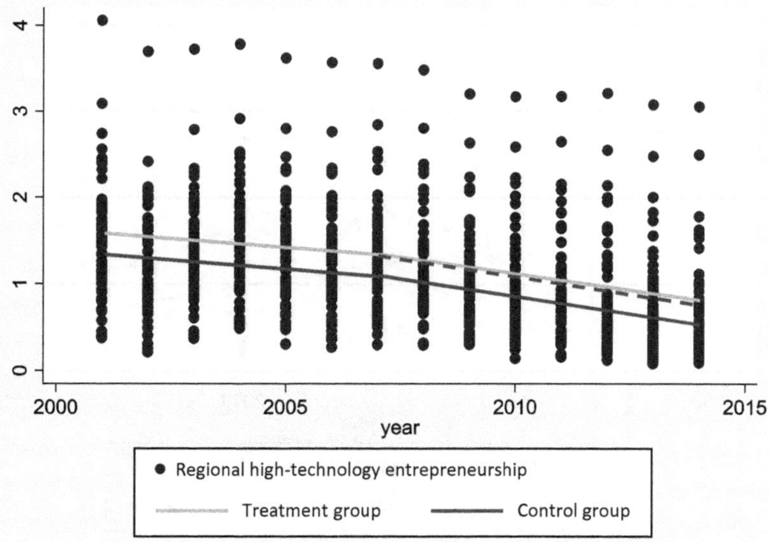

Appendix 2. Common trends assumption | graduate schools.

Note: This figure visualises the development of our dependent variable regional high-technology entrepreneurship measured by the logarithmized number of high-technology start-ups over time. The treatment group classifies all regions that have been funded in the first funding line (Graduate Schools).

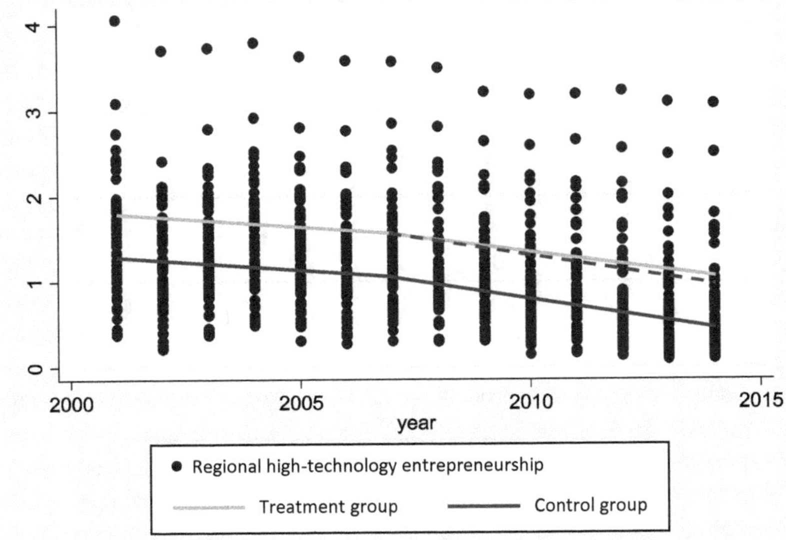

Appendix 3. Common trends assumption | clusters of excellence.

Note: This figure visualises the development of our dependent variable regional high-technology entrepreneurship measured by the logarithmized number of high-technology start-ups over time. The treatment group classifies all regions that have been funded in the second funding line (Clusters of Excellence).

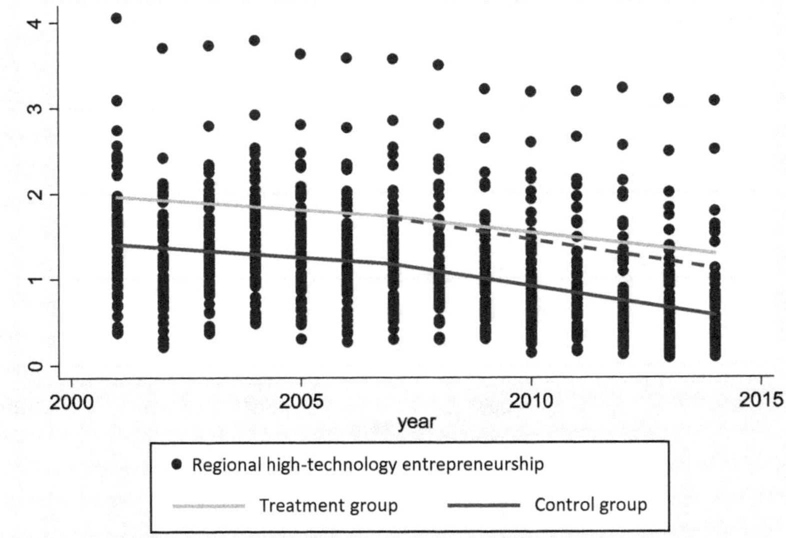

Appendix 4. Common trends assumption | institutional strategies.

Note: This figure visualises the development of our dependent variable regional high-technology entrepreneurship measured by the logarithmized number of high-technology start-ups over time. The treatment group classifies all regions that have been funded in the third funding line (Institutional Strategies).

Looking inside the determinants and the effects of entrepreneurial innovation projects in an emerging economy

Maribel Guerrero and David Urbano

ABSTRACT

Ongoing research agendas regarding the intersection between entrepreneurship and innovation in academia still demand analysis about the antecedents/consequences of enterprise-university collaborations. On the one hand, little is known about how enterprise-university collaborations manage their resources/capabilities to develop entrepreneurial innovation projects, as well as how do enterprises-university collaborations capture economic benefits. On the other hand, regarding the context, there is also a gap concerning the effect of institutional voids on entrepreneurship/innovation strategies in emerging economies. This paper analyses the determinants and the consequences of entrepreneurial innovation projects within enterprise-university collaborations in an emerging economy. By using a sample of 514 Mexican enterprises, our proposed framework offers insights into the remarkable effect in the transformation of enterprises-universities' capabilities and state funds into the generation of economic value from entrepreneurial innovation projects. This paper contributes to the thought-provoking discussion about a future research agenda and implications for triple-helix actors in emerging economies.

1. Introduction

Ongoing research agendas regarding the intersection between entrepreneurship and innovation in the academia (Audretsch, Lehmann, and Link 2019) still demand more analysis about the antecedents and the consequences of enterprise-university collaborations, as well as a better understanding of entrepreneurial innovations in the context of emerging economies (Autio et al. 2014; Lehmann and Menter 2016; Feldman, Siegel, and Wright 2019; Guerrero, Herrera, and Urbano 2019).

Regarding the antecedents, the accumulation of knowledge has highlighted the motivations/aims, shared resources/risks, and innovation/business outcomes behind enterprises-universities collaborations (Perkmann et al. 2013). However, little is known about the adequate combination of enterprises-universities capabilities required for developing entrepreneurial innovation (Autio et al. 2014; Guerrero and Urbano 2019b). In this vein, there is also no consensus about the effect of public incentives for fostering entrepreneurship/innovation by engaging enterprise-university collaborations to develop entrepreneurial innovations (García-Quevedo 2004; Zeng, Xie, and Tam 2010; Dimos and Pugh 2016; Guerrero and Urbano 2019b). Indeed, in emerging economies, there is also a gap concerning the effect of institutional voids on enterprise-university strategies towards entrepreneurship and innovation (Liedong, Peprah, and Eyong 2020). Therefore, new insights about the determinants of entrepreneurial innovation projects within enterprise-university are needed.

Regarding the consequences, the term 'entrepreneurial innovations' has emerged without a consensus about the definition (Guerrero and Urbano 2019b), but with certain particularities such as the generation/commercialisation of outstanding/novel innovations developed by entrepreneurs in co-creation with single/multiple triple-helix agents (Schumpeter 1942; Von Bargen, Freedman, and Pages 2003; Cohen 2006; Norbäck and Persson 2012; Autio et al. 2014; Guerrero and Urbano 2017; Malerba and McKelvey 2018). However, little is known about how enterprises-university collaborations do manage the resources/capabilities to develop entrepreneurial innovation, as well as to capture a value-added (Klofsten et al., 2019; Guerrero, Herrera, and Urbano 2019; Guerrero and Urbano 2019b). Therefore, new metrics/measures are still required to operationalise entrepreneurial innovations and their links with triple-helix agents across the Globe (Guerrero and Urbano 2019b).

Regarding the context, the academic interest in understanding the dynamic roles and contributions of triple-helix actors have increased substantially,[1] particularly in emerging economies, where institutional voids inhibit economic markets' functioning (Mahmood and Mitchell 2004). Although institutional voids can characterise any economy, they are most prevalent in emerging markets (Puffer, McCarthy, and Boisot 2010). The main reason is that institutional voids hamper the mechanisms that allow business/innovation partners to interact, causing higher transaction costs of entrepreneurial activity to rise, as well as diminish incentives for developing innovation and leveraging of unique talent, knowledge, and skills (Liedong, Peprah, and Eyong 2020, p.59). Therefore, institutional voids do not only influence entrepreneurial organisations' strategies but shape innovation governance. It may explain why institutional voids have been considered the primary justification of state intervention via subsidies/incentives to promote entrepreneurship and innovation via enterprise-university collaborations in emerging economies (Hall and Maffioli 2008; Dimos and Pugh 2016; Kochenkova, Grimaldi, and Munari 2016; Guerrero and Urbano 2017).

Inspired by these research gaps, this paper analyses the determinants and the consequences of entrepreneurial innovations within enterprise-university collaborations in the context of an emerging economy. By adopting the theoretical foundations of the triple-helix, dynamic capabilities and institutional economic approaches, we proposed a conceptual model to explore this phenomenon in the context of an emerging economy (Mexico). The criteria for selecting the research setting were: (a) the identification of multiple universities that have

[1]The higher education organisations, the government and the enterprises across industries have been critical participants in the configuration of entrepreneurial and innovation ecosystems (McMullen and Dimov 2013; Autio et al. 2014; Paleari, Donina, and Meoli 2015; Acs et al. 2017; Colombo, Meoli, and Vismara 2019; Urbano et al. 2019).

transformed their capabilities and activities to mitigate the effect of institutional voids as well as have been opened to collaborate with industrial, commercial, and scientific agents (Guerrero, Herrera, and Urbano 2019, Guerrero, Urbano, and Herrera 2019b); (b) the efforts of public administration for implementing incentives and subsidies that promote the development of entrepreneurial innovations via enterprise-university collaborations (OECD 2013); and (c) the evidence of enterprises that have captured favourable/adverse outcomes as part of entrepreneurial innovations developed within collaboration practices with diverse partners (Guerrero and Urbano 2017). The methodological design consisted of a two-step method to explore the determinants and, simultaneously, the effects of innovation projects of 514 Mexican enterprises.

Our findings provide insights about the crucial role of enterprises' capabilities, universities' capabilities, and state support such as determinants of entrepreneurial innovation projects within enterprises-universities collaborations. Without sufficient enterprises' innovation capabilities as well as knowledge of universities' capabilities, enterprises will not be able to run entrepreneurial innovation projects in collaboration with universities, even though the state might provide additional incentives. Consequently, without these determinants, the expected economic return of entrepreneurial innovation projects will be uncertain for enterprises. Although the regional heterogeneity, our findings do not show robust insights about the effect of enterprises' perception of institutional voids on antecedents/consequences of entrepreneurial innovation projects with the universities. The plausible explanation is the lowest variance in the measure of institutional voids across our research setting (only one emerging economy). In this regard, this paper contributes to the ongoing academic debates related to the role of academia in entrepreneurship and innovation (Audretsch, 2007, 2014; Audretsch, Lehmann, and Link 2019); to the determinants of entrepreneurial innovation projects within enterprise-university collaborations (Autio et al. 2014; Guerrero and Urbano 2019b); to the consequences of entrepreneurial innovation projects within enterprise-university collaborations (Lehmann and Menter 2016; Guerrero and Urbano 2019a, 2019b); and the effect of institutional voids on entrepreneurial innovation projects within enterprise-university collaborations (Puffer, McCarthy, and Boisot 2010; Liedong, Peprah, and Eyong 2020).

The paper is organised as follows. Section 2 introduces the theoretical framework. In particular, the determinants and effects of entrepreneurial innovations are explained. Section 3 describes the methodology used in the study. Two methodological steps were designed to analyse the determinants as well as the effects of entrepreneurial innovation in the context of emerging economies. Section 4 addresses the results obtained in this study as well as the discussion about the most provocative findings. Section 5 presents the conclusions and implications for decision-makers as well as further research.

2. Theoretical framework

2.1. Entrepreneurial innovations

According to Guerrero and Urbano (2019b), the term 'entrepreneurial innovations' has been identified in a few published studies without a consensus about what entrepreneurial innovations mean.

The conception of entrepreneurial innovations was introduced by Schumpeter (1942) as an inherent consequence of creative destruction as part of the entrepreneurs' transformation of means in novel and marketable innovations. Several decades later, with the rise of the entrepreneurial society, Von Bargen, Freedman, and Pages (2003, p. 315) and Norbäck and Persson (2012, p. 488) associated this terminology with the contribution of a small group of high-growth, innovative, and new companies on the transformation of the industries where they entered. In this perspective, Cohen (2006, p.1) argued that entrepreneurial innovations also contribute to the configuration of a sustainable society. Furthermore, Autio et al. (2014, p.1100) introduced the intersection of the entrepreneurship ecosystem and innovation ecosystem through multi-level processes, actors, and contexts that regulates where entrepreneurs are developing disruptions of existing industries. In this vein, Guerrero and Urbano (2017, p.295) and Malerba and McKelvey (2018, p.15) expanded the entrepreneurial innovation understanding by introducing the relevance of learning and university-industry collaborations in the generation/diffusion of marketable innovations in the context of emerging economies.

Based on these theoretical foundations, in the context of emerging economies, entrepreneurial innovations could be understood as the primary motivation/outcome of enterprise-university collaboration projects (mostly supported by multiple triple helix-actors) that are looking for sharing resources, capabilities, and risks during the co-create novel and marketable innovations with a economic and societal impact that should be commercialised through entrepreneurial models (Autio et al. 2014; Guerrero and Urbano 2017; Guerrero and Urbano, 2019a, 2019b; Guerrero, Herrera, and Urbano 2019). As a result of this collaboration projects, actors can develop multiple dynamic capabilities oriented to sensing, seizing, and transforming opportunities into entrepreneurial innovations that producing a sustainable performance (Teece, Pisano, and Shuen 1997; Teece 2007, 2010, 2014).

2.2. *Antecedents of entrepreneurial innovation projects in emerging economies*

For enterprises located in emerging economies, the decision for developing collaborative projects with other organisations tends to be moved by the lack of technological capabilities and human capabilities, as well as by reducing costs that allow capturing projected returns (Kogut 1988; Bayona, García-Marco, and Huerta 2001; Becker and Dietz 2004; Zeng, Xie, and Tam 2010). Assuming the existence of enterprises that sharing resources/risks with others to gain maximum returns (Chesbrough 2010, 2012), we believe that enterprises tend to develop innovative capabilities based on the quantity/quality of their collaborations with triple-helix actors involved in the entrepreneurship and innovation ecosystems (Perkmann et al. 2013).

Previous studies have recognised that enterprises typically adopt diverse collaborations patterns with scientific organisations, commercial organisations, and both types of organisations simultaneously (Yamin and Otto 2004). Research suggests that enterprises that only collaborate with scientific organisations intend to expand their general knowledge (Belderbos et al. 2004b) into new technological knowledge (Lundvall 1992). Therefore, in the short term, these enterprise-university collaborations will develop dynamic technological capabilities useful for identifying, generating and transforming technologies/knowledge into entrepreneurial innovations applicable for multiple industries (Nieto and Santamaria 2007; Guerrero and Urbano 2017; Malerba and McKelvey 2018).

Similarly, diversity in collaborations generates multiple economic benefits and higher value-added to the final clients (Chung, Bae, and Kim 2003; Teece 2007). As a result, in the short term, these collaborations will be able to exploit dynamic commercial capabilities for identifying the most entrepreneurial, innovative and valuable opportunities to generate sustainable benefits across their value chain (Autio et al. 2014; Teece 2014; Guerrero and Urbano 2017). Indeed, diversity in partners (scientific and commercial) are also oriented to capture the most profitable outcomes within the collaborations in terms of newest innovations (Becker and Dietz 2004). In the short term, these collaborations will be characterised by sophisticated, advanced, and multiple capabilities that are useful for anticipating solutions for non-existing needs or generate opportunities to capture a highest value-added (Autio et al. 2014; Guerrero and Urbano 2017; Malerba and McKelvey 2018). Assuming that innovation capabilities represent the enterprises' experience/know-how acquired during the developing innovations (products/services or processes or both products and processes), enterprises have the capabilities to explore new business/innovative opportunities (sensing), to look for the most appropriated partner to complement their resources/capabilities (seizing) and to transform them into sustainable outcomes (Teece, Pisano, and Shuen 1997), we propose

H1: Enterprises with innovation capabilities are more likely to develop entrepreneurial innovation projects in collaboration with universities than enterprises without these innovation capabilities

Entrepreneurial innovations demand trust, awareness, and commitment within the collaboration. In the context of emerging economies, to mitigate the effect of institutional voids, any scientific organisation requires an integral transformation of individuals/structures into an entrepreneurial innovation vision where all member be part of a system based on the generation, transference, and commercialisation of sophisticated knowledge updated technologies, and the newest innovations (Clark 2001; Klofsten and Jones-Evans 2000; Lu and Etzkowitz 2008; Etzkowitz et al. 2000; Mian, Fayolle, and Lamine 2012; Guerrero and Urbano, 2009a).

Enterprise-university collaborations generate unique capabilities that are needed for producing economical, societal, and technological impacts. Previous studies have adopted a narrow view of enterprise-university partnership just focusing on the commercialisation of research results (O'Shea et al. 2005; Wright et al. 2007; Grimaldi et al. 2011; O'Kane et al. 2014). However, according to the institutional economic theory, enterprise-university collaborations can contribute via entrepreneurial innovations to sustainable financial and economic performance through the generation of specific capabilities in their human capital during the development of knowledge capital and entrepreneurship capital (Guerrero and Urbano 2014). Therefore, entrepreneurial and innovative organisations like universities contribute through human capital, knowledge capital, technological capital, and entrepreneurial capital (Guerrero and Urbano 2012; Audretsch 2014; Urbano and Guerrero, 2013; Guerrero et al. 2014).

In this perspective, the entrepreneurial and innovative university acts such as node that connects all members enrolled in triple-helix; therefore, the university could be the driver of entrepreneurial innovations (Svensson, Klofsten, and Etzkowitz 2012). In this assumption, entrepreneurial and innovative capabilities are part of the university core activities: teaching, research, and commercialisation. During the development of core activities, universities also acquire specific capabilities that are useful to generate new business/innovative opportunities (sensing), to explore new ways to access the required resources/capabilities (seizing), as well as to transform them into commercialised technological outcomes (Teece 2007, 2010, 2014). Therefore, interested enterprises in collaborating with universities for developing entrepreneurial innovation projects should very well know which universities' capabilities may complement their enterprises' capabilities to achieve the expected objectives/outcomes (Autio et al. 2014; Guerrero and Urbano 2019a). Assuming that a better understanding of the university 'capabilities not only reinforces the trust, awareness, and commitment of enterprises to collaborate with universities but also represents the channel for improving technological capabilities as well as complementing their human and commercialisation capabilities, we propose

H2: Enterprises with knowledge of universities' capabilities are more likely to develop entrepreneurial innovation projects in collaboration with universities than enterprises without knowledge of universities' capabilities

Another determinant of enterprise-university collaborations in the context of an emerging economy is the state intervention. Previous studies have generally recognised that emerging economies' administrations promote entrepreneurial innovation via enterprise-university collaborations as the most effective mechanism to improve regional competitiveness and economic growth (Mian 2011; Guerrero and Urbano 2019b). Traditionally, the government has been viewed as the dominant actor that provides subsidies for fostering enterprise-university collaborations (McAdam et al. 2012) and orchestrating the policies that promote entrepreneurship and innovation (Miller, McAdam, and McAdam 2014). Nowadays, the participation of government has changed to be considered as another actor instead of a funder. In this sense, the public administration participates in the configuration of triple-helix collaborations (Autio et al. 2014).

In emerging economies, it is not strange that governments aim to ensure the well-being and sustainable regional development through the enterprise-university collaborations (Kenney and Richard Goe 2004; Wang and Altinay 2012; Urbano and Guerrero 2013). Although the anecdotal evidence provided by previous studies (Dimos and Pugh 2016; Kochenkova, Grimaldi, and Munari 2016), the effectiveness of subsidies or public incentives could be estimated by the achievement of the objectives of entrepreneurial innovation projects. Assuming the existence of governmental support fostering/improving enterprises-university collaborations as an alternative to capture additional funds for ensuring the entrepreneurial innovation projects, we propose

H3: Enterprises with access to governmental support for improving collaborations with universities are more likely to develop entrepreneurial innovation projects than enterprises without access to governmental support

2.3. Consequences of entrepreneurial innovation projects in emerging economies

Literature has primarily focused on external knowledge and innovation, devoting particular attention to performance issues. In today's economy, it is widely agreed that entrepreneurial innovation plays a significant role in established/new ventures that try to survive in the market, especially by improving entrepreneurial and innovation capabilities required to capturing the sustainable outcomes/performance (Ireland, Covin, and Kuratko 2009; Teece 2012, 2014; Guerrero, Urbano, and Herrera 2019b). By nature, enterprises seem most likely to highlight the tension of trying to exist and survive. Authors like Chesbrough (2010, 2012) and Zott et al. (2011) argue that an innovative business model performs two essential functions: creating value (activities that will yield a new product or service) and capturing a portion of that value (establishing unique resources with the series of activities in which a firm enjoys a competitive advantage). Therefore, either explicitly or implicitly, the entrepreneurial innovation projects connect strategic decisions with value creation to final clients (business/managerial strategy) through the mechanism employed to capture it (innovation/entrepreneurship strategy) and to convert it to sustainable profit (financial/economic strategy) (Zott and Amit 2007).

In this perspective, entrepreneurial innovation projects enable an organisation to be more effective in creating and capturing value, using not only its resources but also sharing resources and risks multiple partners enrolled in triple-helix (Autio et al. 2014). This fact allows enterprises to anticipate to uncertainties, innovate faster, and find entrepreneurial mechanisms to commercialise their innovations (Chesbrough 2010, 2012). As a result, the configurations of entrepreneurial innovation projects in different contexts generate new products and new organisational forms. Therefore, entrepreneurial innovation projects contribute to capturing the highest performance (Autio et al. 2014; Guerrero, Herrera, and Urbano 2019). Assuming that enterprises expect to capture higher economic benefits from the entrepreneurial innovation projects' outcomes with universities, we propose

H4: Enterprises that develop entrepreneurial innovation projects in collaboration with universities are more profitable than enterprises that do not develop entrepreneurial innovation projects with universities

2.4. Proposed model

Figure 1 summarises the main determinants behind entrepreneurial innovation projects (Step 1). We analyse several determinant factors that could influence the enterprise's decision to participate or not participate in entrepreneurial innovation projects with universities. After an understanding of the determinants, we explored the effects of these entrepreneurial innovation projects on enterprises' performance (Step 2).

3. Methodology

3.1. Research setting

Research is setting in Mexico with particular emphasis on enterprises-universities collaborations. As an emerging economy, since the publication of the Mexican Science and Technology Law, the National Council for Science and Technology (CONACYT) has

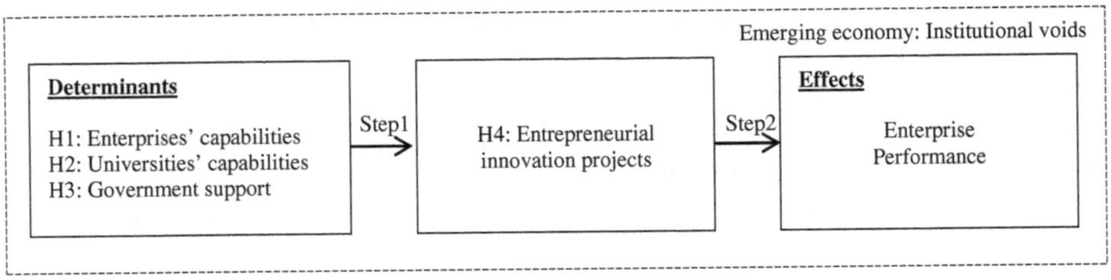

Figure 1. Determinants and effects of entrepreneurial innovation projects.
Source: Authors

implemented several incentive programmes for encouraging growth, competitiveness, enterprise-university collaborations, innovations (new products/services, process) with value-added to strategic sectors, and the creation/protection of intellectual property (Diario Oficial 2014). Similarly, the programs oriented to support entrepreneurship by the public administrations in collaboration with the Ministries of Education and Economy (Hernández, González, and Herrera 2016). However, institutional voids such as corruption and criminal activity have inhibited the quality of institutions and the evolution towards knowledge and entrepreneurial society (Guerrero and Urbano 2017). For a better understanding of the Mexican entrepreneurial and innovation ecosystems see the research developed by Guerrero and Urbano (2017).

3.2. Data Collection

Given the lack of information in emerging economies, we used data from the 2010 Mexican Survey of Enterprise-University. This survey[2] was administered by the Mexican Centre for Research and Teaching in Economics (CIDE) and the Mexican Ministry of Education (SEP) (CIDE and SEP, 2010). The sample was estimated using the enterprise's population registered in the 2004 Economic Census[3] and the 2010 Mexican Business Information System (SIEM).[4] The population was more than 650,000 enterprises from all economic sectors. Therefore, the estimated sample includes 514 enterprises with a 5.32% margin of error and stratified by size, sector, and regions. The respondent was the CEO, and, in average, the enterprises' size is less than five employees (49%) or between 10 to 49 employees (36%) and either a commercial focus (48%) or service focus (37%). We also used secondary sources (official publications and reports) about the Mexican Innovation System.

3.3. Description of variables

The methodological design is divided into two steps. First, we explore the factors that determine the probability that enterprises develop entrepreneurial innovation projects in

[2]For further information about the methodological issues, please consult CIDE and SEP(2010).
[3]In Mexico, the Economic Census is collected every five years. For this reason, the most updated and available information used for calculating the sample was the Economic Census of 2004.
[4]The SIEM primarily comprises data of Mexican companies. The Law of Business Chambers regulates it, its Confederations provide the legal framework, and the Ministry of Economy defines the rules of operation annually.

collaboration with universities. Second, we explore the effect of entrepreneurial innovation projects on enterprises' performance.

3.3.1. Stage 1: Analysing the determinants of entrepreneurial innovation projects in an emerging economy

Based on the literature review, Table 1 summarises the variables used in this step.

The dependent variable is *entrepreneurial innovation projects* is a dummy variable that captures when the enterprise develops both entrepreneurial and innovation projects in collaboration with universities (Guerrero and Urbano, 2009a,b). Conceptually, entrepreneurial innovations are the outcome of enterprise-university collaboration projects characterised by the generation of the newest innovations that should be commercialised by adopting the most innovative business model (Autio et al. 2014; Guerrero and Urbano 2017; Guerrero, Herrera, and Urbano 2019, Guerrero, Urbano, and Herrera 2019b).

Regarding the exploratory variables, we use a set of determinants of entrepreneurial innovation projects within enterprises-universities. The first determinant factor is associated with the enterprises' innovation capabilities. Adopting previous studies (Yamin and Otto 2004; Nieto and Santamaria 2007), we use three dummy variables to capture if the enterprises' innovation capabilities are derivated of their experience of developing innovation of products and processes (*innovation in product and processes*), or only innovation in products (*innovation in products/services)*, or only innovation in processes (*innovation in processes*). The second set of determinants is associated with the enterprises' knowledge of the university's capabilities (Guerrero and Urbano 2014; Klofsten et al., 2019, Guerrero and Urbano 2019a, 2019b). Using a factor analysis for reducing the number of variables, the enterprises' knowledge about the universities' capabilities within entrepreneurial innovation projects are measured in terms of *teaching capabilities* (contributing with qualified human capital), *research capabilities* (contributing with technological and knowledge capital), *and entrepreneurship capabilities* (contributing with entrepreneurship and commercialisation capital). The third determinant is measured by the governmental support towards university-industry collaborations (García-Quevedo 2004; Dimos and Pugh 2016; Kochenkova, Grimaldi, and Munari 2016; Guerrero, Herrera, and Urbano 2019, Guerrero, Urbano, and Herrera 2019b) with subsidies or incentives that are fostering innovative projects (*external funds*).

Using a factor analysis for reducing the number of variables, we also considered several control variables that affect the enterprises' competitiveness: (a) external conditions like infrastructures (*external factors1)* and institutional voids *(external factors2);* and (b) internal conditions like non-technological resources (*internal factors1)* and technological resources *(internal factors2).* Moreover, we controlled by the number of universities' collaborations per enterprise (*university number*), as well as per the university type like research universities (*research university*) or public universities (*public universities*). Finally, we controlled by the enterprises' size, age, sector, capital origin, and market orientation.

3.3.1. Stage 2: Analysing the effects of entrepreneurial innovation projects in an emerging economy

Based on the literature review, Table 2 summarises the variables used in this step.

Our dependent variable (*performance*) is a dummy that captures when the enterprises' profits consecutively increased during the last three years (Zeng, Xie, and Tam 2010; Perkmann et al. 2013). Given the limited access to objective metrics of performance

Table 1. Description of variables (step 1).

	Dimension	Variable	Description
DV	Entrepreneurial innovation projects		Dummy: the enterprises' entrepreneurial innovation projects with universities
IV	Enterprises' innovation capabilities	Innovation in product and processes	Dummy: if the enterprise developed innovations in products and processes
		Innovation in product/ services	Dummy: if the enterprise only developed innovations in products/services
		Innovation in processes	Dummy: if the enterprise only developed innovations in processes
IV	University capabilities	Teaching capabilities	Knowledge about the university's teaching capabilities provided to the industry: human capital through professional practices, students' stays, social services, labour market, etc.
		Research capabilities	Knowledge about the university's research capabilities that provided to the industry: technological capital through academics' stays, R&D services, technological services
		Entrepreneurship capabilities	Knowledge about the university's entrepreneurship capabilities that provided to the industry: entrepreneurship capital through business creation programs, incubation services, alliances with strategic actors
IV	Government support	External funds	Dummy: if the enterprises received public financial support
CV	University	University number	Dummy: simultaneous collaboration with multiple universities
		Research university	Dummy: collaborate only with a research university
		Public university	Dummy: collaborate only with a public university
CV	Competitiveness Factors	Infrastructures (External factor1)	Perception about the role of infrastructures (physical, educational, clusters) on the enterprise competitiveness
		Institutional voids (External factor2)	Perception about the role of institutional voids (security, corruption) on the enterprise competitiveness
		Non-technological resources (Internal factor1)	Perception about the role of internal human, physical resources on the enterprise competitiveness
		Technological resources (Internal factor2)	Perception about the role of internal technological resources on the enterprise competitiveness
CV	Enterprise	Young enterprise	Dummy: young enterprises created in the last five years
		National capital	Percentage of the enterprise's capital that is national
		Domestic market	Percentage of the enterprise's production/services that are intended for the domestic market
		Size	Categorical: 1 = Micro; 2 = Small; 3 = Medium;4 = Large
		Sector	Categorical: 1 = Industry; 2 = Commerce; 3 = Services

Note: DV = Dependent variable; IV = Independent Varible; CV = Control Variable provided by the secondary dataset, we decided to measure the enterprise performance using a dummy variable (one limitation of this study with a natural extension of improving this measure in future research). This dummy variable also highlights the potential high-growth orientation measured by the increment of profits in the last three years (Bosma 2013).

Regarding the exploratory variables, we included our dummy variable *entrepreneurial innovation projects* that capture if the enterprise develops entrepreneurial innovation projects in collaboration with a university in the last three years (Autio, Kanninen, and Gustafsson 2008; Autio et al. 2014; Guerrero and Urbano 2017). It was the dependent variable in step 1; therefore, it allows us to capture the effect of the projects developed.

We also included several control variables. First, we included dummy variables associated with the enterprises' *innovation capacity* acquired from the innovation activities that were developed during the last three years (Carayannis, Alexander, and Ioannidis 2000); as well as per type of innovation (*innovation in product and processes, or innovation in product, or innovation in processes*) developed by these enterprises in the last three years (Yamin and Otto 2004; Nieto and Santamaria 2007). Second, the state supports oriented to enterprise-university collaborations (García-Quevedo 2004; Dimos and Pugh 2016) via subsidies for developing innovative projects (*external funds*). Third, we also considered external factors (*external factors1, external factors2)* and internal factors (*internal factors1, internal factors2)* that affect competitiveness described in step 1. Finally, we included variables related to size, age, sector, capital origin, and focus market.

3.4. Data Analysis

We ran several tests to check the multicollinearity among those variables (Greene 2003). First, the descriptive and correlations do not evidence multicollinearity (Tables 3 and 4). Indeed, the mean-variance inflation factor (VIF) is 1.82, indicating that the entire model is moderately correlated. The rule is that if VIF>10 then multicollinearity is high. The cut off of 5 is also commonly used to denote moderately correlation among independent variables (Aiken, West, and Reno 1991). Second, we did the means test for corroborating differences between enterprises that develop entrepreneurial innovation projects with universities and enterprises that do not develop entrepreneurial innovation projects. This test showed that all the means were significantly different within and between the groups. Third, since both dependent variables are dichotomous, we used two binominal logistic regression methods.

The binominal logistic regression estimates the probability of an event happening; in this case, the determinants (Model 1) and the consequences (Model 2) of entrepreneurial innovations within a university-enterprise partnership. The predicted proportion follows the logistic model of $Ln\ P/(1 - P_i) = \beta X_i$, where P_i is the probability of an enterprise deciding to develop entrepreneurial innovation projects after searching a link with university (Model 1) as well as the probability that their profits (Model 2) will be influenced positively from the development of entrepreneurial innovation projects in collaboration with universities (Hosmer and Lemeshow 1989). The logarithmic odds of these events are held to be linearly affected by a vector of covariates X_i with coefficient vector β. Maximum likelihood estimations were used to calculate the logit coefficients,

Table 2. Description of variables (step 2).

	Dimension	Variable	Description
DV	Enterprise	Performance	Dummy: if profits increased in the last three years
IV	Enterprise-University	Entrepreneurial innovation projects	Dummy: the entrepreneurial innovation projects with the university in the last three years
CV	Enterprise capabilities	Innovation capacity	Dummy: if the enterprise introduced innovations in the last three years
		Innovation in both product and processes	Dummy: if the enterprise introduced innovations in both product and processes in the last three years
		Innovation in product/services	Dummy: if the enterprise only introduced innovations in products in the last three years
		Innovation in processes	Dummy: if the enterprise only introduced innovations in processes the last three years
CV	Government support	External funds	Dummy: if the enterprises received public financial support in the last three years
CV	Competitiveness Factors	Infrastructures (External factor1)	Perception about the role of infrastructures (physical, educational, clusters) on the enterprise competitiveness in the last three years
		Institutional voids (External factor2)	Perception about the role of institutional voids (security, corruption) on the enterprise competitiveness in the last three years
		Non-technological resources (Internal factor1)	Perception about the role of internal human, physical resources on the enterprise competitiveness in the last three years
		Technological resources (Internal factor2)	Perception about the role of internal technological resources on the enterprise competitiveness in the last three years
CV	Enterprise profile	Young enterprise	Dummy: young enterprises created in the last five years
		National capital	Percentage of the enterprise's capital that is national
		Domestic market	Percentage of the enterprise's production/services that are intended for the domestic market
		Size	Categorical: 1 = Micro; 2 = Small; 3 = Medium;4 = Large
		Sector	Categorical: 1 = Industry; 2 = Commerce; 3 = Services

Note: DV = Dependent variable; IV = Independent Varible; CV = Control Variable

Table 3. Descriptive and correlation analysis (step 1).

	Variables	Min	Max	Mean	S.D.	1	2	3	4	5	6	7	8	9	10	11	12	13	14	15
1	Entrepreneurial innovation projects	0	1	0.17	0.38	1														
2	Innovation in products and processes	0	1	0.27	0.44	0.162***	1													
3	Innovation in products	0	1	0.38	0.49	0.031	−0.170***	1												
4	Innovation in process	0	1	0.17	0.38	0.058	−0.080*	−0.038	1											
5	Teaching capabilities	−1.95	2.27	0.00	1.00	0.163***	0.119**	−0.002	−0.023	1										
6	Research capabilities	−3.16	1.10	0.00	1.00	0.146***	0.057	0.002	0.007	0.000	1									
7	Entrepreneurship capabilities	−1.59	2.81	0.00	1.00	0.126***	0.067	0.097**	−0.019	0.000	0.000	1								
8	External funds	0	1	0.04	0.18	0.394***	0.101**	−0.013	0.055	0.111**	0.031	0.021	1							
														1						
10	Universities number	0	1	0.52	0.50	0.195***	0.034	0.078*	0.039	0.135***	0.290***	0.173***	.0120**	0.762***	1					
11	Technological universities	0	1	0.06	0.24	−0.071	0.014	−0.009	0.028	0.032	−0.005	−0.063	−.048	−0.140***	−0.263***	1				
12	Research universities	0	1	0.05	0.22	−0.057	−0.019	0.003	−0.031	−0.044	−0.016	−0.103**	−.044	−0.127***	−0.240***	−0.058	1			
13	Public universities	0	1	0.08	0.27	−0.116**	0.013	−0.084*	−0.040	0.034	0.063	−0.037	−.057	−0.187***	−0.310***	−0.076*	−0.069	1		
14	Private universities	0	1	0.09	0.29	0.004	0.027	0.016	−0.042	−0.077*	0.083*	−0.001	−.023	−0.202***	−0.326***	−0.079*	−0.072*	−0.094**	1	
15	Research centres	0	1	0.00	0.06	0.055	0.033	−0.018	−0.008	−0.010	0.025	0.002	−.012	−0.016	−0.065	−0.016	−0.014	−0.019	−0.020	1
16	Infrastructures (external factor 1)	−2.01	2.61	0.00	1.00	0.033	0.031	−0.035	−0.017	−0.015	−0.051	0.019	.092**	0.011	0.003	−0.065	0.098**	−0.011	−0.015	0.007
17	Institutional voids (external factor 2)	−2.72	2.44	0.00	1.00	0.039	0.033	0.016	−0.005	−0.098**	0.046	0.065	.056	0.039	0.039	0.031	0.041	−0.012	−0.029	−0.012
18	Non-technological resources (internal factor 1)	−2.28	1.99	0.00	1.00	0.085*	−0.034	−0.025	0.043	−0.065	0.042	0.036	.066	0.000	0.020	−0.072	0.030	−0.055	0.057	0.026
19	Technological resources (internal factor 2)	−2.13	2.66	0.00	1.00	0.142***	0.145***	0.026	0.012	0.080*	0.054	0.078*	.151***	0.180***	0.144***	0.001	−0.003	0.020	−0.116	−0.021
20	Size: large, small, medium, micro	1	4	1.70	0.83	0.279***	0.115**	0.023	0.103**	0.049	0.101**	0.022	.185***	0.154***	0.080*	−0.016	−0.023	−0.002	0.000	0.023
21	Young enterprise	0	1	0.24	0.43	−0.076*	−0.108**	−0.005	−0.042	−0.027	0.044	0.036	−.059	−0.085*	−0.019	0.046	−0.070	−0.038	−0.004	−0.036
22	Sector: service, industry and commerce	1	3	2.23	0.68	−0.001	0.034	0.013	−0.067	0.007	0.052	0.012	−.003	0.046	0.047	0.010	−0.013	−0.008	0.054	0.071

(Continued)

Table 3. (Continued).

	Variables	Min	Max	Mean	S.D.	1	2	3	4	5	6	7	8	9	10	11	12	13	14	15
23	National capital	0	100	92.19	23.33	−0.118 **	−0.037	0.005	−0.107 **	0.026	0.022	−0.047	−.020	−0.077	−0.053	0.050	−0.075 *	0.060	0.045	0.021
24	Domestic market	0	100	85.88	30.37	0.000	−0.065	−0.033	−0.036	0.061	−0.033	−0.014	.026	−0.040	−0.089 *	−0.029	0.002	0.024	0.017	−0.022

	Variables	**16**	**17**	**18**	**19**	**20**	**21**	**22**	**23**	**24**
16	Infrastructures (external factor 1)	1								
17	Institutional voids (external factor 2)	0.000	1							
18	Non-technological resources (internal factor 1)	0.604 ***	0.167 ***	1						
19	Technological resources (internal factor 2)	0.243 ***	0.263 ***	0.000	1					
20	Size: large, small, medium, micro	0.095 *	−0.099 **	0.057	0.002	1				
21	Young enterprise	0.023	−0.149 ***	0.000	−0.015	−0.128 ***	1			
22	Sector: service, industry and commerce	0.069	0.007	0.051	−0.016	−0.121 ***	0.053	1		
23	National capital	−0.056	0.144 ***	−0.112 **	0.001	−0.140 ***	−0.073 *	0.079 *	1	
24	Domestic market	0.149 ***	0.057	0.075 *	0.062	−0.042	−0.002	0.013	0.160 ***	1

Note: Level of statistical significance: *** $p \leq 0.000$, ** $p \leq 0.05$, * $p \leq 0.10$.

Table 4. Descriptive and correlation analysis (step 2).

	Variables	Min	Max	Mean	S.D.	1	2	3	4	5	6	7	8	9	10	11	12	13	14	15	16	17
1	Performance	0	1	0.33	0.47	1																
2	Innovation capabilities	0	1	0.61	0.49	0.079 *	1															
3	Innovation in products and processes	0	1	0.27	0.44	0.050	0.487 ***	1														
4	Innovation in products/services	0	1	0.38	0.49	0.068	0.228 ***	−0.170 ***	1													
5	Innovation in processes	0	1	0.17	0.38	0.000	0.108	−0.080 *	−0.038	1												
6	Entrepreneurial innovation projects	0	1	0.17	0.38	−0.011	0.195 ***	0.162 ***	0.031	0.058	1											
7	External funds	0	1	0.02	0.13	0.094 **	0.108 **	0.154 ***	0.019	−0.018	0.296 ***	1										
8	Research university	0	1	0.02	0.14	0.020	0.085 *	0.106 **	0.014	−0.019	0.312 ***	0.626 ***	1									
9	Infrastructures (external factor 1)	−2.01	2.61	0.00	1.00	0.153 ***	0.057	0.031	−0.035	−0.017	0.033	0.023	0.030	1								
10	Institutional voids (external factor 2)	−2.72	2.44	0.00	1.00	−0.034	−0.023	0.033	0.016	−0.005	0.039	0.035	0.047	0.000	1							
11	Non-technological resources (internal factor 1)	−2.28	1.99	0.00	1.00	0.132 **	−0.012	−0.034	−0.025	0.043	0.085 *	0.018	0.033	0.604 ***	0.167 ***	1						
12	Technological resources (internal factor 2)	−2.13	2.66	0.00	1.00	0.098 **	0.171 ***	0.145 ***	0.026	0.012	0.142 ***	0.081 *	0.052	0.243 ***	0.263 ***	0.000	1					
13	Size: large, small, medium, micro	1	4	1.70	0.83	0.013	0.137 ***	0.115 **	0.023	0.103 **	0.279 ***	0.121 **	0.154 ***	0.095 **	−0.099 **	0.057	0.002	1				
14	Young enterprise	0	1	0.24	0.43	0.016	−0.010	−0.108 **	−0.005	−0.042	−0.076 *	−0.042	−0.080 *	0.023	−0.149 ***	0.000	−0.015	−0.128 **	1			
15	Sector: service, industry and commerce	1	3	2.23	0.68	−0.091 **	0.006	0.034	0.013	−0.067	−0.001	−0.002	−0.089 **	0.069	0.007	0.051	−0.016	−0.121 **	0.053	1		
16	National capital	0	100	92.19	23.33	−0.026	−0.019	−0.037	0.005	−0.107 **	−0.118 **	0.045	−0.013	−0.056	0.144 ***	−0.112 **	0.001	−0.140 ***	−0.073 *	0.079 *	1	
17	Domestic market	0	100	85.88	30.37	−0.051	−0.005	−0.065	−0.033	−0.036	0.000	−0.031	−0.095 **	0.149 ***	0.057	0.075 *	0.062	−0.042	−0.002	0.013	0.160 ***	1

Innovation in products and processes
Note: Level of statistical significance: *** p ≤ 0.000, ** p ≤ 0.05, * p ≤ 0.10.

Table 5. Logistic regression [determinants of entrepreneurial innovation projects – Model 1].

	Model 1a					Model 1b				Model 1 c			
Variables	B	S.E.	Sig	Odds		B	S.E.	Sig	Odds	B	S.E.	Sig	Odds
Enterprise innovation capabilities													
Innovation in product and processes						0.539	0.32	*	1.71	0.519	0.23	*	1.68
Innovation in products/services						0.199	0.56		1.22	0.108	0.56		1.11
Innovation in processes						0.029	1.08		1.03	0.237	1.08		1.27
University capabilities													
Teaching capabilities						0.420	0.17	***	1.52	0.507	0.16	***	1.66
Research capabilities						0.851	0.32	***	2.34	0.931	0.32	***	2.54
Enterprise capabilities						0.340	0.14	**	1.40	0.347	0.14	**	1.41
Government supports													
External funds						2.796	1.08	***	2.58	2. 749	1.08	***	2.58
Control variables													
Competitiveness													
Infrastructures (External factor1)	−0.365	0.19	**	0.69		−0.319	0.22		0.22	−0.292	0.22		0.75
Institutional voids (External factor2)	−0.011	0.15		0.99		−0.057	0.17		0.17	−0.089	0.18		1.09
Non-technological resources (Internal factor1)	0.406	0.18	**	1.50		0.430	0.21	**	0.21	0.366	0.21	*	1.44
Technological resources (Internal factor2)	0.450	0.14	***	1.57		0.192	0.16		0.16	0.224	0.17		1.25
University profile													
University number						0.257	0.15	*	1.29				
Research university										1.241	0.54	**	1.14
Public university										−1.796	0.91	*	0.17
Enterprise profile													
Size: Large (ref)													
Micro	−2.065	0.57	***	0.13		−1.163	0.64	*	0.31	−1.184	0.64	*	0.31
Medium	−1.275	0.54	**	0.28		−0.470	0.63		0.63	−0.481	0.63		0.62
Small	−0.446	0.58		0.64		0.186	0.67		1.20	0.210	0.67		1.23
Young enterprise	−0.458	0.35		0.63		−0.499	0.41		0.61	−0.555	0.41		0.57
Sector: Services (ref)													
Industry	0.057	0.35		1.06		0.341	0.40		1.41	0.359	0.40		1.43
Commerce	−1.476	0.33	***	0.23		−1.369	0.37	***	0.25	−1.365	0.37	***	0.26
National capital	−0.009	0.01	*	0.99		−0.010	0.01	*	0.99	−0.011	0.01	*	0.99
Domestic market	0.004	0.00		1.00		0.004	0.01		1.00	0.004	0.01		1.00
Constant	0.796	0.77		2.22		−0.707	0.90		0.49	−0.568	1.00		0.57
−2 Log likelihood	365.871		301.117		296.066								
Cox & Snell R Square	.154		.257		.264								
Nagelkerke R Square	.259		.432		.445								
Chi-square	83.252		148.006		153.057								
Sig.	***		***		***								
N	514		514		514								

Note: Level of statistical significance: *** $p < 0.000$, ** $p < 0.05$, * $p < 0.10$.

which denote changes in *the log odds* of the dependent variable (Greene 2003). We assessed the goodness of fit of the models using the Pearson Chi-square test, the rate of correct classification, and the *pseudo-R-square*. The significance of each independent variable was tested using Wald statistics.

The robustness test was developed with the structural equation modelling for corroborating the results obtained using the logistic regressions. This statistical technique allows the examination of a set of relationships between one or more independent or dependent variables, either continuous or discrete (Tabachnick and Fidell 1996; Shook et al. 2004). This statistical technique also allows seeing the direct and indirect contributions, as well as testing potential mediation effects (Fox 1980; Sobel 1982; Cheung and Lau 2008). To perform the SEM, we corroborate the correlations, reliability and validity of the constructs using the confirmatory factor analysis and the Cronbach alpha. These analyses showed acceptable parameters between 0.6 and 0.7. Additionally, we tested the correlation between constructs and we did not find a significant co-variance. We simultaneously tested Model 1 and Model 2 with the entire sample (Model 3).

4. Results and Discussion

4.1. Determinants of entrepreneurial innovation projects

Table 5 shows the determinants of entrepreneurial innovation projects.

Regarding enterprises' innovation capabilities, 17% of the Mexican enterprises of the sample have manifested their participation in entrepreneurial innovation projects. Similarly, 27% of these enterprises recognised the improvement of their capabilities through the implementation of innovation mixed practices, 38% through innovation in product/services, and 17% through innovation in processes. Model 1 shows that when Mexican enterprises are developing capabilities through their simultaneous participation in both the innovation product and innovation in processes. The probability of developing entrepreneurial innovation projects increases when enterprises have developed innovation' capabilities in products and processes [0.539; 0.100]. We do not find strong support about the effect of enterprises' capabilities associated with the development of only innovation in products/services or only innovation in processes. In this vein, innovation' capabilities in products and process represent highest returns for enterprises interested to enhance innovation capabilities and to acquire resources/skills during the development of collaboration project (Yamin and Otto 2004; Nieto and Santamaria 2007). Therefore, these results support H1.

Concerning the knowledge of university' capabilities, results show that having a better understanding of universities' research capabilities increases the probability of developing entrepreneurial innovation projects with universities [0.851; 0.001]. Similarly, having a better understanding of universities' teaching capabilities [0.420; 0.001] and universities' entrepreneurial capabilities [0.340; 0.001] increases the probability that Mexican enterprises develop entrepreneurial innovation projects with universities. Concretely, these findings demonstrate that Mexican enterprises are more interested in developing entrepreneurial innovation project when their partner (i.e., university) contributes to the most robust research and technological capabilities. Enterprises do not valuate the qualified human capital and the incubation capabilities provided by the university.

Table 6. Logistic regression [effects of entrepreneurial innovation projects on enterprise performance – Model 2].

	Model 2a				Model 2b				Model 2 c			
Variables	B	S.E.	Sig	Odds	B	S.E.	Sig	Odds	B	S.E.	Sig	Odds
Enterprise-University												
Entrepreneurial innovation projects	0.32	0.13	*	1.38	0.39	0.12	*	1.48	0.59	0.16	*	2.68
Control variables												
Government support												
External funds					1.99	0.62	**	1.90	1.94	0.52	**	1.90
Enterprise capabilities												
Innovation capacity					0.32	0.13	*	1.38				
Innovation in product and processes									0.75	0.37	**	2.11
Innovation in products/services									0.26	0.24		1.30
Innovation in processes									0.02	0.76		1.02
Enterprise profile												
Size: Large (ref)												
Micro	0.41	0.51		0.13	0.52	0.53		1.69	0.49	0.53		1.62
Medium	0.24	0.51		0.28	0.26	0.53		1.30	0.22	0.53		1.25
Small	0.40	0.56		0.64	0.64	0.57		1.90	0.59	0.58		1.80
Young enterprise	0.05	0.23		0.63	0.02	0.24		1.02	0.05	0.24		1.05
Sector: Services (ref)												
Industry	0.66	0.31	**	1.06	0.76	0.32	**	2.13	0.78	0.32	***	2.18
Commerce	0.11	0.22		0.23	0.05	0.23		1.05	0.07	0.23		1.07
National capital	0.00	0.00		0.99	0.00	0.00		1.00	0.00	0.00		1.00
Domestic market	−0.01	0.00	*	1.00	−0.01	0.00	*	0.99	−0.01	0.00	*	0.99
Competitiveness												
Infrastructures (External factor1)	0.23	0.13	*	1.25	0.23	0.13	*	1.26	0.24	0.14	*	1.27
Institutional voids (External factor2)	−0.17	0.11		0.84	−0.16	0.11		0.85	−0.18	0.11		0.84
Non-technological resources (Internal factor1)	0.21	0.13		1.23	0.22	0.13	*	1.25	0.23	0.13	*	1.25
Technological resources (Internal factor2)	0.19	0.11	*	1.21	0.16	0.11		1.18	0.17	0.11		1.19
Constant	−0.85	0.63		0.43	−0.93	0.68		0.40	−0.88	0.69		0.41
−2 Log likelihood		606.85			595.39					593.106		
Cox & Snell R Square		.053			.075					.079		
Nagelkerke R Square		.074			.104					.109		
Chi-square		27.12			38.57					40.862		
Sig.		**			***					.002		
N		514			514					514		

Note: Level of statistical significance: *** $p \le 0.000$, ** $p \le 0.05$, * $p \le 0.10$.

A plausible explanation is that enterprises collaborate with another partner that could contribute to business capabilities (i.e., collaborate with other enterprises across their value chain). Intuitively, although we do not find evidence per type of university (i.e., technological university, technological institutes, public university, private university, or research centre), previous findings debate that Mexican universities are facing a transformation process to become more entrepreneurial and innovative organisations (Guerrero and Urbano 2012; McAdam et al. 2012). Therefore, these results support H2.

Concerning state intervention, the probability of participating in entrepreneurial innovation projects increased when the partnership has received public funds [2.796; 0.001]. In this regard, our findings provide insights that one critical determinant of entrepreneurial innovation projects is the support provided by the government. Although the role of the Mexican government has changed across time/spaces, our results debate the active role of government in the context of emerging economies (Miller, McAdam, and McAdam 2014). Indirectly, our findings are providing insights into the positive effects of public incentives towards the development of entrepreneurial innovations in the context of emerging economies (Guerrero and Urbano 2019b). Therefore, these results support H3.

Our results show the effects of control variables. Regarding the enterprises' perception of institutional voids, our result does not show strong evidence about its effect on entrepreneurial innovation projects. Although Mexico's regional heterogeneity, this result may be capture lower variance on the enterprises' perception of institutional voids because there are located within the same emerging economy. Another explanation may be the measurement used in the survey for capturing this perception, as well as its transformation during our analysis. Notably, the probability that an enterprise participates in entrepreneurial innovation projects increases when enterprises perceive lacks in human and physical resources that are relevant for their competitiveness [0.406; 0.05] and when perceiving lacks on technological resources [0.450; 0.001]. Our findings are similar than previous studies (Bayona, García-Marco, and Huerta 2001; Kogut 1988) that found that when enterprises perceived resource scarcity tried to appropriate value and resources through collaborations. Regarding an enterprise's size, respect large firms, the probability decreases when an enterprise is a micro-enterprise with less than five employees [−2.065; 0.001]. By their nature, Mexican enterprises are focused on survival, reducing costs without exploring alternatives to be more competitive (Ruelas 2004). The probability of being involved in entrepreneurial innovation projects decreases when enterprises are enrolled in commercial activities [−1.476; 0.001]. Maybe the commercial orientation demands specific types of innovations and demands specific returns. Regarding the age and market orientation, the results do not provide strong evidence. A plausible explanation is that almost 80% of the sample is characterised by established firms oriented to the domestic market.

4.2. Consequences of entrepreneurial innovation projects

Table 6 shows the consequences of entrepreneurial innovation projects. In our sample, 33% of the enterprises have recognised an increment of profits in the last three years. By nature, their collaboration objective is reducing the tension of survival in uncertainty market. As a consequence, enterprises' strategies are oriented towards developing

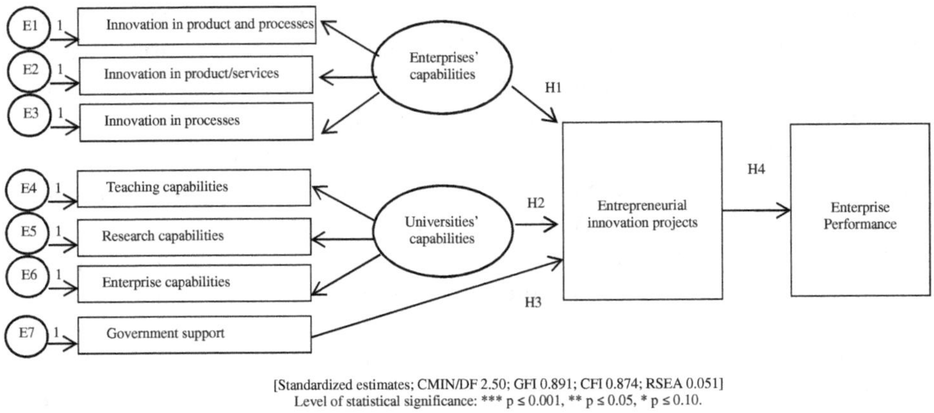

Figure 2. Structural equation modelling.
Source: Authors

entrepreneurial innovation projects in collaboration with universities to capture the value-added that improves their performance.

Model 2 shows the effect of entrepreneurial innovation projects on higher enterprises' performance. The probability that entrepreneurial innovation project with universities generate a significant effect on enterprises' performance depends on the enterprises' innovation capabilities, the enterprises' access to public support, and the enterprises' knowledge of universities' capabilities. First, the probability that the enterprises' performance increases depends on the enterprises' innovation' capabilities acquired in the three previous years. Second, based on our findings, the effect of entrepreneurial innovations on performance is conditioned by the state funds. It means that the probability that the enterprises gain higher performance increases when the enterprise-university collaboration has received public funds to support their entrepreneurial innovation projects. Third, our results also show that enterprises looking for collaborations not only to create value but also to capture a portion of this value in economic terms as well as improving their entrepreneurial innovation capabilities (Zott and Amit 2007; Zott et al., 2011; Autio et al. 2014; Guerrero and Urbano 2017). Therefore, these results support H4.

Regarding the control variable, although the expected regional heterogeneity, the enterprises' perception of institutional voids, our results do not show insights about the effect on enterprises' performance. The potential explanation behind this result is that the positive/negative effect is disseminated by the lower differences in the enterprises' perceptions of institutional voids across Mexico.

4.3. Robustness tests

Figure 2 and Table 7 show the determinants and the consequences of entrepreneurial innovation projects using structural equation modelling as a robustness test.

As a robustness test, the structural equation analysis helps to confirm the patterns observed to test our hypotheses (Model 3). Regarding the determinants, the results show a positive and direct effect of the enterprises' innovation capabilities on entrepreneurial innovation projects [0.704; $p < 0.001$] supporting H1. This variable shows a positive and

Table 7. Structural equation modelling [determinants and consequences of entrepreneurial innovation projects – Model 3].

	Relationships			Model 3 Coef.	S.E.	P
H1	Entrepreneurial innovations	< –	Enterprise capabilities	0.704	0.136	***
H2	Entrepreneurial innovations	< –	University capabilities	1.875	0.344	***
H3	Entrepreneurial innovations	< –	Government support	2.749	1.080	***
H4	Enterprise performance	< –	Entrepreneurial innovation projects	1.549	0.800	*
Enterprise capabilities	Innovation in product and processes	< –	Enterprise capabilities	3.051	0.057	***
	Innovation in product/services	< –	Enterprise capabilities	1.620	0.192	***
	Innovation in processes	< –	Enterprise capabilities	0.952	0.052	***
University capabilities	Teaching capabilities	< –	University capabilities	1.416	2.479	***
	Research capabilities	< –	University capabilities	3.035	0.660	***
	Entrepreneurial capabilities	< –	University capabilities	1.019	0.400	**

The direct and indirect effect

H	Relationships	Entire Sample Direct	Indirect
H1	Enterprise capabilities → Enterprise performance	0.704 ***	0.320 ***
H2	University capabilities → Enterprise performance	1.875 **	0.750 **
H3	Government support → Enterprise performance	2.749 **	1.940 **

indirect effect on enterprise performance [0.320; p < 0.001]. Second, results also show the positive effect of the university's capabilities as the determinant of entrepreneurial innovation project [1.875; p < 0.001, as well as their indirect effect on enterprise performance [0.750; p < 0.001]; supporting H2. Indeed, we found a positive effect of state support on entrepreneurial innovation projects [2.749; p < 0.001], as well as an indirect effect on enterprise performance [1.940; p < 0.001]; supporting H3. Finally, results also show the contribution of entrepreneurial innovation projects on enterprises' performance [1.549; p < 0.100]; supporting H4.

5. Conclusions

The objective of this paper was to provide insights into the determinants and the consequences of entrepreneurial innovation projects within enterprise-university collaborations in an emerging economy. Based on the theoretical basis of triple-helix, dynamic capabilities and institutional economic approaches, we developed hypotheses about the effect of enterprises' innovation capabilities (H1), the knowledge of universities' capabilities (H2), and the access to state support (H3) on the likelihood of enterprises for developing entrepreneurial innovation projects in collaboration with universities, as well as the effect of these entrepreneurial innovation projects on enterprises' performance (H4). In this regard, this paper contributes to the ongoing academic debate on entrepreneurship and innovation.

The first contribution relates to the role of academia in entrepreneurship and innovation (Audretsch 2014; Audretsch, Lehmann, and Link 2019). Our results show that the universities' capabilities were relevant determinants for developing simultaneously entrepreneurial and innovation projects within enterprises-universities collaborations. In our empirical setting, for confidential agreements, it was very complicated to identify the universities' name to include objective measures of their capabilities. However, the enterprises' perception of universities' capabilities helps us to understand the relevance of knowing/understanding which are potential contributions of universities into entrepreneurial innovation projects based on their capabilities. In this regard, Klofsten et al. (2019) and Guerrero and Urbano (2019a) highlighted the lack of insights about the identification/management of capabilities that universities have acquired from their core activities: teaching capabilities, the research capabilities, and knowledge commercialisation capabilities. Although than previous studies have contributed with relevant insights about the motivations and determinants of enterprise-university collaborations (Perkmann et al. 2013), a better identification/measurement of universities' capabilities allows us to test and legitimise their contribution on the development of entrepreneurial initiatives with an innovative impact in collaboration with diverse agents, as well as innovation initiatives with an entrepreneurial impact in diverse contexts (Colombo, Meoli, and Vismara 2019; Feldman, Siegel, and Wright 2019).

The second contribution relates to the determinants of entrepreneurial innovation projects within enterprise-university collaborations (Autio et al. 2014; Guerrero and Urbano 2019b). Our results show that enterprises' innovation capabilities, knowing universities' capabilities, and the access to additional state funds increase the probability that enterprises develop entrepreneurial innovation projects in collaboration with universities. In our theoretical/empirical analyses, adopting the theoretical foundations of dynamic capabilities and triple-helix approaches, we assumed that enterprises, universities, and the state acquire capabilities during the development of their core activities. In this vein, these organisational' capabilities are useful to explore/exploit new business/innovative opportunities (sensing), to try new ways to access to the required resources/capabilities for developing these opportunities (seizing), as well as to transform them into commercialised technological outcomes (Teece 2014). Therefore, it helps to operationalise the contribution of each triple-helix agents on the development of entrepreneurial innovations by adopting the dynamic capabilities perspective (Heaton et al., 2019). At the same time, the study provides insights into the operationalisation of entrepreneurial innovations within a collaboration partnership between enterprises and universities towards projects with a unique entrepreneurial and innovative orientation (Guerrero and Urbano 2019a), as well as provide insights into the positive effect of state incentives towards entrepreneurial innovations (Dimos and Pugh 2016; Guerrero and Urbano 2019b).

The third contribution relates to the consequences of entrepreneurial innovation projects within enterprise-university collaborations (Lehmann and Menter 2016; Guerrero and Urbano 2019a; Guerrero and Urbano 2019b). Previous studies have shown the regional contributions of industry-university collaborations (Lehmann and Menter 2016) as well as the impact of cooperation networks on enterprises' innovation performance (Zott and Amit 2007; Zeng, Xie, and Tam 2010). In this vein, our study show insights about the economic benefits captured by the enterprises' from the development of entrepreneurial innovation projects within enterprise-university collaborations. Although the lack of longitudinal dataset, our study tested the economic benefits of entrepreneurial innovation projects with universities captured by enterprises in the last three years. Therefore, a natural extension of this study should be testing the effects of entrepreneurial innovations by using longitudinal case studies or panel datasets.

The last contribution relates to the effect of institutional voids on entrepreneurial innovation projects within enterprise-university collaborations (Liedong, Peprah, and Eyong 2020). By considering the particularities of emerging economies in terms of institutional voids and how they could affect entrepreneurship and innovation strategies, we introduced as a control variable the measure of 'institutional voids' that captured the perception of enterprises about their positive/negative effects of institutional voids on their strategies. Our results do not provide significant insights into the effect of this variable on both the antecedents and the consequences of entrepreneurial innovation projects within an enterprise-university collaboration. Potential explanations emerged from this result. On the one hand, by considering that we analysed enterprises located in one emerging economy, the perception about the institutional voids (corruption, criminality) could be generalised across all enterprises. We may assume the existence of heterogeneity at the regional level. However, given the confidential agreements, we do not have access to regional level information to avoid the potential identification of enterprises. Although our results do not provide significant insights, the state orientation towards supporting entrepreneurial innovation via enterprise-university collaborations is reducing the transactional costs generated by institutional voids that diminish organisational incentives for developing innovation and leveraging of talent (Mahmood and Mitchell 2004; Puffer, McCarthy, and Boisot 2010; Liedong, Peprah, and Eyong 2020). This issue could also explain the effect captured by the institutional voids proxy.

This study has several limitations that provide research opportunities. *The first limitation* was the use of secondary datasets for exploring this phenomenon. Concretely, the lack of information in emerging economies limitate the implementation of quantitative analysis. A natural extension of this research requires an in-depth exploration of entrepreneurial innovation projects using qualitative/quantitative longitudinal analysis of the determinants and the impacts. *The second limitation* was the number of observations and the proxies used in our models. It is the most common problem faced by previous studies that have used secondary sources. In this vein, we need to improve the measures of performance with an objective and lagged measures, as well as include variables that capture the organisational and regional dimensions. *The third limitation* was the restriction in the implementation of sophisticated methods. Given the nature of the dependent variables, we adopted logistic regressions. However, panel data analysis demands longitudinal datasets that allow capturing the effects and implementing robustness tests. *The fourth limitation* was the theory development also restringed by the nature of our dataset. More theory development combining several theoretical approaches and empirical testing across the globe are still needed to advance in this academic field. In this sense, theoretical perspectives such as the knowledge spillover theory, institutional theory, endogenous economic theory, and dynamic capabilities could help to understand the dynamic entrepreneurial and innovation process (Audretsch and Lehmann 2005; Audretsch et al. 2016; Chang, Hughes, and Hotho 2011; Huizingh 2011; Thornton, Ribeiro-Soriano, and Urbano 2011; Landström, Åström, and Harirchi 2013). Therefore, future research should consider the theoretical foundations of these approaches for exploring the determinants and the impacts of entrepreneurial innovations. *The fifth limitation* was the lack of a dynamic vision of time/context. As an agent who recognise opportunity, mobilise resources and create value, enterprises have the responsibility of creating organisations as well as building capacities to sustain regional economic development

(Feldman 2014). It means that enterprises obtain benefits from their contexts, but enterprises are also agents of change who also transform their contexts. The literature recognises that knowledge-intensive scenarios are good examples to understand the reciprocal relationship between triple-helix agents (Etzkowitz and Leydesdorff 2000; Lu and Etzkowitz 2008; McAdam et al. 2012; Miller, McAdam, and McAdam 2014; Audretsch, Lehmann, and Link 2019). However, it requires an evolutionary process that demands time and contextual dimension. For this reason, future research should also consider an evolutionary perspective that also combines the ecosystem approach for a better understanding of reverse relationships between triple-helix agents and the context.

Even though the results of this study apply to our research setting, some implications for triple-helix agents emerged of this study. *For policymakers*, this study exhibits the determinants of enterprises-universities participation in entrepreneurial innovation projects. Contextualising these results within an emergent economy, if policymakers expect a transition towards a knowledge-based economy, they should enhance not only public supports towards on collaborations between enterprises-universities but also enhance collaboration with other organisations (e.g. private investors, educational system actors, labour market regulators, research centres, incubators). The orchestration of multiple actors could enhance capabilities, resources, and mitigate the effects of institutional voids (e.g., corruption, criminal activity, insecurity). Moreover, the paper provides some insights into the positive effect of public policies that could legitimise the role of public intervention. *For enterprise managers*, this study offers insights about the best mechanisms/practices for generating/capturing value through entrepreneurial innovation practices. In particular, managers could be able to evaluate the costs and the benefits of participating in sustainable innovative and entrepreneurial projects that enhance capabilities, reduce risks, sharing resources, and income expectations through collaborations with scientific actors. *For university managers*, could adopt the entrepreneurial university model as a good practice for transforming organisations and enhancing teaching, research, and entrepreneurial capabilities. Becoming an entrepreneurial university could be actively contributing to the well-being and regional development through entrepreneurial innovation processes in collaboration with multiple societal and economic agents. Therefore, this practice could be a benchmark reference to develop similar strategies because legitimising the role of universities in societies.

Disclosure statement

No potential conflict of interest was reported by the authors.

Funding

David Urbano acknowledges the financial support from the Spanish Ministry of Economy & Competitiveness [Project ECO2017-87885-P], the Economy & Knowledge Department—Catalan Government [project 2017-SGR-1056] and ICREA under the ICREA Academia Programme.

ORCID

Maribel Guerrero http://orcid.org/0000-0001-7387-1999
David Urbano http://orcid.org/0000-0001-7600-8656

References

Acs, Z. J., E. Stam, D. B. Audretsch, and A. O'Connor. 2017. "The Lineages of the Entrepreneurial Ecosystem Approach." *Small Business Economics* 49 (1): 1–10. doi:10.1007/s11187-017-9864-8.

Aiken, L. S., S. G. West, and R. R. Reno. 1991. *Multiple Regression: Testing and Interpreting Interactions.* US: Sage.

Audretsch, D. 2007. *The Entrepreneurial Society.* USA: Oxford University Press.

Audretsch, D. 2014. "From the Entrepreneurial University to the University for the Entrepreneurial Society." *Journal of Technology Transfer* 39 (3): 313–321.

Audretsch, D., E. Lehmann, M. Meoli, and S. Vismara, Eds.. 2016. *University Evolution, Entrepreneurial Activity and Regional Competitiveness.* Basel: Springer International Publishing.

Audretsch, D. B., and E. E. Lehmann. 2005. "Does the Knowledge Spillover Theory of Entrepreneurship Hold for Regions?" *Research Policy* 34 (8): 1191–1202.

Audretsch, D. B., E. E. Lehmann, and A. N. Link. 2019. "A Research Agenda for Entrepreneurship and Innovation." *Edward Elgar Publishing.*

Autio, E., M. Kenney, P. Mustar, D. Siegel, and M. Wright. 2014. "Entrepreneurial Innovation: The Importance of Context." *Research Policy.* doi:10.1016/j.respol.2014.01.015.

Autio, E., S. Kanninen, and R. Gustafsson. 2008. "First-and Second-order Additionality and Learning Outcomes in Collaborative R&D Programs." *Research Policy* 37 (1): 59–76.

Bayona, C., T. García-Marco, and E. Huerta. 2001. "Firms' Motivations for Cooperative R&D: An Empirical Analysis of Spanish Firms." *Research Policy* 30: 1289–1307.

Becker, W., and J. Dietz. 2004. "R&D Cooperation and Innovation Activities of Firms—evidence for the German Manufacturing Industry." *Research Policy* 33 (2): 209–223.

Belderbos, R., M. Carree, B. Diederen, B. Lokshin, and R. Veugelers. 2004b. "Heterogeneity in R&D Cooperation Strategies." *International Journal of Industrial Organization* 22 (8): 1237–1263.

Bosma, N. 2013. "The Global Entrepreneurship Monitor (GEM) and Its Impact on Entrepreneurship Research." *Foundations and Trends in Entrepreneurship* 9 (2): 143–248.

Carayannis, E. G., J. Alexander, and A. Ioannidis. 2000. "Leveraging Knowledge, Learning, and Innovation in Forming a Strategic Government–university-industry (GUI) R&D Partnerships in the US, Germany, and France." *Technovation* 20 (9): 477–488.

Centro de Investigación y Docencia Económica (CIDE), Secretaria de Educación Pública (SEP). 2010. *Encuesta Nacional de Vinculación Empresas, ENAVES.* México: CIDE/SEP.

Chang, Y. Y., M. Hughes, and S. Hotho. 2011. "Internal and External Antecedents of SMEs' Innovation Ambidexterity Outcomes." *Management Decision* 49 (10): 1658–1676.

Chesbrough, H. 2010. "Business Model Innovation: Opportunities and Barriers." *Long Range Planning* 43: 354–363.

Chesbrough, H. 2012. "Why Companies Should Have Open Business Models." *MIT Sloan Management Review* 48 (2): 21–28.

Cheung, G. W., and R. S. Lau. 2008. "Testing Mediation and Suppression Effects of Latent Variables: Bootstrapping with Structural Equation Models." *Organizational Research Methods* 11 (2): 296–325.

Chung, J. W., Z. T. Bae, and J. S. Kim. 2003. "Changing Patterns of Technological Cooperation Activities of Innovative Small Firms along Technological Development Stages in the Korean Telecommunication Sector." *Technovation* 23 (2): 163–173.

Clark, B. 2001. "The Entrepreneurial University: New Foundations for Collegiality, Autonomy, and Achievement." *Higher Education Management* 13: 2.

Cohen, B. 2006. "Sustainable Valley Entrepreneurial Ecosystems." *Business Strategy and the Environment* 15 (1): 1–14.

Colombo, M. G., M. Meoli, and S. Vismara. 2019. "Signalling in Science-based IPOs: The Combined Effect of Affiliation with Prestigious Universities, Underwriters, and Venture Capitalists." *Journal of Business Venturing* 34 (1): 141–177.

Diario Oficial. 2014. Consejo Nacional de Ciencia y Tecnología. Estados Unidos Mexicanos: Presidencia de la Republica. Accessed October 2015. http://www.fiderh.org.mx/21_ciencia_y_tecnologia.pdf

Dimos, C., and G. Pugh. 2016. "The Effectiveness of R&D Subsidies: A Meta-regression Analysis of the Evaluation Literature." *Research Policy* 45 (4): 797–815.

Etzkowitz, H., A. Webster, C. Gebhardt, and B. R. C. Terra. 2000. "The Future of the University and the University of the Future: Evolution of Ivory Tower to Entrepreneurial Paradigm." *Research Policy* 29 (2): 313–330.

Etzkowitz, H., and L. Leydesdorff. 2000. "The Dynamics of Innovation: From National Systems and "Mode 2" to a Triple Helix of University-industry–government Relations." *Research Policy* 29 (2): 109–123.

Feldman, M., D. S. Siegel, and M. Wright. 2019. "New Developments in Innovation and Entrepreneurial Ecosystems." *Industrial and Corporate Change* 28 (4): 817–826.

Feldman, M. P. 2014. "The Character of Innovative Places: Entrepreneurial Strategy." *Economic Development, and Prosperity. Small Business Economics* 43 (1): 9–20.

Fox, J. 1980. "Effects Analysis in Structural Equation Models." *Sociological Methods and Research* 9: 3–28.

García-Quevedo, J. 2004. "Do Public Subsidies Complement Business R&D? A Meta-analysis of the Econometric Evidence." *Kyklos* 57 (1): 87–102.

Greene, W. H. 2003. *Econometric Analysis*. New York: Prentice-Hall.

Grimaldi, R., M. Kenney, D. Siegel, and M. Wright. 2011. "30 Years after Bayh-Dole: Reassessing Academic Entrepreneurship." *Research Policy* 40 (8): 1045–1057.

Guerrero, M., and D. Urbano. 2019a. "A Research Agenda for Entrepreneurship and Innovation: The Role of Entrepreneurial Universities." In *A Research Agenda for Entrepreneurship and Innovation*, edited by D. Audrestsch, A. Link, and E. Lehmann, 107.

Guerrero, M., and D. Urbano. 2012. "The Development of an Entrepreneurial University." *Journal of Technology Transfer* 37 (1): 43–74.

Guerrero, M., and D. Urbano. 2014. "Academics' Start-up Intentions and Knowledge Filters: An Individual Perspective of the Knowledge Spillover Theory of Entrepreneurship." *Small Business Economics* 43 (1): 57–74.

Guerrero, M., and D. Urbano. 2017. "The Impact of Triple Helix Agents on Entrepreneurial Innovations' Performance: An inside Look at Enterprises Located in an Emerging Economy." *Technological Forecasting & Social Change*. doi:10.1016/j.techfore.2016.06.015.

Guerrero, M., and D. Urbano. 2019b. "Effectiveness of Technology Transfer Policies and Legislation in Fostering Entrepreneurial Innovations across Continents: An Overview." *The Journal of Technology Transfer* 44 (5): 1347–1366.

Guerrero, M., D. Urbano, and F. Herrera. 2019b. "Innovation Practices in Emerging Economies: Do University Partnerships Matter?" *The Journal of Technology Transfer* 44 (2): 615–646.

Guerrero, M., D. Urbano, J. Cunnigham, and D. Organ. 2014. "Entrepreneurial Universities: A Case Study Comparison in Two European Regions." *Journal of Technology Transfer* 39 (3): 415–434.

Guerrero, M., F. Herrera, and D. Urbano. 2019. "Strategic Knowledge Management Within Subsidised Entrepreneurial University-industry Partnerships." *Management Decision* 57 (12): 3280–3300.

Hall, B. H., and A. Maffioli. 2008. "Evaluating the Impact of Technology Development Funds in Emerging Economies: Evidence from Latin America." *The European Journal of Development Research* 20 (2): 172–198.

Hernández, K., L. González, and M. Herrera. 2016. Regional Repot 2015, Global Entrepreneurship Monitor. Mexico: Tecnológico de Monterrey.

Hosmer, D., and S. Lemeshow. 1989. *Applied Logistic Regression*. New York: John Wiley and Sons.

Huizingh, E. K. R. E. 2011. "Open Innovation: State of the Art and Future Perspectives." *Technovation* 31 (1): 2–9.

Ireland, R. D., J. G. Covin, and D. F. Kuratko. 2009. "Conceptualizing Corporate Entrepreneurship Strategy." *Entrepreneurship: Theory & Practice* 33 (1): 19–46.

Kenney, M., and W. Richard Goe. 2004. "The Role of Social Embeddedness in Professorial Entrepreneurship: A Comparison of Electrical Engineering and Computer Science at UC Berkeley and Stanford." *Research Policy* 33 (5): 691–707.

Klofsten, M., A. Fayolle, M. Guerrero, S. Mian, D. Urbano, and M. Wright. 2019. "The Entrepreneurial University as Driver for Economic Growth and Social change-Key Strategic Challenges." *Technological Forecasting and Social Change* 141: 149–158.

Klofsten, M., and D. Jones-Evans. 2000. "Comparing Academic Entrepreneurship in Europe—the Case of Sweden and Ireland." *Small Business Economics* 14 (4): 299–310.

Kochenkova, A., R. Grimaldi, and F. Munari. 2016. "Public Policy Measures in Support of Knowledge Transfer Activities: A Review of Academic Literature." *The Journal of Technology Transfer* 41 (3): 407–429.

Kogut, B. 1988. "Joint Ventures: Theoretical and Empirical Perspectives." *Strategic Management Journal* 9 (4): 319–332.

Landström, H., F. Åström, and G. Harirchi. 2013. "Innovation and Entrepreneurship Studies: One or Two Fields of Research?" *International Entrepreneurship and Management Journal.* doi:10.1007/s11365-013-0282-3.

Lehmann, E. E., and M. Menter. 2016. "University-industry Collaboration and Regional Wealth." *The Journal of Technology Transfer* 41 (6): 1284–1307.

Liedong, T. A., A. A. Peprah, and J. E. Eyong. 2020. "Institutional Voids and Innovation Governance: A Conceptual Exposition of the Open versus Closed Architecture Choice." *Strategic Change* 29 (1): 57–66.

Lu, L., and H. Etzkowitz. 2008. "Strategic Challenges for Creating Knowledge-based Innovation in China: Transforming Triple Helix University-government-industry Relations." *Journal of Technology Management in China* 3 (1): 5–11.

Lundvall, B. A. 1992. "User-producer Relationships, National Systems of Innovation and Internationalisation." National systems of innovation: towards a theory of innovation and interactive learning. London: Pinter Publishers, 45–67.

Mahmood, I. P., and W. Mitchell. 2004. "Two Faces: Effects of Business Groups on Innovation in Emerging Economies." *Management Science* 50 (10): 1348–1365.

Malerba, F., and M. McKelvey. 2018. "Knowledge-intensive Innovative Entrepreneurship Integrating Schumpeter, Evolutionary Economics, and Innovation Systems." *Small Business Economics.* doi:10.1007/s11187-018-0060-2.

McAdam, R., K. Miller, M. McAdam, and S. Teague. 2012. "The Development of University Technology Transfer Stakeholder Relationships at a Regional Level: Lessons for the Future." *Technovation* 32 (1): 57–67.

McMullen, J. S., and D. Dimov. 2013. "Time and the Entrepreneurial Journey: The Problems and Promise of Studying Entrepreneurship as a Process." *Journal of Management Studies* 50 (8): 1481–1512.

Mian, S., A. Fayolle, and W. Lamine. 2012. "Building Sustainable Regional Platforms for Incubating Science and Technology Businesses Evidence from US and French Science and Technology Parks." *The International Journal of Entrepreneurship and Innovation* 13 (4): 235–247.

Mian, S. A. 2011. "University's Involvement in Technology Business Incubation: What Theory and Practice Tell Us?" *International Journal of Entrepreneurship and Innovation Management* 13 (2): 113–121.

Miller, K., M. McAdam, and R. McAdam. 2014. "The Changing University Business Model: A Stakeholder Perspective." *R&D Management* 44 (3): 265–287.

Nieto, M. J., and L. Santamaria. 2007. "The Importance of Diverse Collaborative Networks for the Novelty of Product Innovation." *Technovation* 27 (6): 367–377.

Norbäck, P. J., and L. Persson. 2012. "Entrepreneurial Innovations, Competition and Competition Policy." *European Economic Review* 56 (3): 488–506.

O'Kane, C., V. Mangematin, W. Geoghegan, and C. Fitzgerald. 2014. "University Technology Transfer Offices: The Search for Identity to Build Legitimacy." Research Policy. forthcoming.

O'Shea, R., T. J. Allen, A. Chevalier, and F. Roche. 2005. "Entrepreneurial Orientation, Technology Transfer and Spin-off Performance of US Universities." *Research Policy* 34: 994–1009.

OECD. 2013. OECD Science, Technology and Industry Scoreboard 2013. Accessed 22 May 2016 www.oecd-ilibrary.org/docserver/download/9213051e.pdf_

Paleari, S., D. Donina, and M. Meoli. 2015. "The Role of the University in Twenty-first-century European Society." *The Journal of Technology Transfer* 40 (3): 369–379.

Perkmann, M., V. Tartari, M. McKelvey, E. Autio, A. Broström, P. D'Este, R. Fini, et al. 2013. "Academic Engagement and Commercialisation: A Review of the Literature on University-industry Relations." *Research Policy* 42: 423–442.

Puffer, S. M., D. J. McCarthy, and M. Boisot. 2010. "Entrepreneurship in Russia and China: The Impact of Formal Institutional Voids." *Entrepreneurship Theory and Practice* 34 (3): 441–467.

Ruelas, A. 2004. "Innovar en Mercados Emergentes: el paradigma de la T grande." *Harvard Business Review* 82 (2): 54–63.

Schumpeter, J. A. 1942. *Capitalism, Socialism and Democracy*. New York: Harper & Brothers Publishers.

Shook, C. L., D. J. Ketchen, G. T. Hult, and K. M. Kacmar. 2004. "An Assessment of the Use of Structural Equation Modelling in Strategic Management Research." *Strategic Management Journal* 25: 397–404.

Sobel, M. 1982. "Asymptotic Confidence Intervals for Indirect Effects in Structural Equation Models." In *Sociological Methodology*, edited by S. Leinhardt, 290–312. San Francisco: Jossey-Bass.

Svensson, P., M. Klofsten, and H. Etzkowitz. 2012. "An Entrepreneurial University Strategy for Renewing a Declining Industrial City: The Norrköping Way." *European Planning Studies* 20 (4): 505–525.

Tabachnick, B. G., and L. S. Fidell. 1996. *Using Multivariate Statistics*. New York: Harper Collins.

Teece, D. J. 2007. "Explicating Dynamic Capabilities: The Nature and Micro-foundations of (Sustainable) Enterprise Performance." *Strategic Management Journal* 28 (13): 1319–1350.

Teece, D. J. 2010. "Business Models, Business Strategy and Innovation." *Long Range Planning* 43 (2): 172–194.

Teece, D. J. 2012. "Dynamic Capabilities: Routines versus Entrepreneurial Action." *Journal of Management Studies* 49 (8): 1395–1401.

Teece, D. J. 2014. "The Foundations of Enterprise Performance: Dynamic and Ordinary Capabilities in an (Economic) Theory of Firms." *Academy of Management Perspectives* 28 (4): 328–352.

Teece, D. J., G. Pisano, and A. Shuen. 1997. "Dynamic Capabilities and Strategic Management." *Strategic Management Journal* 18 (7): 509–533.

Thornton, P., D. Ribeiro-Soriano, and D. Urbano. 2011. "Socio-cultural Factors and Entrepreneurial Activity: An Overview." *International Small Business Journal* 29 (2): 105–118.

Urbano, D., and M. Guerrero. 2013. "Entrepreneurial Universities Socioeconomic Impacts of Academic Entrepreneurship in a European Region." *Economic Development Quarterly* 27 (1): 40–55.

Urbano, D., M. Guerrero, J. J. Ferreira, and C. I. Fernandes. 2019. "New Technology Entrepreneurship Initiatives: Which Strategic Orientations and Environmental Conditions Matter in the New Socio-economic Landscape?" *The Journal of Technology Transfer* 44 (5): 1577–1602.

Von Bargen, P., D. Freedman, and E. R. Pages. 2003. "The Rise of the Entrepreneurial Society." *Economic Development Quarterly* 17 (4): 315–324.

Wang, C. L., and L. Altinay. 2012. "Social Embeddedness, Entrepreneurial Orientation and Firm Growth in Ethnic Minority Small Businesses in The." *UK.International Small Business Journal* 30 (1): 3–23.

Wright, M., B. Clarysse, P. Mustar, and A. Lockett. 2007. *Academic Entrepreneurship in Europe*. Massachusetts: Edward Elgar Publishing.

Yamin, M., and J. Otto. 2004. "Patterns of Knowledge Flows and MNE Innovative Performance." *Journal of International Management* 10: 239–258.

Zeng, S. X., X. M. Xie, and C. M. Tam. 2010. "Relationship between Cooperation Networks and Innovation Performance of SMEs." *Technovation* 30 (3): 181–194.

Zott, C., and R. Amit. 2007. "Business Model Design and the Performance of Entrepreneurial Firms." *Organization Science* 18 (2): 181–199.

Zott, C., R. Amit, and L. Massa. 2011. "The Business Model: Recent Developments and Future Research." *Journal of Management* 37 (4): 1019-1042.

Index

Note: Page numbers followed by "n" denote notes.

For Product Safety Concerns and Information please contact our EU
representative GPSR@taylorandfrancis.com
Taylor & Francis Verlag GmbH, Kaufingerstraße 24, 80331 München, Germany

www.ingramcontent.com/pod-product-compliance
Lightning Source LLC
LaVergne TN
LVHW080655011026
849160LV00014B/1435
* 9 7 8 1 0 3 2 1 5 8 7 9 2 *